The McGraw-Hill
36-Hour
Management
Course

The McGraw-Hill
36-Hour
Management
Course

Lester R. Bittel

McGraw-Hill Publishing Company

New York   St. Louis   San Francisco   Auckland
Bogotá   Hamburg   London   Madrid   Mexico
Milan   Montreal   New Delhi   Panama
Paris   São Paulo   Singapore
Sydney   Tokyo   Toronto

Library of Congress Cataloging-in-Publication Data

Bittel, Lester R.
  The McGraw-Hill 36-hour management course/Lester R. Bittel.
    p.   cm.
  Includes index.
  ISBN 0-07-005579-3 : ISBN 0-07-005578-5 (pbk.) :
  1. Management. 2. Management—Case studies. I. McGraw-Hill Book
Company. II. Title. III. Title: McGraw-Hill thirty-six-hour
management course.
HD31.B512 1988   88-26030
658.4—dc19   CIP

  234567890   DOC/DOC   895432109

ISBN 0-07-005579-3

*The editors for this book were Martha Jewett and Georgia Kornbluth, the
designer was Naomi Auerbach, and the production supervisor was Suzanne W.
Babeuf. This book was set in Baskerville. It was composed by the McGraw-Hill
Publishing Company Professional & Reference Division composition unit.*

Printed and bound by R. R. Donnelley & Sons Company.

Contents

Introduction   vii

Your Program of Study   ix

Part I. What's Expected of Managers

Coordinating efforts and results in an organizational setting.

1. The Unique Nature of Managerial Work   3

Comprehension-Check Case: The Harassed Plant Superintendent   20

2. Coping with Environmental Forces   23

Comprehension-Check Case: The Underflown Airline   39

3. The Power of Human Resources   43

Comprehension-Check Case: The Contrary Claims Department   65

Part II. What Managers Do

The five key functions that all managers must perform.

**4. Planning: Setting Goals and Creating Plans
and Programs**   71

Comprehension-Check Case: The Burgeoning Cosmetics Company   93

5. **Organizing: Dividing Up the Work in a Structured Framework** **97**

Comprehension-Check Case: The Shrinking Lumber Company 119

6. **Staffing: Placing the Right People in the Right Jobs** **123**

Comprehension-Check Case: The Expanding World of Kite 'n' Games 148

7. **Directing: Providing Communications, Motivation, and Leadership** **153**

Comprehension-Check Case: The Take-Charge CEO 175

8. **Controlling: Monitoring Progress and Exercising Control** **179**

Comprehension-Check Case: Spectacular Ski Company 198

Part III. Skills That Managers Develop and Apply

Conceptual, interpersonal, and technical.

9. **Problem Solving, Decision Making, and Innovation** **205**

Comprehension-Check Case: The Puzzled Bank Manager 224

10. **Information Management** **229**

Comprehension-Check Case: Coleman Memorial Hospital 245

11. **Developing Interpersonal Skills** **249**

Comprehension-Check Case: The Lively Advertising Agency 266

12. **Productivity Improvement** **269**

Comprehension-Check Case: The Declining Productivity at Carrie's Crafts 285

Answer Key to Comprehension-Check Cases **288**

Index **299**

Final Examination (following Index) **1**

Introduction

Management is a rewarding profession. This is true for the individual as well as for society as a whole. Wherever people join together in an organized fashion to work toward a common goal, management assumes a pivotal role. Little is accomplished in business, government, or public service without management.

Promotion to or advancement in a managerial position helps an individual not only to advance along the road toward financial success, but also to find a sense of personal achievement that is difficult to find in many other careers.

Proficiency in management, however, does not come easily. It requires a foundation of basic study, and it is enhanced through experience. Without a firm grasp of management principles and practices, success in a managerial position may prove to be elusive. It is the intent of this course to provide you with the comprehensive knowledge that you need in order to become a proficient manager.

A Body of Practical Knowledge

Effective management today is practiced according to an established body of knowledge which has evolved over the past 100 years into a set of generally accepted principles, practices, and terminology.

In this course, the body of management knowledge has been carefully distilled into 60 clearly stated concepts, each presented along with its supporting terminology. These concepts have been arranged in 12 chapters containing 5 concepts each.

All the essentials that are normally presented in a university-level course in management are included here. In this text, however, they are (1) presented in a format especially designed for independent study and (2) enhanced by an emphasis upon their practical application.

The author of this text has had over 25 years of experience as a practicing supervisor, manager, and executive in a number of Fortune 500 businesses. He has taught this particular management course at a leading university for the last 10 years. His award-winning writings in this field have played an important part in the education and development of hundreds of thousands of effective managers around the world.

Your Program of Study

To obtain maximum benefit from this course will require a total of 36 hours of your dedicated attention, not counting the time you may spend on the "Final Examination." You should be prepared to devote 3 hours to each of the 12 chapters. Ideally, you can plan to complete 1 chapter a week for 12 weeks. That follows the university semester plan. If, however, you can devote a greater portion of your time to your studies and you are a quick learner, you can finish the course in 6 weeks or even sooner.

Understanding the Chapter Format

This course is divided into 12 lessons or chapters. Each chapter is laid out in modular style. That is, each chapter contains several major features, and these features appear in the same sequence in every chapter. Each chapter includes the following features in the same order:

1. *The five concepts.* A preliminary overview of the concepts that you will study in the chapter.
2. *Key terms.* A list of the important terms associated with the five concepts.

3. *Concept lesson.*   Five lesson segments, each including the following:
   - A reiteration of the concept
   - A textual discussion in which the key terms are highlighted and explained
   - A "Practical Implications" case study which (a) illustrates a realistic application of the concept, (b) poses questions for you to consider, and (c) provides immediate answers along with practical insights

4. *The "Comprehension-Check Case."*   A five-part case study which concludes the chapter. The case method of study is well established as an effective method for adults to acquire a practical knowledge of management. Each case-study part is designed to relate to one of the concept lessons in the chapter. The purpose of the "Comprehension-Check Case" is to allow you to check your understanding of each concept and its associated terminology. This is accomplished through five sets of *assignment questions,* one set for each concept. The "Answer Key" (giving "solutions" to problems that emerge in the cases) is provided at the end of the book, along with "Comments" that explain potential ambiguities and add other insights.

The Final Examination

To provide evidence of successful completion of this course, the optional "Final Examination" appears at the end of the book. This examination consists of 200 multiple-choice questions. You may take the examination and send it to the McGraw-Hill certification examiner for grading. A score of 70 percent or better (140 correct answers) entitles you to a handsome certificate of accomplishment presented by McGraw-Hill, Inc. Details are provided with the "Final Examination" at the end of the book.

A Recommended Study Plan

The author has had extensive experience with independent-study programs. They succeed because the individuals who use them (1) lay out a plan of study, (2) commit themselves to that plan, and (3) persist until the course is completed. This particular course has been designed to simplify your study plan and to assist you in your commitment to it. The author recommends the plan outlined below, although you may vary its elements to suit both your time and the ease with which you acquire knowledge.

1. Don't be tempted to complete the course overnight. The text can probably be skimmed by a rapid reader in a few hours. The concept lessons will not have been learned this way, however. Neither will the value of the "Comprehension-Check Cases" have been exploited. Most important, you will not have gained the true value of the material. Nor will you have prepared yourself for taking the "Final Examination"—to prove to yourself and others your genuine understanding of management.

2. Plan to allot 12 weeks for this course of study. If you find that more time is available to you or that you are moving more quickly, you can always shorten your period of study to 8 or 6 or even 4 weeks.

3. Each week, set aside 3 study periods of 1 hour each. Learning is easier and information more likely to be assimilated when study is broken into segments that allow for reflection between them. Cramming your study into a 3-hour block of time can be self-defeating.

4. Proportion your time for each chapter this way:

First hour

20 minutes to read and absorb the introductory preview pages (the concept statements and list of key terms)
20 minutes to study the first concept
20 minutes to study the second concept

Second hour

20 minutes to study the third concept
20 minutes to study the fourth concept
20 minutes to study the fifth concept

Third hour

20 minutes to read the "Comprehension-Check Case"
20 minutes to answer the "Assignment Questions"
20 minutes to compare your answers with the "Answer Key to Comprehension-Check Cases"

5. Do not proceed to the next chapter until you fully understand the reasons for the correct answers to the questions about the "Comprehension-Check Case."

6. Do not skip chapters. Each succeeding chapter builds upon the previous ones. Management is an integrated practice; you will not have mastered it until you can pull it all together in your mind.

7. When you have completed all 12 chapters, consider taking the "Final Examination" and mailing it to the McGraw-Hill certification examiner for grading.

PART I

What's Expected of Managers

1
The Unique Nature of Managerial Work

The practice of management is difficult, demanding, and unique. Managers — the practitioners of management — exert tremendous leverage in helping groups of people — organizations — to become effective and productive. Paradoxically, managers do not perform work, in the ordinary sense. Instead, they perform five unique functions for an organization — and in so doing, they play three important roles and practice three vital skills. Their effectiveness is judged, not by their own performance, but by how well their organizations do. Finally, managers do not go "by the book" so much as they choose methods and techniques that are appropriate to the demands of a given situation.

Key Concepts Regarding Managerial Work

Figure 1.1 represents graphically the five key concepts that relate to managerial work. They are:

1. The tasks and services that managers perform are uniquely different from those of others in an organization.
2. In carrying out their work, managers perform five unique functions for an organization.
3. Managers play three important roles in an organization and apply three basic skills.

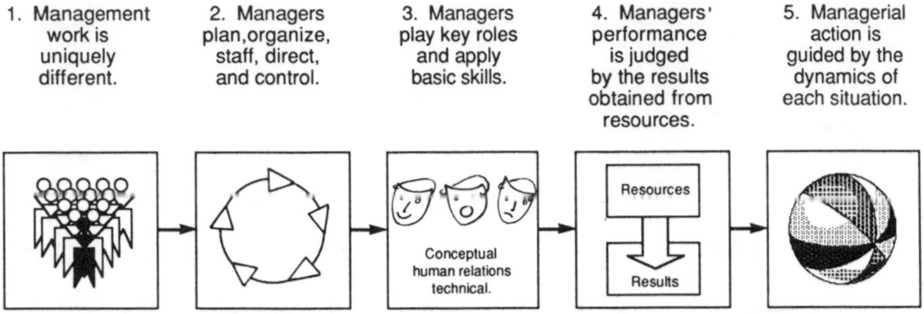

| 1. Management work is uniquely different. | 2. Managers plan, organize, staff, direct, and control. | 3. Managers play key roles and apply basic skills. | 4. Managers' performance is judged by the results obtained from resources. | 5. Managerial action is guided by the dynamics of each situation. |

Figure 1.1. Concepts 1–5.

4. The effectiveness of managers is judged by the results that they obtain for the organization by using the resources available to them.

5. Effective managers are able to discern differences between situations and to apply methods whose appropriateness is contingent upon the dominant factors in each situation.

Key Terms

To make full use of the key concepts, you will need to understand the following terms:

Management
Manager
Management process, or management cycle
Role
Conversion process
Resources

Results
Profitability
Cost benefits
Optimum
Situational management or contingency management

Concept 1

The tasks and services that managers perform are uniquely different from those of others in an organization.

When you think of work, you are likely to conceive of men and women using their hands to manipulate tools, such as word processors or paintbrushes. They pick up and manipulate materials and goods, as when a checkout clerk places groceries in a shopper's bag. Quite literally, these people put their hands on the work they are doing. Other people don't work so much with their hands as they do with their minds. An accountant, for instance, adds up and interprets a column of figures. A salesperson uses logic to persuade a customer to buy. An engineer studies a design problem to find the best solution. These people "put their minds on" the work that they are doing.

Most people in an organization touch the work with either their hands or their minds, or with both. These people make up the majority of employees in an organization. And their work is very important, since they actually produce the goods or services of the organization.

Managerial Work

Managers do none of the above. They do not put either their hands or their minds directly on the work — the products or services — that are being produced. They do not produce anything except management. What is management?

Management is the process of obtaining, deploying, and utilizing a variety of essential resources in support of an organization's objectives. One of the most essential resources of an organization is its employees. **Managers** devote a large portion of their efforts to planning, directing, and controlling the work of these human resources. One clear distinction between managers and other employees, however, is that managers direct the work of others rather than performing the actual work themselves. This is not to say that managers do not put their hands on the work when they instruct, teach, and coach. They do, of course. Managers do this, however, not as a productive effort of their own but to develop the skills of their employees.

Managerial Levels

Managers are designated by many titles. These titles may be misleading, although within any organization they are intended to indicate where a particular manager's position falls within the organization's hierarchy, as shown in Figure 1.2. Managers at the top of the hierarchy, or pyramid, are usually called "executives." Their titles include president, general manager, and vice president. Managers at the bottom of the hierarchy are conveniently described as "first-level managers." Their titles most often include "supervisor," as in "billing supervisor" or "assembly supervisor." The large body of managers whose positions lie between the top and the bottom are called "middle managers." Their titles are

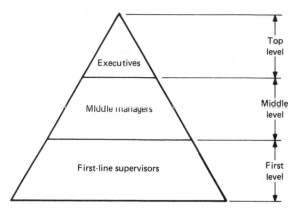

Figure 1.2. Levels of management.

likely to vary most, but are usually connected with a functional, or departmental, descriptor. They may be called "manager of accounts receivables," "manager of manufacturing," "director of engineering," "merchandising manager," and the like.

Note that executives and middle managers often have other managers or supervisors reporting to them. As such, the upper-level managers will be directing the work, not only of nonmanagers but of other managers. Supervisors usually direct only the work of rank-and-file, or nonmanagerial, employees.

Practical Implications

The Situation.   Betty is the supervisor of a sportswear section of a department store. Just when Betty is in the midst of planning her purchases for the next month, a shipment of new merchandise is delivered to her floor. This merchandise should be unpacked, and its contents should be verified against the shipping ticket and then placed on the appropriate display racks. The last time such a shipment arrived, the salesclerks—whose job it is to unpack, check, and display the merchandise—failed to catch an important mistake. The shipment called for 6 gross of small sizes and 3 gross of large, but the quantities were exactly reversed. By the time the error was caught, Betty's section was stuck with too many large sizes and had to reduce prices to unload the excess inventory in that size. Betty doesn't want this to happen again.

Question.   Should Betty check this shipment herself or direct one of the salesclerks to handle it?

Answer. Unpacking, checking, and displaying is clearly the work of a nonmanagerial employee. It is a temptation for Betty to check this particular shipment because she wants to make sure that there is no mistake. Nevertheless, if Betty regularly performs such nonmanagerial tasks, she won't be able to complete her managerial work. The best solution is for Betty to assign this job to a salesclerk—but before doing so, Betty should instruct the clerk to take special care to verify the contents of the shipment, and should also say that if there is some doubt about the correctness of the shipment, the clerk can ask for Betty's advice before putting the merchandise on the display racks.

In general, managers should differentiate between managerial work and other tasks, and should devote their time and energy to the former and avoid the latter. When managers perform nonmanagerial work, the organization is likely to suffer in the long run.

Concept 2

In carrying out their work, managers perform five unique functions for an organization.

You've seen what nonmanagerial work is. Now let's look more closely at the nature of managerial work to see exactly how it differs. *First of all, managers not only direct the work of others, they are also responsible for the work of others.* That is, if maintenance manager Tom assigns pipefitter supervisor Peter to have his crew install a new piping system, and the system leaks, Tom's boss will hold Tom responsible, even though Tom was out of town when the system was installed. Similarly, Tom will hold Peter responsible for the leaks, even though Peter never picked up a wrench.

You may well ask: How can that be fair, since neither Tom nor Peter did the actual work? The answer is that the managerial work of Tom and Peter involves five specific functions. Each of these has either a direct or an indirect impact—for better or worse—on those who actually perform the hands-on work. The five functions that managers perform and how these functions affect the work of others are discussed below.

1. Planning. Rather than allowing each employee of an organization to work, willy-nilly, toward a goal that she or he feels is important, a manager is responsible for setting an overall objective to unify employee efforts. As an extension of such goal setting, managers also design the plans and schedules that will help to move everyone toward the goal on time. Supervisors establish short-term goals and plans, such as how many widgets the group must make today. Middle-level managers are more likely to think in terms of goals and plans for the next month or year. Executives set broad goals and plans for the entire organization, and these will typically look ahead for 1 to 5 years.

2. Organizing. In any organization, there is always the question of who should do what. When managers carry out the organizing function, they make that decision. It is their responsibility to specify the tasks and duties that are to be performed so that the organization can meet its objectives. Organizing also requires that the manager establish the relationships between tasks—or positions. These relationships determine which position will have priority over others and which will be dependent upon others. In other words, the various claims sections of an insurance company may all be on the same level of an organization chart, but the claims department itself may be placed at a lower level than the underwriting or sales department.

3. Staffing. Positions on an organization chart have little consequence until they have been filled with individuals who are qualified to perform the duties associated with those positions. When managers fill these positions, they are performing the staffing function.

4. Directing. Once the plans have been set, the organization created, and the positions filled, the organization is ready to be set in motion. In effect, the organization is waiting for someone to ring the starting bell. That is the manager's responsibility, and it is carried out by the directing function. Managers direct (command or instruct) employees to go about their assignments. Directing, of course, requires much more of managers. They must not only be expert communicators; they must also provide the motivation and leadership that give purpose and spirit to the employees who report to them.

5. Controlling. Once an organization's wheels are in motion, the hope is that all members will do their jobs well, that plans will run smoothly, and that goals will be met. This is not often the case. Someone must keep an eye on things, regularly checking to see whether or not things are going according to plan. That is the manager's controlling responsibility. Managers must know when plans are faltering and results are off-target. When these things *do* go awry, it is the manager's control responsibility to take the necessary corrective action to put the plan back on track.

The Management Process

Managers routinely perform the five unique functions just described. In principle, they perform these functions in the sequence in which they are discussed above and shown in Figure 1.3. That is, it is rational for managers first to develop plans, then to create and staff an organization, next to direct it into action, and finally to exercise controls as the organization proceeds toward its goals. Conceptually, these five steps, taken in order, have been described as the **management process**.

In actual practice, any of the functions may be taken independently and in any sequence that circumstances dictate. A manager may go through all five functions in a day and repeat all five the next day. Or a manager may spend months in planning before an organization is developed and staffed. The plan may then remain in place for months while it is being activated and its progress monitored and controlled. Because the management process can be—and is—repeated over and

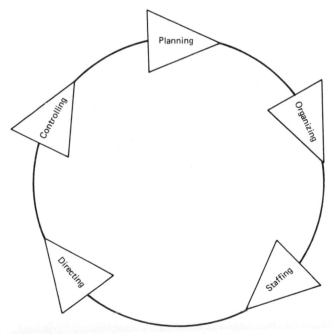

Figure 1.3. Management process, or cycle.

over again, as managers are continually engaged in performing its functions, the process is sometimes called the **management cycle**.

Practical Implications

The Situation.   In the previous situation—the case of Tom, the maintenance department head, and Peter, the pipe-fitter supervisor—Peter's crew made a faulty installation of a piping system.

Question.   How and why can Tom and Peter—as managers—be held responsible for the crew's faulty work?

Answer.   They can be held responsible because they did not perform their managerial functions properly. For instance:

1. *Planning*.   Either Tom or Peter may have (a) set too tight a time schedule (goal) for the job or (b) set up the job in the wrong way (according to a poor plan).

2. *Organizing*.   Tom may have organized the department in such a way that Peter couldn't demand proper time estimates from the job schedulers. Or Peter may have organized his pipe-fitter section so that there were not enough first-class mechanics to handle a critical assignment.

3. *Staffing*.   Tom may have chosen the wrong person (Peter) to be pipe-fitter supervisor. Or Peter may have staffed his section with untrained or otherwise unqualified personnel.

4. *Directing*.   Tom may not have provided enough motivation for Peter to *want* to have his crew do a difficult job in faultless fashion. Or Peter may not have made his instructions clear to the mechanics who were handling this installation.

5. *Controlling*.   Tom may not have checked the time estimates that were issued to see that they were realistic. Or Peter may have allowed his crew to work far too long without having an inspection made of their work.

When work is not performed properly by rank and file employees, there is a good chance that the managers in charge haven't performed their functions properly in the first place. Conversely, when jobs are well done, it's a good sign that managers are performing their special functions well, too.

```
┌─────────────────────────────────────────────────────────────┐
│                                                               │
│   Concept 3                                                   │
│                                                               │
│   Managers play three important roles in an organization and apply │
│   three basic skills.                                         │
│                                                               │
└─────────────────────────────────────────────────────────────┘
```

Managers not only perform functions; they also fulfill roles. A **role**, in this sense, is a social role, a part that others in an organization come to expect a particular person to play. People within an organization, as well as those who have contact with it only from the outside, tend to view its managers in a highly personalized way. These managerial roles are very real, even though they are often informal roles and do not have titles.

Managerial Roles

Managerial roles have been characterized as (1) interpersonal, (2) informational, and (3) decisional.

In the *interpersonal role,* the manager may act as a figurehead by representing the organization at formal functions, or may act as liaison between departments, or, most frequently, may play an important part as the leader who inspires others.

In the *informational role,* the manager may be the person who is the source of important data and, as such, the disseminator of that information to others. Or the manager may be viewed by the public, for example, as its spokesperson.

In the *decisional role,* the manager often acts as a crisis handler, deciding what to do, for example, when the power fails or a competitor cuts its prices. The manager also acts as a negotiator between the firm and its suppliers. The most common and most difficult decisional role is that of allocator of resources, as, for example, when a decision must be made about who in the department will get a computer terminal and who will not.

Managerial Skills

As if performing key functions and playing a variety of roles were not enough, managers must also acquire, develop, and apply three basic kinds of expertise. These have been identified as (1) conceptual skills, (2) human relations, or interpersonal skills, and (3) technical skills.

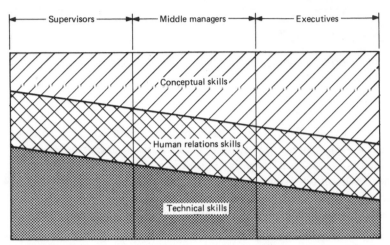

Figure 1.4. How requirements for basic managerial skills vary at different levels of management.

1. *Conceptual skills.*   The ability to analyze, interpret, and solve problems becomes increasingly important as you move up the managerial ladder, as shown in Figure 1.4.

2. *Human relations skills.*   These are important at all levels of management, although they differ in nature and intensity at different levels.

3. *Technical skills.*   Related to the specific operating requirements of a particular organization, technical skills tend to be more important at lower levels of management than at upper levels.

Practical Implications

The Situation.   Marie, as superintendent for a paper plant, must go before the local water-control board to defend a charge that the plant is discharging pollutants into the river. Oliver, the engineering manager, is asked to coordinate his department's activities with the marketing department's plans. Ralph, the production control manager, has just been informed that the vendor upon whom the plant depends for its daily supply of packing cartons has suffered a damaging fire and won't be able to ship for at least a month. The packaging department at the mill wants to know what it is supposed to do in the meanwhile. Ralph says that he'll take care of the problem. Finally, there is Rose, supervisor of the word processing section. She has just been asked to settle a dispute among her employees about who should occupy the quietest workplace, farthest from the printers.

Question. What roles are Marie, Oliver, Ralph, and Rose fulfilling for the organization?

Answer. Marie is fulfilling an *informational role* as spokesperson. Oliver is carrying out an *interpersonal role* in liaison. Ralph is playing a *decisional role* as crisis handler. Rose is in the difficult *decisional role* as allocator of resources.

Concept 4

The effectiveness of managers is judged by the results that they obtain for the organization by using the resources available to them.

If you recall the definition of management given earlier in this chapter, it should be apparent that managers are in charge of a process that converts resources into results, or inputs into outputs. This process, called the **conversion process**, is illustrated in Figure 1.5.The greater the results (or outputs) are as compared with the resources (or inputs) needed to attain them, the better a manager is judged to be. If, for example, a manager of an automobile-parts store spends $3000 a week on labor, merchandise, rent, and utilities, and the store takes in $4000, that manager will be judged as doing a better job than one who spends $3000 and takes in only $3300. Or, to turn it around, if both managers sell an equal amount of merchandise for $4000 and one spends only $2500 while the other spends $3000, the former will be judged a better manager than the latter.

The same concept will prevail for managers of departments within a large organizations, where money may never pass through a particular manager's hands. The manager's effectiveness will be gauged by com-

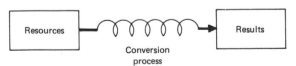

Figure 1.5. Conversion process.

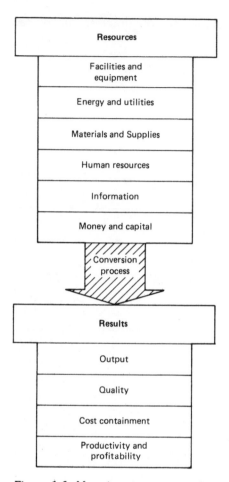

Figure 1.6. Managing resources to attain results.

paring (1) the output of a department—in terms of units processed—
with (2) the total of all expenses charged by the corporation to that department.

Let's look more closely at what might constitute resources and results
(Figure 1.6).

Resources

When you are appointed manager of a particular operation, there is a
tendency to take many things for granted. Your focus might be drawn
mainly to the machines and employees at your disposal. These are very

important, but the total available resources usually go far beyond them. Managerial **resources** include all the things — tangible and intangible — needed by an organization to meet its objectives. Typically, these resources can be classified as follows:

Facilities and equipment. These include floor space, desks, benches, tools, production machinery, cash registers, computer terminals, and microfiche readers.

Energy, power, and other utilities. Heat, light, air conditioning, electricity, steam, water, compressed air, and telephone lines are included in this category.

Materials and supplies. Raw materials, parts, and assemblies that actually go into a final manufactured product (or merchandise for wholesaling or retailing operations) are in this classification, as well as operating supplies such as lubricants, stationery, masking tape, computer ribbons, and anything else that gets used up during the conversion process rather than becoming part of the end product.

Human resources. Included here are the work force in general, including employees of varying capabilities, but most specifically, those employees who are assigned to a manager's operations.

Information and data. All sources — internal and external — of data are in this category, but most important is that information that is relevant to the conversion process for which the manager is responsible.

Money or capital. This includes financial resources available, either directly or indirectly, for use in acquiring and supporting all the other resources.

Generally speaking, it is assumed that if these resources are managed well, then the desired goals of the organization will be met.

Results

Terms like "results" and "outputs" are rather general. By definition, **results** (or outcomes) are the end products of the conversion process. They are the direct consequence of the management process and are affected by how well a manager has acquired, deployed and utilized the resources needed to meet an organization's objectives. Results become most meaningful when they are expressed in specific terms related directly to a particular organization. To put it another way, *results should meet or exceed an organization's objectives.*

Typically, the results expected from managers can be placed into four different, but closely dependent, groups:

1. Output. A manager's operations or department will be expected to turn out a certain amount of work — often referred to as "production" — per day, per week, per month, or per year. Output can be measured in units of product made or units of service provided, as in number of orders processed, clients cared for, or telephone calls answered. Time, too, is an essential dimension of output. The specified output must take place within a given time period; delivery schedules must be adhered to, and project deadlines met. Note that "output" is not the same as "productivity," which is explored in Chapter 12.

2. Quality. Often called "craft," quality is not an absolute: It is a set of standards of performance — or product or service — specified by management in response to customers' requirements. Quality is measured by such things as the number of product defects, service errors, and customer complaints.

3. Cost Containment. Costs are a measure of how effectively the output and quality results have been obtained. The expectation is that output and quality objectives will be met within established cost constraints. These constraints are usually established by an expense budget given to a manager. The typical expense budget is based directly upon the expected output and quality results.

4. Profitability, Cost Benefits, or Productivity. Each of these measures is, essentially, a comparison of results obtained with resources expended. For highly placed managers, profitability is often the ultimate measure of their effectiveness. For a business firm, **profitability** is the difference between (1) all its results, as measured by its revenues and (2) all the resources expended, as measured by their cost. In public and not-for-profit institutions, there is a similar measure, called **cost benefits**. The components of this measure have been turned around so that the cost of resources is stated before the value of results. Otherwise, managers in the nonprofit sector are judged similarly to those in the profit-seeking sector. That is, the performance of public-sector managers is evaluated on the basis of the value of their results (expressed as "benefits") as compared with the cost of obtaining these benefits.

Productivity is a far broader measure of the relationship of results obtained to resources expended. It will be explored in greater detail in Chapter 12.

Practical Implications

The Situation. Anne B. manages the "telling" activities for six branches of the Farmer's State Bank. She is disturbed because there is so little consistency of results between branches. She has asked her assistant to prepare a table showing comparative results. This is what the report looked like:

Branch name	Average number of transactions	Average monthly expenses	Number of transactions per dollar
Alport	32,000	$4000	_____
Centerville	25,000	3000	_____
LaCross	36,000	5000	_____
Media	30,000	4000	_____
Valdosta	42,000	5000	_____
Zanesville	24,000	3000	_____

Question. Based upon this information, the manager of which branch is most effective? Least effective?

Answer. A comparison of the results, as measured by the number of transactions with the input resources, as measured by the monthly expenses shows the following:

Best. Valdosta with 8.4 transactions per dollar (42,000 ÷ $5000)

Worst. LaCross with 7.2

Others. Alport, 8.0; Centerville, 8.3; Media, 7.5; and Zanesville, 8.0

Question. What factors other than the number of transactions might affect Anne's evaluation of the effectiveness of the different branches?

Answer. This report does not tell Anne whether or not the transactions varied: i.e., were some more difficult and more time-consuming than others? Nor does this report tell Anne how many errors were made in these transactions, or the extent of delays while customers were waiting for service.

Concept 5

Effective managers are able to discern differences between situations and to apply methods whose appropriateness is contingent upon the dominant factors in each situation.

Because of the unique relationship that results and resources have in determining organizational effectiveness, managers must carefully balance both factors. The temptation is to seek to obtain maximum results from minimum resources. This requires a precarious balancing act, often leading to failure. Accordingly, the most effective managers manage for optimum — not maximum — results. **Optimum** implies the most favorable outcome under specified, or limited, circumstances. In other words, results tend to be largely dependent upon the adequacy, capability, and utilization of the resources employed. Consequently, effective managers focus their attention on resources as well as results.

Implications of Situational Variations

Recognition that the goal of optimum results is more realistic than that of maximum results has led managers, in general, to another, related guideline. It is this: *Of the many methods and techniques available to managers, there is no single one that works well in all situations.*

If each theory, concept, or technique were universally applicable, there would be no need for managers. Everything could be programmed into a computer, and problems would be solved and decisions made automatically. It is the *difference* between situations that is so critical to managerial success or failure.

Few situations are exactly alike. Most situations have so many contributing factors that the potential differences become enormous. Variables include such factors as the degree of motivation and capability of the participants, the money and facilities available, the clarity of communications, and the urgency of the situation. Accordingly, experience has shown that the effectiveness of a concept, guideline, or technique is dependent upon the factors that dominate a particular situation. The approach, then, that a wise manager chooses to use is dependent — or contingent — upon the situation.

Two descriptive terms for this approach, which are used interchangeably, are **situational management** and **contingency management**. The contingency aspect of management is what makes the work of managers so difficult. The ability to analyze a particular situation so as to identify its dominant features and to differentiate it from others — and then to choose the most appropriate approach — is what separates ordinary managers from superior ones.

Practical Implications

The Situation. Rauel, manager of frozen-foods purchases for a major grocery chain, is negotiating with a large supplier. He is concerned because the chain's store managers are continually asking that purchase volumes be limited so as to avoid building up the store's inventories. Rauel's boss has also cautioned him in the past about buying too much at one time. On the other hand, Sam, the salesperson for the supplier, always pushes for large orders, holding out lower prices as an incentive. The last time the salesperson called, however, Rauel got burned. He placed a large order at a low price, but it sat around in the warehouse for weeks before it was depleted.

This time, Rauel feels that he will have the advantage, since he isn't under pressure from his boss or the store manager to buy. Accordingly, Rauel makes a low-price offer for a minimum purchase. Sam contacts his home office, and they say, "No dice." Rauel shrugs and says, "Too bad, then. We won't order today. We'll wait until you come again and we can order in larger units at lower prices." A week later, Rauel gets a call from his boss, who says, "The stores are crying for frozen foods. At least three of them have run out of stock. What happened?"

Question.   What do you think may have happened to put Rauel behind the eight ball?

Answer.   Rauel might wisely have given a number of factors more consideration. He should realize that his performance will be judged by how well his results compare with the resources expended. In his mind, his job is simply to get the most goods for the least money. Unfortunately, that measure must be tempered by other considerations. First, it's tempting fate to allow inventories to become so low that the stores will run out of stock—and lose sales. Second, the time that Rauel got burned by ordering too much may have been during a period of slow sales for the stores; the current period may include an approaching holiday. Third, the store managers may have been reflecting pressure they were feeling to reduce inventories and may have been all too willing to shift the responsibility for stocking to Rauel. Fourth, the supplier may have been eager to make deals during a period of slow demand but less likely to do so in periods of rising demand.

Had Rauel sought an *optimum* result, his decisions about how much to purchase at one time would have been *contingent* upon the time of year, the attitudes of the store managers, the risk entailed in running out of stock, and the demand for the supplier's goods.

Comprehension-Check Case for Chapter 1

The Case of the Harassed Plant Superintendent

For easy reference, the text of the comprehension-check case is numbered to correspond to the assignment questions that follow

The Lock Stock & Barrel Company manufactures a variety of home-building supply specialties in a small plant in the midwest.

1. Brady is the plant superintendent, and his boss is the company president. The assembly supervisor, Charlie, reports to Brady. Reporting to Charlie are seven employees who assemble locks.

2. One day last spring, the company president called Brady into his office and said, "We've had a number of complaints about our locks being improperly assembled." After investigating the problem, Brady told his boss, "I'm glad that I wasn't responsible for those poor assemblies. I found that Charlie, our assembly supervisor, has been failing to make sure that his employees follow the proper assembly procedures."

That same day, Brady also found himself engaged in the following activities: (a) drawing up the production schedule for the fall, (b) filling in on the packaging line for a couple of hours while the operator went to the doctor, (c) instructing the shipping crew on the loading dock about the use of a new lift truck, (d) interviewing a candidate for the position of quality-control manager, (e) checking with the chief accountant about an overrun on the plant's expense budget, and (f) making a change in organizational structure, with the result that the plant engineer began to report directly to the plant superintendent instead of to the chief engineer.

3. During the previous week, Brady had also (a) settled a grievance with the labor union, (b) attended the local Rotary meeting as the company's representative, (c) explained proposed changes in compensation policies to the plant's supervisors, (d) discussed product changes with the marketing manager, (e) called suppliers to find a replacement for a critical processing machine that had broken down and couldn't be repaired, and (f) thought up ideas for improving manufacturing methods in the plant.

4. When the end of the year approached, Brady examined the records to see just how well the plant had done as a whole. This is what the records showed:

Expenses

Equipment repair and depreciation	$ 100,000
Utilities	210,000
Raw materials	1,100,000
Operating supplies	50,000
Labor	500,000

Computer programs	30,000
Cash for out-of-pocket expenditures	10,000
Total expenses	$2,000,000

Outputs

PRODUCTION: 100,000 units, valued, if perfect, at $5 each
DEFECTS RETURNED: 20,000 of the above units returned by dealers and scrapped

5. Looking ahead to next year, Brady decided that, by expending a little more on labor for inspection, the number of defects could be cut to 5000, although total production would also drop to 395,000. He calculated that labor costs would rise from $500,000 to $510,000, but all other costs would remain the same. Brady felt that this approach was a good one since it balanced anticipated expenditures against results that seemed reasonable to attain.

Brady took his plan to the company president, who asked just how sure Brady was that the results he predicted from it would actually materialize. Brady said that *if* prices of raw materials, supplies, and utilities did not rise and *if* there were no changes in product specifications, his plan would work. On the other hand, Brady said, *if* these prices did rise or *if* there were changes in product specifications, he would have to look for cost-cutting methods in assembly rather than concentrating on closer inspections alone.

Assignment Questions

1 (a) Brady appears to be at the _____ level of management, Charlie at the _____ level.
    _____ *a.* executive; first
    _____ *b.* middle; first
    _____ *c.* executive; middle
    _____ *d.* middle; middle
1 (b) The company expects that Brady and Charlie should perform _____ work, while the assemblers and all other employees should perform _____ work.
    _____ *a.* mental; physical
    _____ *b.* easy; hard
    _____ *c.* important; unimportant
    _____ *d.* management; hands-on

2 (a) Whom should the company president hold responsible for improperly assembled locks?
    _____ *a.* Charlie, the assembly supervisor
    _____ *b.* Brady, the plant superintendent
    _____ *c.* The workers in the assembly department
    _____ *d.* No one should be held responsible.
2 (b) For each of the lettered items in part 2, describing Brady's activities for

the day, write the proper managerial *function* designation (planning, organizing, staffing, directing, controlling) in the space provided.

a. _____   d. _____
b. _____   e. _____
c. _____   f. _____

3 (a)   For each of the lettered activities in part 3, describing Brady's activities
for the previous week, enter the name of Brady's *role* (informational, decisional,
interpersonal) in the space provided.

a. _____   d. _____
b. _____   e. _____
c. _____   f. _____

3 (b)   Which basic *skill* classifications would you associate with each of the
lettered activities? Enter your answer (conceptual, human relations, technical) in
the spaces provided here:

a. _____   d. _____
b. _____   e. _____
c. _____   f. _____

4 (a)   The record shows that, at year's end, the results (net value of outputs)
of Brady's plant operations will be:

_____   a. $2 million
_____   b. $2,100,000
_____   c. $1,900,000
_____   d. $1 million

4 (b)   Brady's effectiveness, as measured by comparing results attained with
resources expended, yield a figure of _____ percent.

_____   a. 100
_____   b. 105
_____   c. 95
_____   d. 50

5 (a)   Brady's plan for next year seems to be aiming for_____
results.

_____   a. maximum
_____   b. minimum
_____   c. optimum
_____   d. best-chance

5 (b)   When Brady explained to the company president the chances for his
plan's success, Brady was reflecting what management approach?

_____   a. Contingency management
_____   b. Tight-fisted management
_____   c. Riskfree management
_____   d. Speculative management

2
Coping with Environmental Forces

The practice of management may have a conceptual, or theoretical, underpinning, but it is carried on in a very real world. Managers must deal not only with members of their own departments, but also with managers and members of other departments in the organization. They must also learn to contend with, and gain support from, managers above and below them in the organization's hierarchy. And it doesn't stop there: they must do their managing in the spheres of contending and supporting forces that surround the inner world of their own organization. To understand and conquer this real-world environment, managers must learn to optimize their interactions by integrating three time-tested approaches, described later under concept 10.

Key Concepts Regarding the Managerial Environment

Figure 2.1 illustrates the five concepts that relate to the managerial environment. They are:

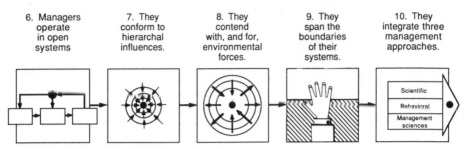

Figure 2.1. Concepts 6–10.

6. Managers perform their work in an open system that restricts their freedom to act indiscriminately but enlarges their opportunities to seek outside resources and support.

7. The internal constituents of a manager's organizational system represent a source of both support and conflict.

8. Managers compete with, as well as look for support from, independent forces in the external environment in which the parent organization exists and which it depends upon for survival.

9. Successful managers span the boundaries of the systems in which they operate so as to optimize support and minimize resistance from, and conflict with, contending factions and forces.

10. Managers accomplish their work in an ever-changing environment by integrating three time-tested approaches.

Key Terms

To make full use of the concepts, you must understand the following terms:

System
Closed system
Open system
Strategic influence
Partisanship
Factionalism
Directly interactive environmental forces

Indirectly interactive environmental forces
Boundary spanning
Scientific management
Behavioral management
Management sciences
Integrative approach

Concept 6

Managers perform their work in an open system that restricts their freedom to act indiscriminately but enlarges their opportunities to seek outside resources and support.

Management was described in Chapter 1 as the process of obtaining, deploying, and utilizing a variety of essential resources in support of an organization's objectives. This definition was elaborated upon to imply that managers are in charge of a process whereby an organization converts its resources (or inputs) into useful results (or outputs). When this conversion process is placed in context with the manager and the environment, it looks like Figure 2.2.

Closed Systems

To clarify the manager's part in this process, the manager in Figure 2.2 is placed above the process, in a position to receive information (or feedback) about results so that he or she can make changes and improvements in either the supply of resources or the process itself if the results aren't satisfactory. Observe that the arrows connect the resources, the conversion process, the results, and the manager in an endless loop. That loop, tying all four elements together, depicts a system. A **system** is an interrelated set of elements functioning as a whole. Each

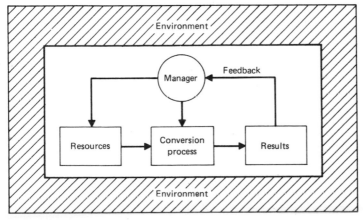

Figure 2.2. Closed system.

part is dependent upon the others: a change in one part will affect the other parts. The human body is an example of a system; so is a clock or an automobile engine.

If you will look at Figure 2.2 again, you'll note that the management system is enclosed by a rectangle, or box. Placing the management system in a box makes it a **closed system**. This means that the manager in charge can manipulate anything within the system without interference from any person, or anything, outside the system. The manager is king or queen of everything inside the closed system. Uninformed observers and, indeed, inexperienced managers mistakenly think that managers work in such a closed system. They do not. They are subject to a great many relatively uncontrollable factors that break into, or open up, their little world. Money to buy new equipment isn't forthcoming. Employees run into problems at home and don't report to work. A supplier is late in making a shipment of raw materials. A customer refuses to accept a shoddy product or service. That's the real world of management, open on both the input and the output sides.

Open Systems

In Figure 2.3, the management system has been redrawn to reflect reality. The changes in the drawing are slight but very, very significant. The heart of the original system—the conversion, or transformation, process—is the only element that remains within the rectangle. Both the input and the output elements are now exposed to the environment. The manager is still in charge of the conversion process, but must now respond to the environment in which the process exists. The manager is

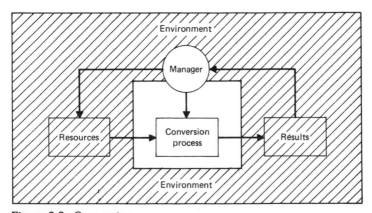

Figure 2.3. Open system.

now functioning in an open system. In an **open system**, managers must continually seek and compete for resources, just as they must continually respond to customers' or clients' demands. Organizations survive when their managers conduct successful searches and make intelligent responses to the environment. Companies and institutions fail when their managers do not cope effectively in such open systems.

Practical Implications

The Situation. John Paul manages the processing department of a mail-order service company, one that inserts material into, and addresses, envelopes for clients. The company has just accepted a major job from an important client. It has to be in the mail by next weekend. John posts a schedule that calls for his staff to work overtime every night next week. He also asks the purchasing department to double the normal purchase of mailing-label forms. By the middle of next week, John finds the order running far behind schedule, for two reasons: First, two of his best employees have declared that they can't possibly work overtime; they have family emergencies. Second, the purchasing department advises John that the regular supplier of labels can't double the order, because of a failure in a printing machine.

John rants and raves at the two employees who can't work overtime. "You'll have to work every night this week if you want to keep your job," he says. "You don't own us," is their reply, "and these emergencies are beyond our control." In his frustration, John turns to the purchasing manager and says, "If that's the best you can do, the company ought to find a new purchasing manager." The purchasing manager retorts, "The company is more likely to be looking for a new processing manager!"

Question. Is this the end of the line for John Paul? Where has he been particularly shortsighted?

Answer. John Paul is awakening to the harsh fact that he manages in an open system and cannot control all the environmental factors that can influence his effectiveness, for better or, as in this case, for worse. He does have options, of course. An open system not only restricts some of John Paul's control but also offers opportunities to seek additional resources. There is always the possibility that temporary employees hired from a commercial agency can fill in during this emergency. And, if John Paul is wise enough to use, rather than abuse, the purchasing manager, the purchasing manager may just be able to find another supplier to fill the label order. Furthermore, other possibilities might also be explored, such as persuading the customer to accept an extension of the delivery date or a partial shipment. It is important to remember that at the results end of the conversion process, too, an open system can present opportunities as well as restrictions.

Concept 7

The internal constituents of a manager's organizational system represent a source of both support and conflict.

Managers' organizations—the companies, institutions, or agencies for which they work—shape their internal systems. These are open systems, in that each manager must look to (1) managers above or below, or both above and below, for support or constraints and (2) managers at the same level for cooperation or competition for the organization's resources.

Hierarchal Spheres of Influence

Just as there are three levels of management in an organization's hierarchy, so are there three levels—or spheres—of influence. This is illustrated in Figure 2.4. Each sphere offers a different kind of perspective on the organization's performance.

1. **Strategic influence** emanates from the executives at the top of the pyramid. They are charged with seeing the bigger picture and looking toward the longer-range horizons. They plot the master, overriding strategy that sets the overall goals and constraints of the organization.

2. *Administrative influence* cascades down through the organization mainly from the offices of its middle managers. Their tasks are to convert major goals and long-range plans into operational plans for each activity of the organization. They lay out the plans and procedures that govern the work of supervisors at the operational level.

3. *Operational influence* focuses on carrying out the plans and procedures—passed down from above—that will enable the organization to meet its goals. Supervisors at the first level of management have

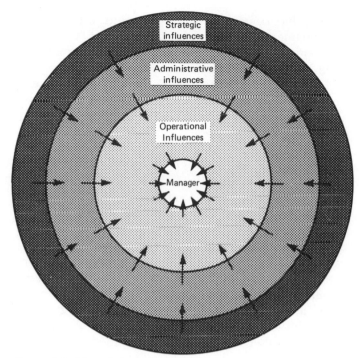

Figure 2.4. Hierarchal spheres of influence.

direct influence over the employees who do the hands-on work of the organization.

It is clear that managers at the middle and lower levels are greatly influenced by the decisions made at the strategic level. It may not be so clear that executives at the strategic level are greatly restrained by the performance and attitudes of the middle-level managers who are, in turn, even more greatly restrained by the capabilities, know-how, and attitudes of managers and supervisors at the lower levels.

At any level, managers must be alert to what's happening in each sphere of influence. They must seek to win favor for their ideas and to reduce resistance to their directions. Neither cooperation nor compliance is a given.

Internal Factions

In every organization, there is a form of internal **partisanship**. That is, people who are joined together in a single activity—as in a sales, or accounting, or purchasing department, for example—tend to form close relationships. As a department, they develop an attitude of "us against them," in which "they" are the other departments in the organization. All too often, partisanship causes development of warring factions. For a manager, this can become a no-win situation. Each department needs the assistance and cooperation of other departments if its goals, and especially the organization's goals, are to be met. **Factionalism**—warring on partisanship grounds—is to be avoided.

Managers must be aware of a reasonable degree of "party loyalty" among members of a particular department—from top to bottom. A vice president in charge of marketing, for example, is likely to be as strongly protective of a salesperson's travel expenses as the salesperson is. An accounting manager who fusses about a salesperson's overrun of expenses may find the marketing vice president on his or her back.

To minimize friction and conflict, managers engage in "hand washing" and "horse trading." All organizations have strong political undertones. An effective manager learns to sense when to make an issue and when to look the other way. Cooperation between departments is very much a two-way street and is highly dependent upon a willingness to give as well as take. Tactics such as pulling rank or going to the top for a ruling are rarely effective, almost certainly not over the long run.

Practical Implications

The Situation. Muriel F., personnel manager of the Blowing Rock Mutual Insurance Company, regularly sends the best job candidates to Dianne J., who manages the claims department. Bill B., manager of the actuarial department, complains that he gets sent all the potential misfits to interview. The personnel manager would probably deny that she plays favorites, but when pressed, she has an explanation. "Dianne knows how to cooperate; Bill doesn't. They are both nice people, but they don't approach their jobs the same way."

Question. What are some of the "political" things that Dianne may do that Bill doesn't?

Answer. When Dianne thinks about other departments that can influence her performance for better or worse, she focuses her attention on what she can do (1) to make their jobs easier and (2) to make them look better. For instance, when the personnel manager was launching a training program that was meeting resistance from other department heads, Dianne volunteered to have several of her employees attend. Another time, when one of the candidates whom Dianne hired turned out poorly, she discussed the problem privately with the personnel manager to find ways to avoid recurrence of such a problem in the future. In many other ways, Dianne avoids embarrassing other department heads in the eyes of their superiors. Conversely, she finds ways to acknowledge publicly when an employee of another department has provided her department with an exceptional service.

Concept 8

Managers compete with, as well as look for support from, independent forces in the external environment in which the parent organization exists and which it depends upon for survival.

If you look beyond the systems of the separate managers in an organization to the larger system of the organization of the organization itself, you will see that it too is an open system. The organization — a company, institution, or public agency — must perform its conversion process while exposed to the environment outside itself. This environment is the external world, and it can be conceived of as having two levels, or spheres, of power: (1) the closer level with which the managers in the organization have regular and direct interactions and (2) a more remote, but equally powerful level — the external environment — with which managers must indirectly interact.

Directly Interactive Forces

The external forces, or **directly interactive environmental forces**, with which the managers of an organization have regular contact are its customers and clients, its suppliers, and its competitors.

The *customer or client group* consists of the people and companies that purchase (or receive, in the case of public agencies) the products and services produced by the organization. Obviously, without satisfied customers, the organization is heading for trouble. It is the customers' cry for lower prices and higher quality that puts the pressure on managers within the organization.

The *supplier group* is closely related to the resources that a firm draws upon. It includes not only raw materials but all kinds of resources — from money to labor. When financial markets are tight and interest rates high, this puts pressure on the internal managers of an organization to compensate by cutting costs. Similarly, when there is a shortage of qualified help available, the internal managers suffer from the comparatively poor performance of the employees they can hire in such a market.

The *competitor group* is one that most managers are keenly aware of. Organizations that compete for the same customers—by offering either lower prices, higher quality, or greater convenience—put the squeeze on the internal managers to improve their performance so as to meet competitive conditions.

It should be acknowledged that, depending upon present circumstances, all the above represent opportunities as well as threats. A business can't get along without a bank or without customers. Sometimes, even competitors can be a help, if their presence brings customers to your area and their advertising creates an awareness of the generic usefulness of your product or service.

Indirectly Interactive Forces

Most of us take the weather for granted. Farmers don't. They understand it as an uncontrollable force upon which they are completely dependent. And they reckon it into their goals, plans, and operations. There are several environmental conditions, or **indirectly interactive environmental forces**, that business managers worry about, even though they may consider them remote and mostly uncontrollable. There are six classes of these forces in the outermost sphere of the environment.

1. *The economy.* Lying in the wings, unpredictable, but a force that influences the cost and availability of just about every resource that a manager needs, is the economy. And, of course, the economy affects consumer spending at the results end of the system. Managers try to forecast shifts in the economy, but there is practically nothing that they can do to control it.

2. *Technology.* All sorts of technology, not just the "high-tech" of electronics and chemistry, threatens a business with change on the one hand and offers it competitive advantages on the other. Alert managers maintain a constant search for the possible uses of technology in their activities.

3. *The legal and political environment.* An ever-growing web of regulations and restrictions that managers must learn to maneuver in with care is woven by the legal and political environment.

4. *Social and cultural forces.* Swift changes in consumers' buying

habits are brought about by social and cultural forces, and they also subtly influence the way in which an organization is allowed to function. These forces generate the values that govern what the public will accept, or not accept, in the way of corporate practices, consumer safety, and damage to the physical environment.

5. *The physical environment.* Not only weather, of course, but also energy sources, the land, water, and minerals are part of the physical environment. Most managers are acutely aware of this dependence and the public's determination to conserve it.

6. *The international environment.* During the post-World War II years, what once was a closed system for major industrial nations like the United States has been broken up by the international environment. The world is encroaching on internal managers everywhere, as both small and large nations jostle each other in the marketplace.

Practical Implications

The Situation. A small manufacturing company in Michigan considers itself the prime source of machined metal parts for a major automobile builder.

One day, Michelle, the company's sales manager, enters the office of Mark, the chief engineer, and throws a machined part on his desk.

MICHELLE: How good is this part?

MARK: I don't know, but it looks exactly like the model we make. Is it one of ours?

MICHELLE: No, it's made by a Japanese firm.

MARK: What do they charge for it?

MICHELLE: Twenty percent less than we do, and the auto builder tells me that this part meets all their quality specifications!

MARK: And this is made in Japan — and shipped here! How can they do it at that price?

MICHELLE: I don't know, but we won't live long as a supplier if we don't do something about it.

Two months later, Mark calls Michelle to his office, saying, "I want to show you something." When the sales manager arrives, the engineer hands her a nicely machined plastic model of the metal part.

MARK: What do you think of it?

MICHELLE: Hey! It weighs a lot less than the other part.

MARK: And it costs a lot less to make, too.

MICHELLE: But will it do the same job as the metal one?

MARK: It sure will. We've put it to every imaginable test. Do you think you can sell it?

MICHELLE: You bet I can. The auto builder is looking for lightweight parts right now.

The next day, at a meeting of the company's managerial staff, Harry, the machine-shop superintendent, is asked to comment upon any problems he foresees with making the plastic part. "Problems?" he says, "lots of them. We don't have the machines to do that kind of work, nor the know-how. We can get the machines and learn how to make these parts, but it will take money, time, and training."

Question.   What are some of the implications of the various comments of these three managers?

Answer.   These exchanges represent the impact upon the company and its managers from (1) their *direct interactions* with the environment—their customers—and from (2) their *indirect interactions* with technology and international competitors.

Concept 9

Successful managers span the boundaries of the systems in which they operate so as to optimize support and minimize resistance from, and conflict with, contending factions and forces.

When threatened by the environment, managers don't just lie there and take it. Instead, they monitor the perimeter of their departments, or of the company as a whole, warding off invasion from hostile forces and scanning the horizon for friendly assistance. Such surveillance beyond the boundaries of their functional responsibilities, in order to detect changing conditions and prepare to adapt their own operations to accommodate them, is called **boundary spanning**. A manager of a construction firm, for example, may have to check the weather every morning before dispatching crews, verify that the truckloads of cement are on their way from the concrete supplier, and call ahead to the work site to make sure that the customer is ready to allow the construction to begin. Such boundary spanning entails three key managerial activities.

1. Monitoring the Boundaries.   An extension of a manager's informational role involves monitoring the boundaries. He or she must constantly seek out news and information that indicate changes in (a) customers' or clients' needs, (b) suppliers' prices or delivery dates, and (c) competitors' policies and practices. Such surveillance takes place internally as well as externally. The manager of a data processing department, for example, must look to the changing requirements of the other departments serviced, the adequacy and timing of the supply of data from the reporting departments, and the possibility of the company's replacing the data processing department with a commercial data processing firm.

2. Developing Relationships.   You may sometimes wonder how an executive can justify a corporate membership in a golf club, for example. The justification, if the membership is properly exploited, is that it provides a basis for informal relationships with other executives so that information regarding operations can be exchanged casually. Companies join trade associations for the same reason. At the administrative and operating levels, it is a good idea for managers to go to lunch together. Internal relationships between managers, formed casually and informally, help to minimize conflict and encourage cooperation. The most important relationships, both internal and external, are built on the basis of service and mutual trust. Managers will exchange information and assistance when they know that confidentiality will be respected and favors will be returned.

3. Adapting to Change.   The purpose of maintaining surveillance of the boundaries is to become alert to the need for change. It is not enough to know about this need; actions must be planned and taken by the organization to accommodate it. If the data processing manager discovers that the firm's operating departments need processed data before business begins in the morning, the manager may have to put on a night shift to meet this requirement. Becoming aware of, and satisfying, the needs of other departments in an organization reduces factionalism and encourages cooperation.

Practical Implications

Commentary.   The ramifications of the need for boundary spanning are endless. A production supervisor needs the help of the maintenance supervisor; otherwise machine repair is delayed. An operating department manager won't be particularly effective without the interested cooperation of the purchasing department—and the personnel department—and the accounting department. A marketing manager depends upon good relationships with the research and development department; otherwise the new products developed won't match market expectations. The factory superintendent must be alert to changing local ordinances or federal regulations affecting disposal of wastes. The financial manager must keep on top of interest rates and the bank's attitude toward loans. The human resources manager checks in regularly with local employment agencies to determine the state of the labor market. And the company president must know what other members of the trade association are saying about international competition.

Concept 10

Managers accomplish their work in an ever-changing environment by integrating three time-tested approaches.

The ultimate consequence of ever-changing conditions in both the internal and external environments is that managers, themselves, must be adaptive. Since the turn of this century, managers have become more and more flexible in their approaches to carrying out their functions and roles. They began the century, however, with a conviction that there was "one best way." Gradually, this hope yielded to a grudging acknowledgment that, for managers to be effective, employees must be treated as human beings, not as machines. And, for a brief period, many managers were convinced that the whole process could, with the aid of mathematics and science, be programmed on computers. Alas, none of these three approaches worked out very well in practice. Yet, none was a total failure. Each approach had its merits in certain situations. Managers have thus come to rely on all three approaches, mixing and matching them to suit a particular situation.

The three approaches have been known, variously, as (1) scientific management, (2) behavioral management, and (3) management sciences. You will need a basic understanding of each if you are to mix and match these approaches yourself.

Scientific Management.   This approach has been known by many names: classic, traditional, systematic, rational. The terms "systematic" and "rational" are, perhaps, most descriptive. **Scientific management** bases its approach on: (1) making no assumptions about any matter until it has first been studied and measured, (2) seeking to minimize the time and energy needed to perform a particular task, (3) relying upon carefully prescribed procedures and controls, and (4) believing that wages are the driving force in human motivation. The weak link in this approach is its dependence upon money as a motivator and its reluctance to allow employees to make their own decisions about how the work will be performed.

Behavioral Management. While the **behavioral management** approach was triggered by extensive studies of organizational behavior and of human psychology in work situations, it is often described simply as the "human relations" approach. In its original practice, this approach was oversimplified. Managers were led to believe that "if you treat people right, they will respond productively." This belief turned out to be poorly founded. Some people when treated "properly" did work harder; many, however, did not. As managers became more sophisticated in applying the human relations approach, they began to recognize that human behavior is a complicated matter. It is even more complicated when it involves interactions of a diverse group of individuals. Accordingly, the practice of behavioral management is far more sophisticated and realistic today. Nevertheless, to be applied successfully, it requires great sensitivity toward human behavior and organizational interactions.

Management Sciences. This approach should not be confused with "scientific management," although it springs from the same conceptual roots. **Management sciences** (once known as "operations research") are actually a conglomerate of approaches involving statistics, quantitative methods, and the decision sciences (see Chapter 9). Their underpinning is mathematical, and they are often impractical without a computer. They have had their greatest successes in applications involving measurable, tangible objects and conditions. They have been very effective, for instance, in devising operating schedules, optimizing the allocation of resources, managing inventories, and helping to control product quality. Management sciences have been considerably less helpful in the management of human affairs. And, of course, that is where a great deal of a manager's action takes place.

It has become painfully clear that managers cannot rely upon the use of only one, or even two, approaches. Effective managers are confronted with such a great variety of situations that they must be able to call upon any or all of these approaches selectively. As was iterated in Chapter 1, *no single method or technique works well in all situations*.

Application of these three management approaches in concert to solve a problem might be described as an **integrative approach**. As such, an integrative approach represents a practical application of contingency management, as described on page 18. This is so, since it emphasizes the selective use of, one approach to fit a particular situation, but without ruling out use of the other two in conjunction with the primary one chosen.

Practical Implications

The Situation.   Janet H. is credit manager of the Ultra Office Equipment Company. In the course of her work last week, Janet was faced with three problems:

1. The sales manager complained that credit had been refused a customer for whom it ought to have been routinely approved. Upon checking with the clerks in her department, Janet discovered that each had his or her own idea of how the credit criteria should be applied.

Question.   Which approach should Janet use to solve this problem: scientific, behavioral, or management sciences?

Answer.   The systematic, procedural characteristics of scientific management would seem to suit this situation best. Janet should establish a clear-cut procedure and put it in writing. If that doesn't work, she might then try a behavioral approach involving employee motivation and training. Even a management sciences approach might apply, if it leads to a way of programming all routine credit applications so as to eliminate errors of interpretation.

2. A study of absence records in Janet's department showed Janet that one clerk, in particular, was absent far more than other employees during peak periods of the month.

Question.   Which approach should Janet use to solve this problem?

Answer.   A behavioral approach would appear to be most appropriate. Absenteeism is related to personality factors, motivation, and job conditions, and it responds to counseling. On the other hand, Janet cannot rule out the possibility that quantitative methods (management sciences) might be used to level out peak-period schedules to reduce pressure on the employees at that time and, thus, to render the work more attractive and less conducive to absences.

3. The company announced a plan to install an office automation sys-

tem that would greatly affect operation of Janet's department. Dozens of factors would have to be juggled for this project—factors such as numbers and types of equipment, workplace layouts, costs, installation of telephone lines, and redesign of paperwork forms.

Question. Which managerial approach should Janet use on this problem?

Answer. This is a natural for the management sciences—in particular, program evaluation and review technique (PERT), critical path method (CPM), or Network Planning (see pages 87–91, for further explanation)—since it involves manipulating a great many variables. This places ordinary systematic analysis way beyond the capability of the human mind unless aided by mathematical techniques and computer processes. Here again, however, the systematic approaches of scientific management would be needed to prepare for the application of a management science. Additionally, the inevitable disruptions in this change will greatly affect the performance of the department's employees unless they are counseled throughout this period by an appropriate behavioral management technique.

Comprehension-Check Case for Chapter 2
The Case of the Underflown Airline

*For easy reference, the text of the comprehension-check case is
numbered to correspond to the assignment questions that follow.*

Falcon Flight Aero (FFA), a small regional airline, is having a bad year. Passenger miles are down, and so are profits. Flight crews are looking for other jobs, and the ground crews and reservation clerks are threatening to strike. To top it off, the federal regulatory agency is complaining about FFA's poor on-time arrivals and departures record. Alicia, an airlines consultant, has been called in to look at the problem. Here are some of the conditions that she uncovered.

1. Each department seems to be operating in a vacuum, concerned mainly with how well it runs its own operation, with little or no thought to how well it serves the needs of the other departments.

2. The operations manager continues to prepare schedules that conform to obsolete policies formulated when the airline had as its goal profits generated by low-cost operations. To compete in today's environment, the company president has said that FFA's first priority is to serve passengers' convenience; profits will have to be sacrificed until passenger miles increase.

Furthermore, there is evidence of continual feuding between ground crews and flight crews. The flight attendants complain about planes that haven't been serviced properly, and the catering crews say that they aren't given enough advance notice when special-diet meals are requested.

3. Bookings made by travel agents have deteriorated; the agents' explanation is that their clients feel that departure times are too early and arrival times too late. The agents point to the convenient schedules offered by Commuter Sky, another airline based at the same field.

The consultant also notes that FFA's schedules do not tie in closely with major airline schedules at Denver, the regional hub where most longer flights originate. "Since deregulation," says the consultant, "everyone should know that big-city hubs have become the gathering point of all air travel. Apparently, FFA has been asleep while this was happening. Lots of FFA's potential passengers want to get to South America from here, and a 4-hour wait at Denver doesn't make them very happy."

4. After reporting the above conditions, Alicia recommended that FFA appoint someone to coordinate its environment surveillance activities.

5. Among other conditions noted, the consultant also reported three situations which she felt were poorly handled by the managers in charge:

- Scheduling of times to take a plane out of service to have its motors reconditioned is haphazard. Compared with other airlines, FFA gets 18 percent less utilization of its aircraft due to unscheduled maintenance. "With some sophisticated planning, instead of this do-it-when-it-is-urgent approach," the consultant says, "use of this valuable resource would be greatly improved."

- The operations manager was overheard being abusive to ground crews when they were slow getting planes towed to the departure gates on a snowy day in February. Alicia remarked, "It looked to me as if the ground crew was understaffed for those conditions."

- When she asked how much time—on average—FFA takes to refuel a plane, the consultant was given several conflicting answers. "How can you plan anything at all without knowing how much time is required for each major task?" she asked.

Assignment Questions

1   Managers at FFA appear to be operating as if their departments exist in a:
    _____   *a.* closed system.
    _____   *b.* open system.
    _____   *c.* integrated system.
    _____   *d.* vacuum.

2 (a)   The operations manager seems unaware of and not responsive to the
    _____ influences affecting the operations department.
           _____   *a.* operational

_____ *b.* administrative
_____ *c.* strategic
_____ *d.* personal

2 (b) Internally, the flight crews and the ground crews seem to be suffering from:

_____ *a.* partisanship.
_____ *b.* factionalism.
_____ *c.* both partisanship and factionalism.
_____ *d.* neither partisanship nor factionalism.

3 (a) According to the travel agents, FFA has been slow to react to two forces in its *directly interactive* environment. Which are they?

_____ *a.* Technology; legal and political factors
_____ *b.* Economy; social and cultural factors
_____ *c.* Customers or clients; competitor
_____ *d.* Supplier; competitor

3 (b) According to the consultant, the failure of FFA's schedules to mesh with those of the Denver hub was an indication that the company was slow to react to the implications of a change in the _____ segment of its external _____ environment.

_____ *a.* customer or client; directly interactive
_____ *b.* competitor; directly interactive
_____ *c.* legal and political; indirectly interactive
_____ *d.* physical; indirectly interactive

4 What is the term commonly applied to surveillance of, and reaction to, the external environment?

_____ *a.* Adapting to change
_____ *b.* Developing relationships
_____ *c.* Boundary spanning
_____ *d.* Territory guarding

5 (a) Which managerial approach might be most suitable for improving the scheduling of motor reconditioning?

_____ *a.* Scientific management
_____ *b.* Behavioral management
_____ *c.* Management sciences
_____ *d.* Partisan management

5 (b) Which managerial approach might be most suitable for improving the performance of the ground crews?

_____ *a.* Partisan management
_____ *b.* Management sciences
_____ *c.* Scientific management
_____ *d.* Behavioral management

5 (c) Which managerial approach might be most suitable for finding the average time it takes to refuel a plane?

_____ *a.* Scientific management
_____ *b.* Cost-benefit management
_____ *c.* Behavioral management
_____ *d.* Management sciences

3
The Power of Human Resources

Managers get their jobs done through the efforts undertaken and the results accomplished by other people. These other human beings represent a powerful resource — perhaps the most powerful one available to management. The human resource, however, is an extraordinarily complex one; accordingly, managers must deploy it with care and wisdom. Employees must be told precisely what is expected of them. In return, managers must become aware of, and must respect, each employee's individuality. At the same time, managers must provide an atmosphere that encourages and nurtures each person's potential and productivity. As a further challenge, managers must also understand and harness the power of employees in their normal roles as members of formal and informal work groups.

Key Concepts Regarding the Management of Human Resources

Figure 3.1 shows the key concepts relating to human resources management. The five concepts are:

11. Organizational productivity begins with employees who know what is expected of them in terms of performance and cooperation. It is the manager's responsibility to convey this information.

12. An individual's performance is deeply dependent upon his or her unique perceptions, potential, and personality. Managers must ac-

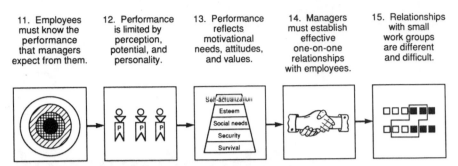

Figure 3.1. Concepts 11–15.

cept these differences between people as "givens," since they are re-lated to individuals' heredity, environment, and experience, and there is little that can be done to change them.

13. An individual's performance also reflects his or her personal needs, attitudes, and values. Managers must be sensitive to these qualities and respond to them in such a way as to create conditions that en-courage the release of each person's potential.

14. Productive one-on-one relationships with individual employees form the elements of a manager's effective relationship with the en-tire organization.

15. A manager's relationships with groups of employees take on a dif-ferent character from relationships with individual employees. Re-lationships with groups are perhaps the most difficult to create and sustain in a productive manner.

Key Terms

To make full use of these concepts, it is essential that you understand the following terms.

Performance	Theory X
Cooperation	Theory Y
Perception	Dissatisfiers
Potential	Job enhancement
Personality	Formal work groups
Hierarchy of human needs	Informal work groups
Attitudes	Homogeneous groups
Values	Stable groups

Small work groups   Roles
Group norms

Concept 11

Organizational productivity begins with employees who know what is expected of them in terms of performance and cooperation. It is the manager's responsibility to convey this information.

The foundation stone for productive relationships with employees is the employees' precise knowledge of what management and the organization expects of them in the way of performance and cooperation (Figure 3.2). Both "performance" and "cooperation" are complex concepts that require closer examination in order to grasp their full ramifications.

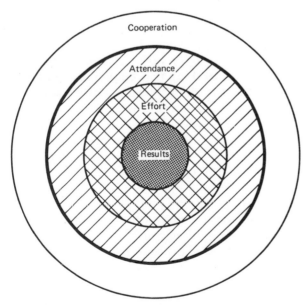

Figure 3.2. Performance expectations.

Performance

While managers are judged by the results they accomplish, employees are judged not only by their results but also by how hard they try to attain them. This is an important difference for two reasons: (1) employees do not have control over the resources that are made available to them, and (2) employees do what they do mostly at the direction of their managers.

Performance—so far as employees are concerned—is a combination of behaviors and results that are specified by management. If employees proceed as directed and accomplish the results required, then their performance can be judged as good. It should be kept in mind, however, that both the specified behavior and the expected results must be reasonable with regard to all factors affecting a particular situation.

Specification of employees' performance has three important dimensions, or measurements.

1. Attendance and Promptness.   Clearly, an organization cannot function effectively without the regular and prompt attendance of all its members. Starting times, hours of work, the need to remain at workstations, and the dependence of others on each employee's contribution to the joint effort should be stressed.

2. Effort.   Employees rarely have full control over their resources, or free choice of the methods they can use. They do, however, have control over the extent to which they apply themselves vigorously to the work at hand. The old adage of "a fair day's work for a fair day's pay" holds true. It is a mistake, however, to think that employees will know instinctively what a reasonable effort is; it must be demonstrated by example. This is relatively easy for physical tasks; it is more difficult, but still possible, for so-called knowledge work. You can, for example, readily show a laborer unloading a truck how fast to move; it takes more thought to show an accountant how fast to tally a column of figures or a salesclerk how quickly to approach a customer. Nevertheless, it can and should be done.

3. Results.   Because of the difficulty in demonstrating what makes for an acceptable effort, the practitioners of scientific management conceived of the value of specifying results. This is done by providing employees with standards with which they are expected to comply, as follows.

Output.   Simply "how many" or "how much." An engineer, for example, may be given a standard of designing 5 components a week. A claims adjuster for an insurance company, 8 claims a day. A word processing operator, 24 forms an hour. A press operator in a stamping shop, 200 units a minute.

Time.   Note that each output unit mentioned above is related to a time period. An output standard that is not related to time carries little meaning. Consequently, time is an important standard, but it must always be connected to an output figure.

Quality.   A specification of "how good." The quality of performance becomes increasingly meaningful as it relates to output. The engineer's output standard should contain a clause that states the acceptable number of incorrect calculations (zero?) or the percentage of field changes that may be tolerated. The claims adjuster might be advised that, of every 1000 claims handled, no more than 35 should result in legal suits. The quality standard for the word processor might be 1 returned form for every 200 processed. And the standard for the press operator could be 15 rejects by an inspector for every 1000 units stamped.

Cooperation

"Cooperation" is a trite word, and purists don't feel that it is fully descriptive, but it still carries a clear meaning to most managers and employees. In the sense of expectations of an employee's conduct in the workplace, **cooperation** implies three related behaviors:

1. *A ready willingness to join the common effort—sometimes called "teamwork."*   The implication is that each individual must be reasonably agreeable to working along with and giving support to others in the immediate work group. This is made clear when a manager says, for example, "You are to work each day with Mary and George, giving them a hand when they need it or when I ask you to."

2. *An acceptance of reasonable direction and instruction.*   While only a foolish manager will declare, "I'm boss and what I say goes," it should be made clear that during the normal work time, an employee will accept orders and instructions without undue questioning or outright refusals.

3. *A commitment to the job.*   Employees cannot be expected to dedicate their lives to their employers, but they can be expected to devote their attention to the work at hand and its purpose. In effect, a manager must say to employees, "When you're here—and I want you to be here during working hours—you've got a job to do that is important to me and to the organization and, I hope, to you. In any event,

during your working hours, I'll expect you to keep your eyes and mind on what you're doing."

Practical Implications

The Situation.   When Bill Dobbs took over as manager of a retail chain store for a major distributor of electronic parts, he was disturbed by a number of things. For starters, the two salesclerks routinely took turns each morning going to the cafeteria next door for coffee and donuts. During the absence of a clerk, it was common to see customers waiting for service. What was even more disturbing was that sales volume was below the company's averages. When Bill spoke to the clerks about both matters, he was rebuffed with the reply, "For what the company pays us, what do you expect?"

Question.   What should Bill say in reply?

Answer.   First of all, Bill should get his own act together—to be certain of the facts of the situation and certain, too, of the standards and expectations he wants to convey to the salesclerks. Having done that, Bill should say something like this: "Before we can discuss the matter of pay in a meaningful way, it's important for you to know exactly what I expect from you on the job. Let me make three things clear. First, no one is to leave the store during scheduled working hours. Your lunch hour, of course, is yours to do with as you please. Second, if this store is to be kept open and not moved to another location, we must average $1000 in sales a day. The company records show that sales average about $5 per customer. That's 200 customers a day. With two salesclerks on duty, I expect that each of you should, on average, handle 100 customers a day. Third, there's the matter of how you talk to customers. I expect that you'll be attentive and courteous, and that you'll provide the information that they need.

   "Are these three things clear? If so, let's take a look at your pay package and see what's wrong with it and what can be done to make it satisfactory in light of the expectations of this job."

Concept 12

An individual's performance is deeply dependent upon his or her unique perceptions, potential, and personality. Managers must accept these differences between people as "givens," since they are related to individuals' heredity, environment, and experience, and there is little that can be done to change them.

Perhaps the biggest temptation that managers face is the desire to change the basic nature of another human being—in this case, an employee. This desire is based upon the misconception that, by some mysterious process, a manager should try to imbue an employee with viewpoints, capabilities, and characteristics that nature did not bestow on that employee. Management cannot—and should not try to—change the essential nature of an individual. Management's responsibility is to find ways and to establish conditions that will enable an employee to fulfill his or her potential—so far as a particular job is concerned.

The immutable fact seems to be that nature shapes each individual in a unique way. (That's why stereotyping is so misleading when it comes to assessing and dealing with different people with superficially similar characteristics.) Three highly personal qualities are especially significant in determining how an individual copes with the world: perceptions, capabilities or potential, and personality. It is important for managers to recognize that, in any person, these qualities have already been firmly established, by the time the person reports for work. They have been shaped by the individual's heredity, by the home and cultural environment of the formative years, and by other social and job-related experiences.

Perception refers to how a person sees the world. One person will perceive a job as "boring," another as "interesting." One employee may find the boss "a tyrant," while a coworker may see the same boss as "challenging." Such differences are not a matter of truth so much as they are a matter of interpretation. We interpret what we are confronted with in such a way that it conforms to our pattern of how we think the world turns. Such patterns can help us to cope, but they can also weaken us if we insist on putting a "halo" around things we perceive as "right" and on clinging to biased assessments of things we have conditioned ourselves to view as "wrong." In an instance of *self-fulfilling prophecy*, for example, if a manager believes that an employee is irresponsible, that employee—in subtle response to the manager's assessment—will, in fact, prove to be irresponsible.

Potential covers such characteristics as "aptitude" or a person's innate capabilities to do something if properly prepared and given a chance to perform. Closely related to this is a person's learning pattern: some people are fast learners while others are slow studies. Taken together, these aptitudes and ability to learn (or to assimilate knowledge and skills) add up to a person's potential. In harsh fact, there are enormous differences in potential among the population. For many, their potential is a severely limiting factor in what kinds of jobs they can perform and the kinds of careers that they can pursue. But managers are likely to underestimate, rather than overestimate, an employee's potential; both misperceptions should be guarded against. The self-fulfilling prophecy is almost certain to work when a subordinate's potential has been undervalued by superiors.

Personality has been likened to the sum total of everything an individual is or does. In a work-related situation, however, four personality characteristics are especially important. These characteristics have great range, in that at one extreme they may be highly favorable and at the other, very undesirable.

Risk taking.   How venturesome is an individual? Will he or she like to take a crack at a difficult assignment, or prefer to back away from it?

Self-discipline.   People who have a great deal of this quality take responsibility for their own acts, exhibit self-control, and can be relied upon to do things without being told. On the other hand, people who do not have much self-discipline tend to see problems and errors as "someone else's fault."

Tolerance of ambiguity.   Some people can live with uncertainty. They are not upset by changes in routines or by normal disappointments. They are flexible, and this makes them attractive as employees. At the other extreme are inflexible people who can perform only when procedures are rigidly prescribed and when conditions and outcomes are predictable.

Self-centeredness.   This is the "I'm all right, Jack!" type of person who looks out only for number 1. At the extreme, such employees will do anything that is rewarding to them, with little thought of how it affects others. Many, many people display a degree of this quality at one time or another. When self-centeredness becomes the dominant characteristic of an individual's personality, however, it spells trouble for the organization as a whole and for any manager who must deal with it.

Practical Implications

The Situation. The East-West Hotel Corporation has made major changes in the assignments of its managers.

Rowena A., who was judged as being especially deserving for having run one of the chain's solid, traditional units in Boston for 20 years, was given the opportunity of running East-West's new venture in budget motels in Los Angeles.

Charles B., who had a great track record in hotel operations, was moved to an inside spot as director of the chain's reservation-fulfillment system. He had been a severe critic of East-West's reservation system, and it was thought that he'd be a natural to straighten it out.

Andy T., head of the chain's accounting department, was promoted to chief financial officer. There, his main responsibility would be to juggle revenues, expenses, and investments to produce the greatest possible yield on the company's excess working capital.

None of these assignments turned out successfully.

Rowena never got to southern California. After thinking over her new assignment for 2 weeks, she begged off. "That's not really an opportunity," she said. "There will be massive problems with the budget motels, and I'd be crazy to stick my neck out to try to make it work."

Charlie entered his new assignment with great zest, but within 6 months he became hopelessly bogged down in detail. Instead of improving, the reservation system got worse, and Charlie was sent back to an operations job in the field.

Andy worked like a dog, spent 10 hours a day in the office, and poured over attaché cases full of paperwork at home every weekend. By the time he was relieved from his position, he was ready for a nervous breakdown — and the returns he had earned for the company on its working capital were no better than if the money had been kept in a regular savings account.

Question.   What went wrong with these assignments?

Answer.   Rowena's perception of her situation was pessimistic. What the company's executives had envisioned as an opportunity appeared more like a threat to her. People who had worked with Rowena for years were not surprised. "She's never been a risk taker," they said. "Given a chance, she'll always opt for safe and steady."

Charlie simply wasn't a "numbers and systems" man. Charlie could drum up revenues for his operations in the field, but the auditors in the field could have told East-West's top management that Charlie had trouble balancing his books. Charlie's capabilities were in a different direction from systems, which required a kind of conceptual ability that he did not have and had never demonstrated.

Andy's problem was that, intellectually, he knew exactly what needed to be done, but he was neither a risk taker nor a person who could live with the kind of ambiguity that he found was associated with the job. Not only were the financial markets uncertain and hard to forecast, but Andy could never get a clear-cut set of instructions from the company president about how much financial liquidity he was supposed to maintain at a given moment.

Experienced managers conclude that it is vital that each person's perceptions, potential, and personality be matched as closely as possible with the job assignment.

Concept 13

An individual's performance also reflects his or her personal needs, attitudes, and values. Managers must be sensitive to these qualities and respond to them in such a way as to create conditions that encourage the release of each person's potential.

As an outgrowth of innate nature, each person also develops and responds to a set of unique inner forces that greatly affect what he or she chooses to do or not to do and how that individual goes about doing it. These forces, like perception, potential, and personality, are often not clearly understood by the individual. They are often misunderstood, or wrongly assessed, by others. Nevertheless, these are the forces that drive an individual's performance. Specifically, this set of inner forces is represented by an individual's needs (or motivation), attitudes, and values. Unless a manager can perceive the nature of these three forces within an employee—and this is not an easy task—and find a way to direct them toward productive outlets, employees are likely to be neither satisfied with their jobs nor productive in their efforts.

Human Needs

Every action a person takes, no matter how frivolous or impulsive it may appear, is an attempt to satisfy a need. In most instances, a person's actions are not taken for superficial purposes; they are taken in the hope of satisfying needs that the person holds as important. The better that a manager can sense the importance to an employee of a particular need, the more likely the manager will be able to provide conditions that will satisfy that need. By so doing, the manager provides motivation for the employee. When the motivating condition matches the employee's needs *and* the goals of the organization, the result is a productive employee.

A Hierarchy of Needs. Abraham Maslow, a noted psychologist, pointed out that people take action to satisfy needs that are important to them. He further showed that any given individual will not necessarily act in response to the same needs at two different times. What is important to an individual a week before payday may not be so important after the paycheck arrives. Maslow described a **hierarchy of human needs**, consisting of five classifications, which he arranged in order of their ascending order of importance. These needs, as shown in Figure 3.3, are survival, security, socialization, esteem, and self-actualization.

This hierarchy requires interpretation, especially when seeking to motivate employees. Needs low in the hierarchy are satisfied by such conditions as good pay, health insurance, and security from dismissal. These conditions are essentially financial. Higher-level needs are satisfied by such conditions as praise and recognition, and by opportunities to choose the methods used to perform one's own work and to set one's own work goals. These conditions are not created for employees by a company's money; they are the direct result of a manager's action.

A critical aspect of Maslow's concept is that once a need has been sat-

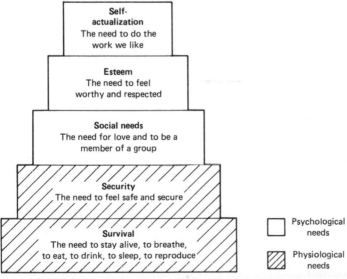

Figure 3.3. Maslow's hierarchy of needs.

isfied, it will no longer motivate an employee's behavior. The manager must then seek to create a condition that responds to an unsatisfied need — usually the lowest need that is still unsatisfied. If Dan is reasonably satisfied with his pay and job security, for example, then a small pay raise or an increase in his company-paid medical benefits isn't likely to motivate Dan to work harder. Dan's manager may have to look toward placing Dan in a position where he especially enjoys his coworkers, or grant him improved status, such as a corner office. If Dan has all those things now, the next motivational step up the hierarchy would be to allow Dan to draw up plans for the way his work should be performed and, ultimately, to set his own work goals.

Attitudes

Often one person says about another, "I don't like his [or her] attitude." What does this mean? The speaker doesn't like what the other person says? Or feels? Or does? From a manager's point of view, the most important expression of an employee's attitude is what that person does! A manager's concern is how an employee's attitude affects performance.

Attitudes are defined as the beliefs, feelings, and behavioral reactions that a person holds toward a person, an object, or an event. If Betty's attitude toward her boss or a coworker is negative, it will almost certainly affect the amount of cooperation extended that person. If Carl hates routine filing work, he is likely to try to avoid that assignment or to botch it when he's asked to do it. Or if Randy feels threatened by a performance appraisal, his conduct during the appraisal will be defensive and not focused on improvement.

A manager's best approach to employees' attitudes is to view them as a "stance," much as a baseball player assumes a unique stance in the batter's box so that he may better hit the pitch. Employees do likewise when they adopt a stance that they think will give them the best chance for dealing effectively with another person or for coping successfully with a work situation.

As you can see, attitudes are related to perceptions. Managers learn to accept a person's perception pattern, but they rightfully try to shape attitudes. Managers do this by focusing on what the employee *does* as a result of his or her attitude. If criticism is directed at the employee, for example, it should be about performance, not attitude. Good performance is praised and otherwise rewarded; poor performance is not rewarded or is discouraged. As a consequence of this approach, behavior improves — and so do attitudes. A baseball coach doesn't try to change the stance of a batter who is a good hitter; but the player who is hitting poorly soon begins to get advice about how to change his stance so as to improve his results.

Values.   A third factor, often a cornerstone upon which an employee's performance is based, is the individual's value system. Don't confuse values with perceptions, attitudes, and needs, although they are closely related. A distinction is made because values go far deeper than specific reactions to other people and outside events. Values are also especially sensitive because they reflect people's most important beliefs about themselves. **Values** are broad, general, enduring beliefs about what's truly important in life—beliefs that govern people's actions and for which they may make great sacrifices. An individual will often defend actions as being in support or defense of "my principles." Values are associated by many people with ethics or morality.

Values can be classified in several ways, as discussed below.

Pragmatic versus Ethical.   A *pragmatic value* regards situations as offering a choice of actions based upon whether or not the result will be satisfying. An *ethical value* considers the choice only as between "right" and "wrong."

An Integrated System.   In this approach, a person is thought of as having to give weight to a number of values so that some are more rigidly adhered to than others. Typical of value catagories in such a system would be values placed upon religion, status, money, quality of work, professionalism, independence, pleasure, love, and service. Thus, one employee might have a personal value-system profile with the highest weight given to money, another employee with professionalism most important, and still another employee with status most vital. Just as perceptions, personalities, and needs vary from individual to individual, so do values. The mistake that many managers make is to project their own value systems onto (expect to see them in) the employees they supervise. For example, think of the manager who says, "I appealed to Mark's sense of pride, and he didn't respond." Or "I offered Peggy a substantial raise in pay if she'd come in off the road and accept a position as head of the sales order department. She refused, saying that she didn't want to give up her independence."

Work Ethic versus Self-fulfillment.   Perhaps nothing distinguishes the younger generation from the older so much as the value placed on work. The older generation of employees was generally raised to believe in the Protestant work ethic. Simply stated, this ethic holds that work is valuable in itself, is important to the person who performs it, and ought to be the center of interest for each person's life. Since the 1960s, however, employees have challenged the validity of this ethic. Younger people, especially, are more likely to believe that work is valuable and important only insofar as it advances their pursuit of self-actualization. Managers, who are held responsible for the accomplishment of specified work, have considerable difficulty in shaping work conditions to suit the growing number of employees who hold this value.

Practical Implications

The Situation.   The Medical Center of Norton County is managed by a professional administrator, Maria Yount. She has been troubled by the high turnover rate among nurse's aides, but not among the licensed practical nurses (LPNs) who work with the registered nurses (RNs). Upon reviewing a number of exit interviews, she concludes that a typical comment from a departing nurse's aide might be: "We have to do everyone else's dirty work, and for pay that is close to the minimum wage." A summing-up statement for the few departing LPNs could be "I stayed here this long only because I liked to wear the LPN uniform and badge, but I've been disappointed by the fact that I'm not allowed to do some of the more important and difficult duties that the RNs can."

Question.   What can—and should—the administrator do to better satisfy the differing needs of the nurse's aides and the LPNs?

Answer.   Most of the LPNs are satisfied with the present working conditions. If conditions were to be changed to provide more motivation, it appears that increased status wouldn't be quite enough to fully satisfy their needs for esteem. Perhaps what they need is to be given greater recognition for the value of their work and to be assigned tasks that provide a greater challenge to their skills. As for the nurse's aides, the administrator should review their pay rates, since there is a strong indication that their survival needs are hardly being met by the Medical Center's current wage scale. Once their survival needs are satisfied by higher wages, the administrator should probably look for a way of increasing the status of the nurse's aides in order to meet their unsatisfied needs for esteem.

Concept 14

Productive one-on-one relationships with individual employees form the elements of a manager's effective relationships with the entire organization.

Satisfied employees are not necessarily more productive than dissatisfied employees. Their attendance, however, is better, and they have fewer complaints. Most important to the manager is a realization that harmonious relationships with all employees can become the elements of a productive organization. With dissatisfied or nonmotivated employees, there will be no foundation for such an organization.

Productive relationships depend to a great extent upon what a manager thinks of employees' motivations. The manager's view can be either positive or negative. With a positive attitude, a manager is ready to build mutual confidence and to encourage good performance by providing realistic rewards and by enhancing the intrinsic motivation in each employee's job.

Employees: For or Against Them?.   A manager's view of the essential nature of human beings, especially as employees, will determine what avenue the manager takes to motivate them. To clarify the choices, Douglas McGregor, professor of management at Massachusetts Institute of Technology, described two contrasting views that may be held about the nature of human beings in relation to work, as shown in Table 3.1. McGregor dubbed these two views "Theory X" (the negative view) and "Theory Y" (the positive view.)

Table 3.1. McGregor's Theory X and Theory Y
Two Contrasting Views of Human Nature in Work Situations

Theory X	Theory Y
The average person	
Dislikes and avoids work.	Finds work as natural as play.
Must be forced or threatened with punishment before making an effort to meet organizational goals.	Is most motivated by the inherent satisfaction of work, not by coercion.
Is passive and likes to be told what to do rather than to accept responsibility.	Becomes committed to goals through rewards for individual initiative and action.
	Accepts and seeks responsibility.
	Is creative in solving an organization's problems.

Theory X holds that people do not like work and that some kind of direct pressure and control must be exerted to get them to work effectively. This view calls for a rigidly managed environment filled with threats of disciplinary action. An underlying belief of Theory X is that monetary rewards are the only incentive to which employees will respond.

Theory Y takes the opposite point of view. It holds that people enjoy work and do it willingly *if* the work appears meaningful to them and *if* they are given the opportunity to become personally involved with its planning. This approach stresses the importance of providing opportunities for decision making and for determining one's own working conditions.

McGregor never claimed that either view is correct. His implication is that a manager's approach to developing relationships and creating motivating conditions will directly reflect the view that he or she holds. Despite McGregor's disclaimers about which view is correct, managers and would-be managers should consider these observations:

- The attitude toward work of today's generation of employees mirrors the Theory Y concept.

- Most managers have little or no control over an organization's compensation practices; accordingly, they have little control over pay as an incentive under Theory X.

- On the other hand, managers have far greater access to the motivational incentives indicated by Theory Y.

The choice to be weighed by a manager is whether to approach employee relationships from a negative or a positive point of view. The question each manager must ask — in each particular situation — is: Which viewpoint will lead to the most productive relationships over the long run?

Productive Relationships

Productive relationships are formed around mutual trust and respect. Few things can be clearer in concept but more difficult to pursue. It is almost impossible to generate trust and respect if a manager's view is based upon Theory X. It cannot be denied, however, that a great many employees may fall into behavior patterns that induce mistrust and disrespect. The implication is that *managers* must initiate the development of mutual confidence. In effect, employees should be deemed interested in performing well and in providing their own self-discipline until proved otherwise.

Such an approach demands much of the manager, whose confidence will be tested many times before it is believed and accepted by reluctant employees. The process is slow, with inevitable backsliding. Without mutual respect and confidence, nothing productive will occur. But, as John W. Gardner wrote in his best-selling book *Self-Renewal,* "The confidence you have in others will in some degree determine the confidence they have in themselves."[1]

Job Enhancement

Another noted sociologist, Frederick Herzberg, gave additional meaning to the work of both Maslow and McGregor. He saw an important link between the two. In effect, Herzberg observed that in an affluent society there is little a manager can do to satisfy the lower levels of Maslow's hierarchy. At the minimum, employees expect survival wages and reasonable security. Without these, Herzberg reasoned, employees will be dissatisfied, but they won't necessarily work harder because they receive them. Herzberg asked, "What *is* left to managers for motivating their employees?" He concluded that only conditions that satisfy higher-level needs are left for motivational purposes. Accordingly, Herzberg set aside appeals to survival, security, and social needs as **dissatisfiers.** That is, without a reasonable set of conditions at those levels, employees will be dissatisfied enough to look elsewhere for work, but they will not work harder because of improvements in these conditions.

Motivation can take place, Herzberg advised, when managers create the following conditions for their employees:

- Work that is challenging and meaningful
- Opportunities to develop and use their skills to the fullest extent
- Involvement in decisions that affect the methods they use and the performance goals they are supposed to attain

Other observers have noted that what Herzberg called his "Two-Factor Theory" matches up fairly well with (1) Maslow's *physiological,* lower-level needs and *psychological,* upper-level needs and (2) McGregor's Theory X at the lower levels and Theory Y at the higher levels, as shown in Figure 3.4.

[1]W. W. Norton & Co., Inc., New York, rev. ed., 1981.

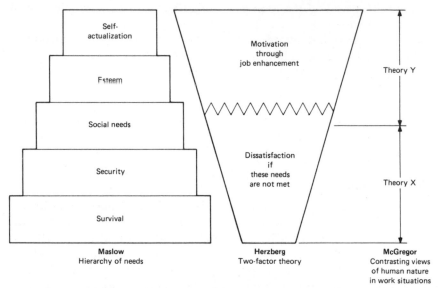

Figure 3.4. Relationships of Maslow's hierarchy of needs to McGregor's Theory X and Theory Y and to Herzberg's Job Enhancement.

Since Herzberg's research took place, many managers have lumped the approaches to satisfying upper-level motivational needs under the term "job enhancement." **Job enhancement** encompasses those actions that a manager takes to incorporate into an employee's work the conditions listed above.

Practical Implications

The Situation.   Fran Burke manages a labor crew that works regularly on highway construction jobs. The pay is comparatively good, but the work is hot, heavy, and repetitive. Despite the good pay, absenteeism is high. Crew members take unauthorized breaks on the job. Long-service employees delight in finding ways to delay the work. Fran is constantly on their case, nagging and pushing to get the day's work done. Fran's crew is looked upon as the least productive one in the company. The site superintendents have been known to declare, "Send any labor crew out on this job except Fran's." When her boss queried her about this, Fran's reply was, "What do you expect me to do with a bunch of dingbats like these?"

Question.   What might Fran do to to improve the productivity of her crew?

Answer. It seems obvious that Fran has a Theory X philosophy about her workers, and it isn't getting results. Since pay is satisfactory and many of the problem employees have the security of long service, Herzberg would direct Fran's attention to the possibility of enhancing the crew's work so as to appeal to their upper-level needs. For instance, Fran might pursue the following course: (1) openly praise workers who stay on the job and don't delay, while ignoring the problem workers; (2) allow the better workers to choose their places on the site each day; (3) invite all workers — problem employees as well as cooperating ones — to discuss each day's job before it begins, seeking the best ways to approach it; and (4) set a daily target goal, slightly higher than what the crew has been achieving in the past, as a challenge.

Because Fran is dealing with a group rather than with individuals, however, the effectiveness of items 1 and 2 above may be lessened, as explained under concept 15.

Concept 15

A manager's relationships with groups of employees take on a different character from relationships with individual employees. Relationships with groups are perhaps the most difficult to create and sustain in a productive manner.

A group of employees is more than just a collection of individuals: a group takes on a character of its own and must be dealt with as an entity. Groups may be established by formal directions from management, or they may coalesce gradually and informally. This distinction is illustrated in Figure 3.5. Whatever their source, groups develop definitive characteristics which may be either a help or a hindrance to management.

Formal work groups are established by management in order to specify exactly who does what and in relation to whom. These are groups that are designated as "divisions," "departments," "sections," "project teams," "committees," and so forth. You'll learn more about the process of forming such groups in Chapter 5.

Informal work groups might better be described as "friendship" groups or "shared-interests" groups. Their purposes and relationships do not necessarily have a work orientation, although such groups can have a strong impact upon a particular work situation. Informal groups come together in a variety of ways. Individuals from different depart-

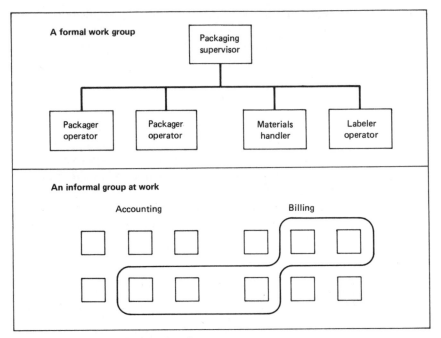

Figure 3.5. Formal and informal work groups.

ments who bowl in the same league, ride in the same carpool, or live in the same neighborhood may be seen at work as having a common interest. Individuals in the same department may form cliques because they use the same kinds of skills, or resent the same boss or coworker, or dislike or prefer a particular kind of work. Often, groups form simply because individuals are attracted to others with similar personalities.

Characteristics of Groups

Groups can be homogeneous or of mixed membership, stable or unstable, large or small.

Homogeneous groups tend to hang together and resist outside influences better than heterogeneous groups. A manager, for example, will encounter greater resistance when trying to impose a change in work rules on a homogeneous group than on a group with mixed membership.

Stable groups have little change in membership. They are likely to act like a closed society—demanding loyalty from members and presenting a strong front to outsiders, such as people with other skills or in other departments. *Unstable groups* tend to be more open, but as a consequence, are less predictable in their behavior. A manager may think, for example, that a group of clerical employees are relatively passive, only to unexpectedly meet opposition to new ideas when new employees are introduced into the department.

Small work groups have been said to be "the building blocks of organizations." This is because, as collective entities, they wield so much influence for good or for harm — or for indifference. Small groups tend to be more tightly knit, to communicate more quickly, and to distribute power more equitably among the members than do large groups. Large groups may have greater resources and, hence greater creativity, but they tend (1) to splinter into smaller factions or (2) to form a number of disruptive leader-subordinate relationships.

Norms and Roles in Small Work Groups

Groups, especially the small groups that a manager organizes formally and the small groups that emerge informally, develop a singular sort of power. Specifically, groups establish norms to which its members are expected to conform and roles that distribute informal responsibilities. These norms and roles may function to assist in or detract from attainment of the formal goals of an organization.

Group norms are standards of acceptable behavior that gradually evolve within a group. Adherence to these norms by group members strengthens the group's cohesiveness and demonstrates it to outsiders. Many norms are essentially innocuous, like wearing similar clothing, styling hair the same way, or talking with the same jargon. Other norms can convey considerable power, as when a group suggests to its members how much work will be produced or how good or poor the quality of work will be. Norms also extend to establishing when and how complaints will be handled — for example, insisting that they be channeled through the group's informal spokesperson (Figure 3.6). Norms about work and about complaints are rarely announced to outsiders; managers become aware of them mainly through observation. Accordingly, norms are not only pervasive within small groups but are also often subtly concealed from management. Members, however, are acutely aware of the norms and will conform even to norms that go counter to their own standards and values.

Roles, as first discussed in Chapter 1, are parts that an individual plays in, or for, an organization. In small work groups, roles are very informal. They emerge as the group, often unconsciously, assigns parts to its various members. One person may be the entertainer, who

Figure 3.6. Examples of group norms being enforced.

tells jokes and keeps the group amused; another may be the enforcer, who makes sure that members respect the norms; and still another the leader, to whom the group looks for direction.

Harnessing the Power of Small Work Groups

A small work group uses its norms and roles to build cohesiveness and to advance or protect the group's interests. Managers must accept this fact of organization life, whether the group has been established as part of the organizational scheme or has simply emerged informally. Group cohesiveness can be viewed by managers as a neutral power—one that can be directed either toward attaining legitimate organizational goals or toward obstructing them. The challenge to a manager, then, is to induce this power to act in a positive direction. How is this accomplished? The guidelines listed below will help most managers to optimize their group relationships.

1. Accept the inevitability of group formation.
2. Avoid confrontations with the group's norms or role players.
3. As far as possible, deal with individuals directly rather than through their informal spokespeople or leaders.
4. Protect the rights of individual employees at all times, but don't ask group members to isolate themselves by becoming management's role models and acting contrary to the group's norms.
5. Introduce opportunities for the group to participate collectively in choosing their work methods and in setting production goals.
6. Do not abdicate a manager's ultimate responsibility for planning, or-

ganizing, staffing, directing, and controlling the work of groups as well as of individuals.

Practical Implications

The Situation. One of the pioneering studies of small-group influence took place in the early 1930s at the Hawthorne Works of Western Electric Company, outside Chicago. The researchers observed, among other things, that workers there would walk behind certain other employees and snap their fingers sharply against the backs of their necks. The workers referred to this practice as "binging."

Question. What was the significance of the practice of binging other workers?

Answer. The bingers were enforcers, whose roles called for them to act on the group's behalf to remind workers who were producing more than the group's agreed-upon daily output that they were violating an important group norm. Workers were paid according to an incentive plan related to how much an individual produced as compared with a production standard. It was in the group's interest not to exceed the standard by so much that the company might raise the standard, requiring everyone to work faster to make the same amount of money as under the existing standard.

Comprehension-Check Case for Chapter 3

The Case of the Contrary Claims Department

For easy reference, the text of the comprehension-check case is numbered to correspond to the assignment questions that follow.

The claims department of the Shawmut Security Insurance Company has had a spotty record. On the one hand, claims payments far exceed the industry's norms; on the other hand, the company's sales agents are complaining that they are losing clients because of slow and discourteous service from the adjusters.

Claims represent an important aspect of the company's business. Claudia H., senior vice president, heads up the entire operation. Two *general managers* report to her—one in charge of *claims investigation,* and the other in charge of *claims services*. Several *claims managers* report to each general manager. In turn, there are dozens of *claims examiners* (who report to the claims-investigation managers) and dozens of *claims adjusters* (who report to the claims-services managers.) The claims-investigation activity is essentially a home-office, inside operation. The claims-services activity is essentially a field, outside activity.

1. Many of the claims examiners are adjusters who have come in from the field. This presents a problem for George J., claims-investigation manager for the southeast region. George has not been a field adjuster, but he does know a lot about the work of the internal claims examiners. Because of travel problems and difficulty in locating clients, field adjusters handle only about 50 claims a week, whereas inside claims examiners can routinely handle more than 4 times that number. Furthermore, adjusters in the field can arrange their own daily schedules, but George plans the schedules for his claims examiners. Marge K., one of the examiners, has become a particular problem for George. Her productivity is far below what George expects from a claims examiner, and when he asks Marge to work through her list of claims in alphabetical sequence, she retorts that she has her own way of arranging her work and will continue to arrange it her own way.

2. It turns out that Marge considers George to be just another authority figure who will push her around if she doesn't set him straight from the beginning. George, for his part, has decided that Marge is only capable of handling claims adjustments in a face-to-face manner and will never be able to handle the paperwork and analysis associated with the inside claims examiner's job. "Besides," George thinks, "Marge isn't capable of providing her own self-discipline, and I have to supervise her closely. Otherwise, she'd never get her work done."

3. George himself, of course, could bear closer examination. He has been a manager of claims investigation for over 10 years and desperately wants to be promoted to general manager. His pay and job benefits are OK, he says, but that isn't enough after all these years.

4. George also feels that he has been around long enough to know that ex-adjusters are a pretty unreliable lot and will take advantage of him whenever they get a chance.

At the end of Marge's first 6 months, she comes up for a performance review. George points out that she is still not producing up to standard. Marge argues that she should get a merit pay increase anyway. George, however, points out that only those whose performance is excellent receive such increases. Marge is unhappy about that. This leaves George puzzled about how to persuade Marge to improve her productivity. He can see that Marge likes her pay and likes the company. She had years of service in the field, and she isn't about to be fired. She also likes the status that goes with the job of claims examiner.

5. As if his problems with Marge aren't enough, George feels that somehow or other he has lost control over the relationship his claims examiners

are having with the field adjusters who report to the manager of claims services. His examiners are supposed to cooperate, but in more than one instance lately, they have let a claim document referred to them from the other department "fall between the desks," and in these instances, not until a sales representative complained has the matter been handled properly. These complaints are making George look bad with his boss.

In querying the examiners about this problem, George gets little information until he talks with Jose X. Jose says, "I don't know what this is all about, but I do know that those field adjusters are trying to pass the buck to us whenever they encounter a difficult case. I suggest that if you want to get to the bottom of this you speak to Marge, who keeps us informed about what the field adjusters are up to." George does speak to Marge, who sheds little light on the situation except to say, "If the field people want any help from us, they'll have to put it in writing. They have been dumping lots of problems over here, and we're not going to lift a finger until they go through the right channels." "Do all of you feel this way?" asks George. "All of us who came in from the field do," replies Marge.

Assignment Questions

1 (a)   In order to get Marge on the right track regarding her performance, George should:

_____   *a.* tell Marge she'll have to shape up or she will face severe disciplinary action.

_____   *b.* specify exactly how many claims must be adjusted during an average week and how many errors could be tolerated.

_____   *c.* tell Marge how much of a problem she has become.

_____   *d.* appeal to Marge's sense of responsibility.

1 (b)   To secure greater cooperation from Marge in accepting instructions, George should:

_____   *a.* strike a compromise about what instructions Marge will or will not comply with.

_____   *b.* because of her experience, allow Marge to arrange her work sequence as she sees fit.

_____   *c.* agree that Marge should discuss with George the appropriateness of each order and instruction as it is issued.

_____   *d.* insist that routine orders and instructions must be followed without debate; unusual ones may be questioned.

2 (a)   Marge's typifying of George as an authority figure is an example of:

_____   *a.* her perception of the world.

_____   *b.* her potential for insight.

_____   *c.* the self-centeredness of her personality.

_____   *d.* her low tolerance of ambiguity.

2 (b)   In assessing Marge's potential, George has probably:

_____   *a.* given her the benefit of any doubt.

_____   *b.* based his judgment upon rational analysis.

_____ *c.* overvalued her potential.

_____ *d.* undervalued her potential.

2 (c)   George's observation about Marge's inability to provide her own self-discipline is an assessment of Marge's:

_____ *a.* personality.

_____ *b.* perceptions.

_____ *c.* attitudes.

_____ *d.* motivation.

3   If you were to satisfy George's most evident unsatisfied need, as classified by Maslow, it would be the _____ need.

_____ *a.* security

_____ *b.* socialization

_____ *c.* esteem

_____ *d.* self-actualization

4 (a)   George appears to be a believer in the _____ philosophy of motivation.

_____ *a.* behavioral

_____ *b.* integrated

_____ *c.* Theory X

_____ *d.* Theory Y

4 (b)   Which of the following approaches might George try to stimulate Marge's productivity?

_____ *a.* Appeal to her lower-level needs.

_____ *b.* Appeal to her physiological needs.

_____ *c.* Follow Herzberg's advice about creating motivational conditions.

_____ *d.* Use a Theory X approach since Marge is obviously a Theory X type of person.

5 (a)   All the claims examiners belong to a(n) _____ work group, but some of those who had previously been field adjusters also belong to a(n) _____ work group.

_____ *a.* homogeneous; heterogeneous

_____ *b.* stable; unstable

_____ *c.* informal; formal

_____ *d.* formal; informal

5 (b)   Marge played an important _____ for the informal group of examiners in establishing and protecting the _____ of not cooperating with the field adjusters. (Choose the terms that the text uses to describe these activities and conditions.)

_____ *a.* role; norm

_____ *b.* norm; role

_____ *c.* part; standard

_____ *d.* position; goal

PART II

What Managers Do

4

Planning: Setting Goals and Creating Plans and Programs

Planning is a comprehensive process in which managers formulate the specific goals of an organization and develop the plans for attaining them. The planning process is critical, since the goals (or objectives) established thereby limit the scope of an organization's activities as well as its plans. Effective planning is future-oriented as well as systematic. In developing their strategies, managers must recognize the limitations placed upon an organization by its environment. Operational planning provides the cutting edge for a company's strategic plans in that it deals with down-the-line specifics of its resources to create specific plans and schedules. Finally, many organizations use a technique called "management by objectives" (MBO) as an incentive, a control, or both, in an effort to bring the plans and actions of its managers closer to its objectives.

Key Concepts Regarding the Planning Process

Figure 4.1 is a graphic representation of the key concepts that relate to the planning process. The five concepts are:

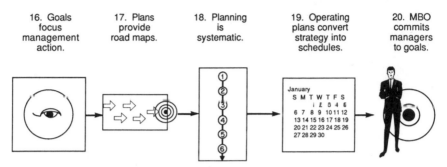

| 16. Goals focus management action. | 17. Plans provide road maps. | 18. Planning is systematic. | 19. Operating plans convert strategy into schedules. | 20. MBO commits managers to goals. |

Figure 4.1. Concepts 16–20.

16. Goals and objectives specify targets that (a) support an organization's survival and (b) provide focus for management's actions and employees' efforts.

17. Strategic and operating plans delineate the paths to be followed in seeking to fulfill an organization's mission and goals.

18. Effective planning follows a systematic process.

19. Operational planning converts strategies into specific timetables by using a variety of forecasting and scheduling techniques.

20. Management by objectives provides a mechanism for encouraging managers to coordinate personal and departmental plans with organizational goals.

Key Terms

To make full use of the key concepts, you will need to understand the following terms:

Mission	Budget
Goals	Planning premise
Mission statement	Survey-method forecast
Goals statement	Historical-trends forecast
Strategic plan	Statistical analysis forecast
Policy	Process capacity
Procedure	Time studies
Rule or regulation	Master schedule
Operating plan	Point-to-point plan
Project	Overlap, or parallel, plans

Gantt chart   Management by objectives
Network plan

Concept 16

Goals and objectives specify targets that (a) support an organization's survival and (b) provide focus for management's actions and employees' efforts.

Goals—or objectives (the terms can be used interchangeably)—state (1) the broad purposes of and (2) the specific targets for an organization. The broad purposes, which become the **mission**, serve as a navigational azimuth, or direction, toward which an organization is steered. The specific targets, usually called **goals**, describe the specific, concrete targets, or standards, that an organization or department is expected to reach in a given period of time.

A complete **mission statement** includes (1) a description of the organization's basic products or services, (2) the functions that it will perform, and (3) the markets or clients it will serve. For example:

- *A food company.* We will prepare and distribute fine-quality packaged foods to national retailers.

- *An insurance company.* We will provide a wide variety of financial services to consumer and commercial customers in northern California.

- *A hospital.* We will provide voluntary health care to all residents of our community.

- *A manufacturing company.* We will design and manufacture metal and plastic valves and fittings, and will market them to home builders through a national network of industrial distributors.

- *A state agency.* We will supervise the equitable distribution of welfare funds to authorized city and county agencies.

A typical **goals statement** will include a range, from rather broad goals at the top of the organization to highly specific goals at the lower levels. At either extreme, goal descriptions are far more specific than mission statements. The time period should be clearly stated and the goals quantified when at all possible. Use of numbers makes it relatively simple to determine whether or not a goal has been reached. Below are some examples of goals statements.

- *A corporate goals statement for a manufacturing company.* Our goal for next year will be to:
  Generate sales revenues of $50 million.
  Make a profit of $5 million, or 10 percent of sales.
  Capture 15 percent of the national market for our product.
- *For the same corporation's production department.* Our goal for next year will be to:
  Manufacture 200,000 units.
  Have fewer than 2 percent defects at inspection.
  Reduce production costs by 7 percent.
- *For the same corporation's purchasing department.* Our goal for next year will be to:
  Reduce cost of raw materials by 3 percent.
  Reduce inventory storage costs by 15 percent.
  Have better than 95 percent of all shipments of raw material arrive on time.
- *For the accounts receivables department of a department store chain.* Our goal for the first quarter of this year will be to:
  Collect 75 percent of all accounts within 30 days.
  Collect 98 percent of all accounts within 90 days.
  Reduce bad debts attributed to uncollected accounts to less than 2 percent.
- *For a small, local welfare agency.* This week, the goals of our social-workers team will be to:
  Make 75 home or on-site visits.
  Conduct 25 verification interviews with employers, pastors, neighbors, etc.
  Seek to release 5 percent of unqualified clients from the agency's caseload, and replace them with qualified applicants from the waiting list.

Characteristic Features of Goals

From a practical standpoint, goals in an organization typically have the following characteristics:

1. There are multiple goals. The number of goals may range from four or five to a dozen. Typically, goals will include sales, profits, production, market share, and a number of measurable targets related to the particular function for which the goals are set.
2. Goals are arranged in a hierarchy. That is, some goals will be, either explicitly or implicitly, more important than others. A sales-revenue

goal, for example, will usually rank higher than a profit or production goal, since each of the latter will be dependent upon the amount of sales generated.

3. The time horizon for goals will vary. A long-range goal for a corporation may extend from 1 year to as many as 10 years. A short-term goal may be anything from a day or a week for an operating section to a month, a quarter, or up to a year for larger departments and divisions of an organization.

4. From an individual manager's point of view, goals are either *dependent* or *controllable*. The great majority of goals will be dependent in that they will be issued to the manager, or, if he or she sets them, the goals will be dependent upon their tying in directly with other goals of the organization. Controllable goals are those that a manager may set independently, as when the head of a maintenance department sets a goal such as "having fewer than 5 percent callbacks on jobs that we have repaired" or when the sales manager establishes a goal of "10 customer calls per salesperson per day."

5. Goals should always specify what, where, and when: *what* is to be accomplished; *where* it should be done, if location is significant; and *when* — by what time or date the goal should be reached.

Practical Implications

The Situation. Neil Borden, division manager of the Family-Farm Foods chain of supermarkets, issued the following message to store managers just before the start of the new year:

> We intend to be the most price-competitive food chain in our market area. To maintain this position, I will expect each store manager to:
>
> - Keep food spoilage to a minimum.
> - Keep overtime charges as low as possible.
> - Maintain minimum inventories of merchandise.
> - Place restocking orders for merchandise far enough in advance to give our purchasing people time to negotiate the best deals.
> - Make sure that newspaper advertising expenses stay in line.
> - Use extra care when accepting coupons.

Six months later, the division manager was unhappy when he was called onto the carpet by the president, Sarah Price. She challenged him on the following issues: (1) profits in his division were not up to expectations, and (2) she thought quality and customer service might be a better way to achieve profits than price cutting. She also showed him the financial analysis of operations of the stores in his district for the first 6 months of the year. Food spoilage and overtime expenses were higher than the company average, and so were advertising expenses. Inventory levels and coupon charges were low, however. But the purchasing department was repeatedly complaining to her about late or rush orders from the store managers.

Question. What was unfair about the president's complaints? What might the division manager have done to make his year-end message more effective?

Answer. A company's mission is more the president's responsibility than the division manager's. Is the company's mission to make the most profits, and if so, by what means? Lower prices? Higher-quality foods? Better service? These aspects of the mission should be made clear before goals can be established meaningfully. Mission precedes goals.

The division manager's goals statement was not clear and quantified. It did not specify the time period in which the goals must be attained. It contained terms like "minimum," "as low as possible," "far enough in advance," "in line," and "extra care." He might have better stated his message as concrete goals to be met "no later than the end of June." For each goal, a specific number would remove all vagueness. For example, food spoilage at "less than 5 percent," overtime "not to exceed 500 hours per store per month," inventory levels at "20 percent lower than monthly sales," orders placed "no later than 3 weeks before merchandise is needed," advertising expenses "at 4 percent of sales," and coupons "99 percent verifiable."

This situation illustrates several things: (1) how a mission provides a framework for establishing goals, (2) that goals need to be time-related and quantified, (3) that multiple goals are present in an organization, and (4) that they occur in a hierarchy. Which goals in this situation, for example, appear more important than others? There is a hierarchy—implied here—that begins with profits, and then descends in this sequence: inventory levels, restocking, advertising, food spoilage, overtime, and coupons.

Concept 17

Strategic and operating plans delineate the paths to be followed in seeking to fulfill an organization's mission and goals.

Plans are the road maps that an organization follows to reach its goals. If plans are well-conceived, they will lead managers and employees to the desired destinations. Well-conceived plans specify at least 10 factors:

1. Resources to be used, such as facilities, equipment, materials, finances, information, and employee staffs
2. Methods, processes, and procedures to be employed
3. Tasks to be performed, often each with its own standard or goal to be attained
4. Sequence, or steps, to be followed
5. Individuals who are to perform the tasks, as well as those who will be held responsible for implementing the plan and accomplishing the goals
6. A reiteration of the related goal, or an extraction or projection of that goal as it applies to the particular plan
7. The location where the plan's activities are to take place
8. Associated deadlines, timetables, and schedules
9. Points along the way at which progress is to be checked
10. Designation of measurements to be used in gauging progress and verifying goal attainment

Plans can be classified according to their relationships to an organization's mission and goals, as shown in Figure 4.2.

Strategic Plans

The plans that frame the big picture painted by the mission statement are called **strategic plans**. Typically, their planning horizon is 5

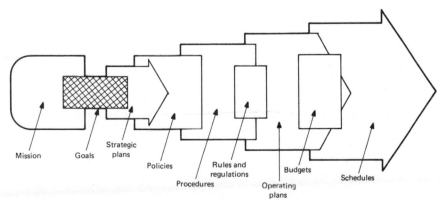

Figure 4.2. How plans interlock: from missions to schedules.

years or more. They are conceptual in nature in that they lay out general guidelines rather than detailed schedules. For example, a manufacturing company may say that its strategy is "to limit investment by purchasing, rather than fabricating, parts, and to assemble them for sale." A computer service company may say that its strategy is "to be the low-priced competitor by processing data only at remote locations where clerical help is inexpensive." A fast-food chain's avowed strategy may be "to maintain our number 1 position by out-advertising all competitors."

Strategic plans are often called "long-range plans," and many companies do not differentiate between their strategies, missions, and long-range plans. Almost all mature companies, however, develop a series of guidelines, called "policies," as an expression of their strategic plans.

A **policy** is a standing plan that provides managers with general guidelines for making decisions. Its main purpose is to assure consistency among an organization's managers and to avoid having to make the same decision over and over again. A policy may be developed for almost any decision area. For example:

- *For personnel administration.*   Our policy is to promote from within.
- *For purchasing.*   Our policy is to have at least three suppliers for each commodity that we buy.
- *For marketing.*   Our policy is to distribute only through wholesalers.
- *For finance.*   Our policy is never to allow our borrowing to exceed 20 percent of our capital financing.

A **procedure** is another form of standing plan. It is far more concrete and detailed than a policy. Typically, a procedure specifies how a recurring task is to be done, enumerating the steps involved and the sequence to be followed. Many organizations establish and maintain a standard operating procedures manual. The procedures in the manual usually describe how a policy is to be carried out. For example, the procedure for the purchasing department in carrying out the policy stated above may be:

1. Before making any purchase commitments, review at least six potential vendors.

2. From among the vendors reviewed, select three vendors, based upon the following criteria:....

3. Proceed with negotiations with these vendors, with final approval required from the company controller.

A **rule** or **regulation** is a further extension of a standing plan. A rule differs from a policy, which is a general guideline, or a procedure, which often allows for some leeway, in that it prescribes a course of action that *must* be followed. As an extension of the purchasing policy and procedure illustrated above, an associated rule may be, "No vendor may supply more than 60 percent of the company's purchases of a particular commodity over a year's period."

Operating Plans

Those plans that focus on short-term objectives are called "tactical plans," or **operating plans**. Their horizon is almost always 1 year or less. Some organizations differentiate between "operating plans" and "operating programs," using the latter term to indicate a plan of broader scope and, perhaps, longer duration. The majority of operating plans are "single-use" plans. That is, a plan is prepared for this week's production, or next month's advertising campaign, or this year's college recruiting. Any of these single-use plans may be repeated with slight variations, but when this occurs, the specific features of dates and people are likely to change. Finally, there are projects. A **project** is a single-use plan, usually of a fixed duration, designed to accomplish a single, often narrowly focused objective.

Probably the most common single-use operating plan is a budget. A **budget** specifies the measurable amount of resources that will be assigned to a particular plan. While budgets are, more often than not, expressed in dollars, they typically encompass equipment, materials, and labor as well.

Five-Point Checklist

Goals and plans are essentially inseparable. Accordingly, a good plan incorporates the three pivotal goal specifications into five vital elements of a plan. As shown in Figure 4.3, this means that all plans should cover the five points *what, where, when, how,* and *who.* Goals designate the "what," "where," and "when"; plans add to these the "how" and "who," as will be demonstrated under concept 18.

Practical Implications

The Situation. Inez was elated. She had just been promoted to divisional vice president on the strength of her performance as manager of the company's client-services department. Inez carefully reviewed in her mind what she had done to make her work there so successful. This is what she could recall:

What	Objectives	Specifications
		Cost/price limits
Where	Locale	Delivery point
When	Time elapsed	Starting date
		Completion date
How	Operating plans	Methods Procedure Sequence
Who	Responsibility	Authority Control Assignment

Figure 4.3. Five-point planning checklist.

The vice president of the division had issued this policy:

Client service should take precedence over routine conveniences; we should attempt to be efficient, but not at the client's discomfort.

Inez had prepared the following memorandum for her staff:

In all contacts with company clients, an attempt should be made to follow this procedure:

1. Introduce yourself and describe your function.
2. Listen carefully to the client to gather information about his or her request.
3. If you have an immediate solution, offer it then; if not, advise the client that you will obtain one within 3 working days.
4. If necessary, obtain the information needed to provide an accurate response.
5. Call the client back within the 3-day period and present your response. Always return the call within the 3-day period, even if you have not obtained the necessary information.
6. If the client is not satisfied with your response, in either instance, refer the client to me. (*Note:* Whatever you do, do not argue with a client!)
7. After closing the interview, make a record of its disposition in your daily file. (*Note:* Since this procedure may be more time-consuming than our past procedure, I've set a new goal of 350 client contacts per week, as compared with the present 400. I've also set a goal of receiving fewer than 1 complaint per 500 contacts with clients.)

At the end of each week, Inez reviewed the daily files with each of her staff (1) to verify that calls had been returned within the 3-day period, and (2) to see whether the client-contact goals were being attained. She also maintained her own file of calls referred to her and of complaints that she or other officials received from clients about the service.

Question. What were the features that Inez incorporated into her plans that made them so effective?

Answer. Inez had accomplished the following:

- Established a memorandum of procedures that would enable the company policy to be implemented.

- Reinforced the policy's intent and a key step of the procedure with two unequivocal rules.

- Set a goal for the staff that would help to assure that, while implementing the policy of customer convenience, the department would also "attempt to be efficient."

- Followed up on her procedure to see if it were being observed by her staff, and if the goal of 350 contacts per week, with only 1 client complaint per 500 contacts, were being met.

Concept 18

Effective planning follows a systematic process.

It has been demonstrated time and again that organizations that engage in systematic planning have better success records than those that do not. While effective planning requires an often uncertain look into the future, the process is, essentially, a logical one. It should proceed, step by step, in an orderly manner so that no important influence or factor is overlooked.

The Planning Process

There are several variations of what consists of a systematic approach to planning. Almost all approaches, however, include the following steps, in the sequence shown here:

Step 1. Determine the objectives. The goal of even the simplest plan or project should be consistent with the goals of the enterprise as a whole. A typical objective statement might read like this: "Reduce the manufactured cost of a 3-inch OD high-carbon steel gear (cat. no. 6 X

571) from $5 per unit to $4 per unit (*what*); deliver it, fully packed and ready for shipment, to the plant warehouse (*where*) by 12 weeks from date of plan initiation (*when*)."

Step 2. Evaluate the situation. Before going ahead with development of a procedure to reach the objective, the circumstances that may affect a plan in any way must be assessed. Such an assessment looks in two directions: outside the immediate organization and inside it. *When assessing the external environment,* a manager looks to see (a) what opportunities there might be (from new technology, for example) to help speed up a plan and (b) what threats there are (from a possible price increase from a supplier, for example) that might prevent the plan from reaching its objective.

When assessing conditions within the enterprise, a manager evaluates the (a) strengths and (b) weaknesses of the resources available for the plan or project, such as facilities, materials, labor, and money.

The assumptions that a manager makes about these external and internal circumstances become the **planning premises** upon which the plan itself will be based. Obviously, the more certain these premises are, the better the chances for the plan to succeed.

Step 3. Establish the procedure. A plan must establish not only the tasks to be performed and the methods for performing them, but also the sequence in which these tasks are to be carried out. The procedure is, of course, the process whereby resources are converted to results. Each step of the procedure should incorporate (a) specifications of what is to be done, (b) a time dimension (a beginning as well as an ending time helps to assure that each step is begun on time), and (c) the person or persons who will be responsible.

Step 4. Set a timetable. This may seem redundant, or out of order, since deadlines are considered when goals are set. It is simply a fact of the planning process, which is somewhat like the chicken-and-egg dilemma. Time that is specified in the objective statement influences the methods selected for the procedure; the methods and other resources available for the procedure will influence the overall deadline and the procedural deadlines. As a consequence, compromise regarding deadlines and timetables must be acknowledged.

Step 5. Assign responsibility. Some one individual (or team of individuals) must have (a) responsibility for, (b) authority over, and (c) control of the plans and resources, and must also be (d) accountable for the results. Furthermore, similar responsibilities, authority, control, and accountability must be assigned for each element in the sequence.

Step 6. Check the plan for feasibility and costs. This step provides a final review before the plan is released for implementation. At this phase of planning, the tentative plan is first assessed to make certain that it (a) has available the resources needed for implementation, (b) allows for the probable influence of uncontrollable external conditions, and (c) includes all the elements of the five previous steps.

Additionally, the plan's feasibility should be checked realistically against the organization's true capabilities. Plans that look good on paper may fail if they cannot be assigned to competent and well-motivated people. Frequently, plans must be modified to reflect the available talent.

The cost of a plan is often its limiting factor. Here again, hard-nosed judgments are made about the total cost of carrying out a plan as compared with the value of its results. Compromises may evolve, such as a lowering of the objectives to match the funds available for attaining them.

Practical Implications

The Situation.   When the trucking and air transportation industries were greatly deregulated during the late 1970s and early 1980s, the Iowa Over-the-Road Transport Corporation (IOTC) set out to expand its operations.

Its plan was to increase its sales revenues to $75 million within 5 years through a strategy of acquiring a number of existing trucking firms in 12 midwestern states. The plan also set a goal of $5 million in profits annually, once the $75 million in annual revenues had been attained. IOTC did acquire several local firms, and it did meet its sales target of $75 million in the alloted time period. Only one thing went wrong: Instead of making a profit of $5 million, IOTC lost nearly $5 million, and the outlook for a turnaround also appeared slight.

Question.   What may have happened to cause IOTC's plan to miss so vital a goal as its profits and by so wide a margin?

Answer.   Deregulation fooled a lot of companies in the transportation industries. Among the more notable were Braniff and Eastern Airlines. Both misread the extent of competition that would ensue. In IOTC's case, the company also failed to assess the external environment correctly. IOTC thought that it could bring its expertise to 12 other states but failed to realize that other major trucking firms would have the same idea. With in-state rates no longer regulated, the competition from both national and small, independent, local firms was intense. Rate cutting became rampant, resulting in negative profit margins on a great many shipments.

IOTC also was slow in anticipating the value of using computer-locator systems for tracking shipments throughout its areas. Use of such systems by other competing national firms gave them a large sales advantage and impressive operating efficiencies. IOTC's plan had not allowed for the expense of adding a computer-locator system. When the company did install such a system, it added significantly to its capital costs without providing a competitive advantage.

Concept 19

Operational planning converts strategies into specific timetables by using a variety of forecasting and scheduling techniques.

Operational planning is concerned, especially, with the process that converts resources into results, inputs into outputs. The emphasis is on concrete details. Forecasts of future conditions can no longer be hypothetical or general; they must settle on numbers that can be placed in schedules and budgets. Dates and times are pinned down. Facilities, equipment, and materials are designated. Personnel assignments are made.

To aid in this process, a number of helpful methods and techniques have evolved and been perfected. Particular attention will be paid here to those involving forecasting, capacity and time planning, and scheduling.

Forecasting Methods

Goals and plans are "premised" upon assumptions of future conditions. In most instances, these assumptions are more nearly forecasts. In the final analysis, most forecasts have to do with specific factors affecting an enterprise's revenues and expenditures. A business firm cannot begin to plan without making a forecast of, for example, next year's sales—for it is these revenues that make resources available for plans. Even a public agency cannot draw up plans without a forecast of revenues it will receive from the legislature, taxes, and license fees.

Three popular techniques are used for business and organizational forecasting. Each has its values and drawbacks.

The **survey-method forecast** is based upon estimates gathered by questionnaires or personal interviews. These may be directed at customers and clients, vendors, a company's own executives and sales personnel, or just about any informed source. Survey methods usually rely upon sampling a small portion of a population. They yield fairly reliable consensus estimates about possible demand for a product or service. These figures are only estimates, however, and are subject to faulty, or biased, opinions.

The **historical-trends forecast** is based upon gathering data from any available record system, plotting it chronologically, and assuming that the established trend will persist into the future. Trend analysis provides reliable data about the past, and the trend charts are easy to follow. The drawback of this method is that the analyst must always make a prediction of whether the trend will continue, accelerate, or slow down. This dilemma is illustrated in Figure 4.4.

The **statistical-analysis forecast** employs mathematical analysis to establish cause-and-effect relationships. A company that sells home furnishings, for example, may find out that when there is a rise in the number of new homes begun, there is a corresponding rise in the sale of the company's products 6 months later. If so, it will forecast its sales revenues in accordance with this relationship.

Capacity and Time Planning

Inherent in the development of all plans is a knowledge of the capacity of the available facilities, equipment, and labor. If Elissa, a manager who is making plans for next month's production, knows that the 5 grinding mills in her department can each handle 1 ton in a 5-day week of 8-hour days, she knows that the process capacity of her department is 5 tons per week or 250 tons per 50-week year. She uses this knowledge of **process capacity** to create schedules. If she is advised that the sales department intends to sell 300 tons of material next year, she will know that she must schedule her operations for more than 5 days a week or more than 8 hours a day sometime during the year. She may, for example, schedule a sixth day for each of the 50 weeks, or 2 hours (⅕ day) of overtime during 200 days of the year.

Capacity is always expressed in units per time period—as in gallons per week, pounds per hour, feet per minute, or copies per second. Capacity, then, is a function of time. Managers and engineers often determine capacity by making **time studies**—measurements of the time taken to accomplish a task, by a process, a machine, or an individual or group of individuals. Data from such time studies or historical records of capacity are the building blocks from which operating schedules are constructed.

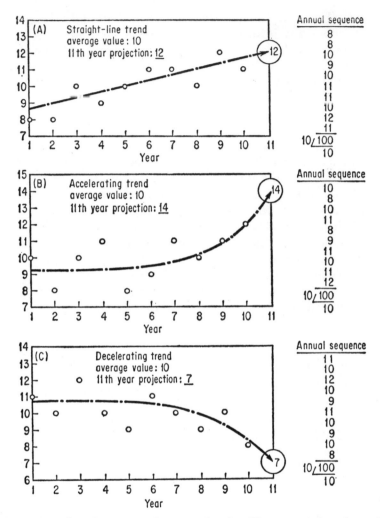

In *A*, *B*, and *C* the numerical average for the 10-year period is always 10. The annual sequence patterns vary, however, indicating projections for the eleventh year of 12, 14, and 7.

Figure 4.4. Historical-trends forecasts: illustrating stable, accelerating, and decelerating trends.

From Master to Departmental Schedules

Operating schedules start at the very top of an organization and then cascade downward to each division, department, section, and individual. The schedule at the top is the **master schedule**, from which all others are derived. If a company's master schedule, for example, calls for producing 2000 widgets a month, this may result in *department schedules* such as: Department A is to make 100 metal parts for each widget, or 200,000 parts; department B, 5 plastic parts for each, or 10,000 parts; department C, 500 fasteners for each, or 1 million fasteners. *Section schedules* may call for section C1 of department C to make 500,000 of one type of fastener, section C2 to make 250,000 of another type, and section C3 to make 250,000 of still another type. *Individual schedules* in section C3 may call for each of its 10 employees to make 25,000 widgets during the month.

A Variety of Useful Scheduling Techniques

Operating schedules range from the simple to the complex, each with its own particular application.

Point-to-point plans arrange for tasks to be performed in sequence: when one task is completed, another one begins, and so on until the overall plan has been completed.

Overlap, or parallel, plans arrange tasks so that one or more tasks may be carried out at the same time, as shown in the lower part of Figure 4.5. This shortens the overall time needed to complete the plan. The most popular overlap plan is the **Gantt chart**, and variations of it can be seen in schedule boards used for scheduling projects, office work, or manufacturing production schedules.

Network plans combine the concept of overlap with a number of time-and-sequence factors to obtain the most efficient scheduling of very complex projects. These schedules are known variously as PERT, CPM, and arrow diagram. Network plans are used mainly for large, complex, one-of-a-kind projects. Typically, construction companies use them for bridges, large apartment complexes, and highway projects; manufacturing companies for fabricating large diesel locomotives; public agencies for installing new administrative procedures; and marketing departments for planning advertising campaigns.

Practical Implications

The Situation. Consider the tasks involved in developing a cost-reduction plan.

PROJECT: Cost Reduction of Product A.

Point-to-point (or straight-line) control chart

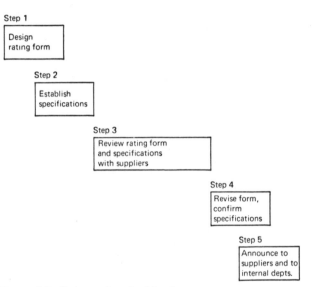

Overlap (or Gantt) control chart

Figure 4.5. Two popular schedule plans.

OBJECTIVE: To redesign product A and revise its manufacturing methods so as to reduce its unit cost (packed ready for shipment from the plant warehouse) from $5 to $4 within 12 months from the project starting date of June 1. Overall responsibility for the project is assigned to senior designer Cudahy.

PROCEDURE: *Step 1.* Initiate value-analysis study to determine design elements (in terms of materials and manufacturing methods) which meet cost targets as well as functional requirements.

TIME ESTIMATE: 4 weeks.

Step 2. Develop new material specifications.

TIME ESTIMATE: 2 weeks.

Step 3. Develop new design for product A.

TIME ESTIMATE: 8 weeks.

Step 4. Prescribe new manufacturing methods.

TIME ESTIMATE: 6 weeks.

Step 5. Requisition and place order for new manufacturing equipment.

TIME ESTIMATE: 10 weeks.
Step 6.   Prepare layout for new manufacturing methods and equipment.
TIME ESTIMATE: 4 weeks.
Step 7.   Install new equipment.
TIME ESTIMATE: 4 weeks.
Step 8.   Requisition new materials and supplies in time for start-up of new manufacturing process.
TIME ESTIMATE: 6 weeks.
Step 9.   Develop new operating procedures and train operators in new methods.
TIME ESTIMATE: 4 weeks.
Step 10.   Start up new manufacturing line. Produce 100 units of product A that meet quality standards of the new design.
TIME ESTIMATE: 4 weeks.

Question.   How can these tasks be scheduled in the most effective fashion?

Answer.   The 10 steps of this plan can be scheduled using any of three techniques, as indicated by the arrangement of data in Figure 4.6. Figure 4.7 illustrates — in simplified fashion — how these 10 tasks, each with its own set of constraints, can be scheduled as (1) a point-to-point plan, (2) an overlap plan, and (3) a network plan. The network plan provides the schedule with the shortest time.

Concept 20

Management by objectives provides a mechanism for encouraging managers to coordinate personal and departmental plans with organizational goals.

The underlying concept of **management by objectives** is that when people are involved in setting their own goals they are likely to be committed to attaining them. This concept has been shown to be most effective when managers assign goals to other managers. Under an MBO system, the higher-level executive does not impose the goals of the organization on a subordinate. Instead, the two work together to examine the organization's goals and then, in light of those goals, arrive at a set of goals for the subordinate manager to attain. This set usually includes self-development goals as well as organizational goals.

There are numerous variants on the MBO system. Most MBO programs, however, include the following elements:

	Time estimate (in weeks) to complete each step	Plan A point to point		Plan B overlap		Plan C network path	
		Week start	Week complete	Week start	Week complete	Week start	Week complete
Step 1 Value analysis study	4						
		1		1		1	
			4		4		4
Step 2 Materials specifications	2						
		5		5		5	
			6		6		6
Step 3 Design specifications	8						
		7		5		1	
			14		12		8
Step 4 Mfg. methods	6						
		15		13		9	
			20		18		14
Step 5 Equipment acquisition	10						
		21		19		15	
			30		28		24
Step 6 Layout	4						
		31		27		9	
			34		30		12
Step 7 Installation	4						
		35		31		25	
			38		34		28
Step 8 Materials acquisition	6						
		39		31		9	
			44		36		14
Step 9 Train operators	4						
		45		35		15	
			48		38		18
Step 10 Start-up	4						
		49		39		29	32
Total time elapsed in weeks	52		52		42		32

Figure 4.6. Progressive shortening of time from point-to-point to network schedules.

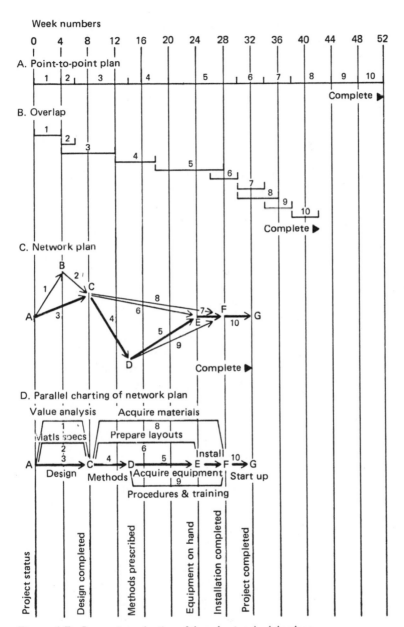

Figure 4.7. Comparison charting of three basic schedule plans.

1. Superior and subordinate examine a possible set of goals for the next 6 months to 1 year.

2. The two negotiate, and agree upon, a challenging but attainable set of goals — often as many as 10 goals.

3. The subordinate is put on his or her own and allowed to select the methods to be used in attaining these goals.

4. The superior remains available for consultation and coaching during the period covered by the set of goals.

5. Periodically, and especially at the end of the time period, the subordinate's performance is evaluated against the established goals. Many MBO programs provide for salary incentives or bonuses related to this performance.

6. The process is repeated for the next time period.

Advantages of MBO are that it ensures that planning takes place, goals are specific, there is commitment on the subordinate's part, goals are tailored to each individual's capacity, and the periodic review provides a built-in control mechanism.

MBO's *disadvantages* are that it is a time-consuming process; there must be genuine leeway in allowing for goal negotiation; it tends to focus on concrete, measurable goals rather than on intangible ones such as creativity; and as its novelty tends to deteriorate over time, participants lose interest.

Practical Implications

The Situation.   Roberta Brown, director of marketing services, was concluding an MBO session with her manager of catalog sales, Ricardo Mount. "Then you agree upon these eight objectives, Ricardo?" "Yes, Roberta, they seem fine to me." "Good," said the director. "I'll see you in 6 months to find out how well you've done."

During the 6-month period, Ricardo encountered difficulty in meeting the objective that called for a reduction of 5 percent in mailing costs. He had planned to meet that objective through bulk mailing of catalogs in lots of 1000 or more to designated postal zones. The trouble was that the sales department was slow in providing customer names for mailing labels, and rather than delay the mailings, Ricardo had sent the catalogs at a premium rate.

When Roberta met with Ricardo at the end of 6 months to discuss his performance, she said that she was greatly disturbed by Ricardo's failure to meet the mailing-expense objective. "If you had come to me at the time, I could have put pressure on the sales department to get you the label data, pronto!" she said. Ricardo replied, "I thought that I had to be on my own for 6 months. I did my best under the circumstances." "Your best wasn't quite good enough," said Ms. Brown.

Question. How could the implementation of this MBO system have been improved?

Answer. Roberta could have emphasized, at the initial session, that she was available for counseling and coaching. In so doing, she should have stressed that she would not be second-guessing but offering counsel or assistance, and that some elements of the MBO system are designed to provide development opportunities for Ricardo. Developing is a form of learning, and it is wise to seek advice when faced by a difficult problem. Roberta could also have been less critical of Ricardo's decision about how to handle the bulk-mailing problem. Instead, she could have accepted his decision as a learning experience, one for which the MBO system makes allowances.

Comprehension-Check Case for Chapter 4

The Case of the Burgeoning Cosmetics Company

For easy reference, the text of the comprehension-check case is numbered to correspond to the assignment questions that follow.

Irene Glassner started her own cosmetics firm when she broke away from a national corporation where she had been a top-flight regional manager of over 250 door-to-door salespeople. She acquired a line of cosmetics from a small Italian perfumery and set up a small bottling and packaging operation in rented space in an old warehouse. Before 3 years were out, Irene Cosmetics was a small success and Ms. Glassner was ready to diversify and expand her product line and distribution network. These are the steps she took:

1. She prepared a mission statement in which she described what she wanted her business to become. This is how it read: "Irene Cosmetics will prepare and market a line of cosmetics for distribution through department and specialty stores in the northeastern United States."

She also established the following long-range objectives: (a) to become a leading distributor of Italian perfumes, (b) to sell only high-quality cosmetics, and (c) to market mainly to upper-income consumers.

2. When Glassner went to the bank for a loan to expand her business, she was asked what would be unique about her operations. She replied that (a) she would distribute only through exclusive department stores and specialty shops, (b) she would offer these shops discounts of 50 percent or better on purchases made 3 months before the Christmas season began, and (c) she would set up an internal system wherein all incoming orders were first checked for credit and then marked for the appropriate discounts, before forwarding to the shipping department.

Upon her return to the plant, Glassner said to her shipping-room supervisor, "You better believe what I'm telling you: Never! Repeat, never, ship anything without first having approval from the credit department."

3. Once she was assured of the availability of the necessary funds, Glassner began to prepare concrete plans. She had one goal, in particular, that she wanted to reach: opening sales offices in 5 major eastern cities. Accordingly, she looked over the situation in each of 10 cities to find the best possible locations, got together with her lawyer and sales manager to establish a procedure for acquiring leases in each of the 5 cities she chose, and set a deadline of having the offices in operation by June 1 of the next year. The deadline was not met, and when she spoke to the lawyer and sales manager, she found out that each thought the other had been expected to finalize the plan and put it into effect.

4. Another goal that Glassner set for Irene Cosmetics was to have sales revenues reach $3 million the next year. Glassner's sales manager said that such an objective was unrealistic. Said Glassner, "If you think my forecast is too optimistic, get me three others that support your view of what a reasonable sales target should be."

Glassner asked the Irene Cosmetics production manager whether the plant would be able to fill orders for $3 million next year, if they materialized. He replied that he'd have to check out his capacity figures before he could give her an answer.

When she checked back with the lawyer and the sales manager about speeding up the opening of the five new sales offices, Glassner was somewhat disappointed. Each emphasized all the details that had to be coordinated before the openings could take place: sign leases, buy furniture, install telephones, hire office help, hire or reassign salespeople, notify customers, prepare new letterheads, etc.

5. Faced with so many goals to be accomplished and decisions to be made, Glassner decided to delegate some of her responsibilities to key department managers. One by one, she met with them and laid out a series of goals to be met. Her goals for the production manager were to increase capacity by 10,000 units per month, reduce breakage by 5 percent, and keep payroll costs within a budget of $500,000. The manager objected, saying that some of these goals were unreasonable. Glassner's reply was, "They may appear that way, but you'll have to do the best you can." At year end, the production manager had reached the first two goals but had overrun the payroll budget by $100,000. "Something had to give," the manager ex-

plained, "and I thought that adding capacity and reducing breakage were more important right now than how much we spent on labor."

Assignment Questions

1 (a)   On the basis of the Irene Cosmetics mission statement, which functions will the firm perform?

_____ *a.* Preparing a line of cosmetics

_____ *b.* Marketing a line of cosmetics

_____ *c.* Neither preparing nor marketing a line of cosmetics

_____ *d.* Both preparing and marketing a line of cosmetics

1 (b)   After reading the company's long-range objectives, how do you think the mission statement might be modified to more fully describe the product line and the market served? Insert the appropriate phrases: _____line of cosmetics to _____ consumers in the northeastern United States.

1 (c)   Which of the following qualifiers might make attainment of the objective of "become a leading distributor" most specific?

_____ *a.* Obtain a very large share of the market.

_____ *b.* Rank among the first four distributors of Italian cosmetics.

_____ *c.* Sell more of the Irene brand each year.

_____ *d.* Make the brand known around the world.

2 (a)   In Glassner's reply to the bank, which of her statements were, essentially, policies?

_____ *a.* Statement *a* only

_____ *b.* Statements *a* and *b*

_____ *c.* Statements *b* and *c*

_____ *d.* Statement *c* only

2 (b)   Which were procedures?

_____ *a.* Statement *a*

_____ *b.* Statements *a* and *b*

_____ *c.* Statements *b* and *c*

_____ *d.* Statement *c* only

2 (c)   When Glassner returned to the plant and spoke to the shipping-room supervisor, she issued a:

_____ *a.* policy.

_____ *b.* procedure.

_____ *c.* rule or regulation.

_____ *d.* goal.

3   What step of the planning process did Glassner's plan for opening the new offices omit?

_____ *a.* Step 1 (Set goals.)

_____ *b.* Step 2 (Evaluate the situation.)

_____ *c.* Step 4 (Set a timetable or deadline.)

_____ *d.* Step 5 (Assign responsibility.)

4 (a)   If the sales manager studied the firm's previous sales records and made a forecast based upon their projection, this would be a:

_____ *a.* survey-method forecast.
_____ *b.* historical-trends forecast.
_____ *c.* statistical-analysis forecast.
_____ *d.* Gantt chart.

4 (b)   The Irene Cosmetics production manager found that the plant could fill $40,000 worth of orders a week working an 8-hour day. In a 50-week year, the plant could fill $_____ worth of orders; to fill $3 million in orders, the plant would have to increase its capacity by _____ percent

_____ *a.* $2,500,000; 25
_____ *b.* $2 million; 25
_____ *c.* $2 million; 50
_____ *d.* $3 million; 0 (would not have to increase capacity)

4 (c)   Which type of schedule is most appropriate and most likely to yield the shortest time needed to open the new offices?

_____ *a.* Point-to-point
_____ *b.* Overlap
_____ *c.* Gantt chart
_____ *d.* Network

5 (a)   In choosing to focus on giving preference to the increased capacity and the reduction of breakage, the production manager had not fully understood Glassner's _____ of goals.

_____ *a.* cascading
_____ *b.* hierarchy
_____ *c.* multiplicity
_____ *d.* strategy

5 (b)   Glassner might have secured a clearer understanding of her goals and a greater commitment to them from the production manager with:

_____ *a.* carefully detailed procedures.
_____ *b.* firmer rules and regulations.
_____ *c.* applying a Theory X approach.
_____ *d.* applying an MBO approach.

5

Organizing: Dividing up the Work in a Structured Framework

Organizing is the process of dividing up the work of an business firm, not-for-profit institution, or public agency into individual tasks and groups of related tasks. Managers specify not only the responsibilities associated with these tasks and groups but also their relationships, one to another. The resulting groups and their relationships form the structure of an organization. The distribution — or delegation — of authority throughout an organization creates the most critical of these relationships. Typically, such delegation follows a chain of command from top to bottom. Authority is greatly affected, however, by the degree of centralized control that an organization retains at the top. Authority within the chain of command is further modified by the extent to which it is extended to support and advisory staffs.

Key Concepts Regarding the Organizing Process and Organization Structures

Figure 5.1 shows the five key concepts that relate to the organizing process and organization structures. They are:

21. Managers divide up the work of an organization so as to define the tasks to be performed in the most effective manner for accomplishing the goals of the organization.

22. Managers collect similar tasks and group them into departments according to a variety of organizational structures that indicate relationships as well as functions.

23. The authority for carrying out tasks, or groups of tasks, is distributed from the top to the bottom of an organization through a chain of command.

24. Authority, or control, over an organization's activities and resources may also be centralized or decentralized.

25. Most large organizations also extend authority to support and advisory staffs and thereby create useful, but often conflicting, relationships with departments that are in the direct chain of command.

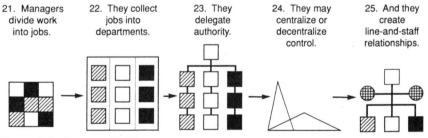

| 21. Managers divide work into jobs. | 22. They collect jobs into departments. | 23. They delegate authority. | 24. They may centralize or decentralize control. | 25. And they create line-and-staff relationships. |

Figure 5.1. Concepts 21–25.

Key Terms

To make the best use of the key concepts, you should understand the following terms:

Division of labor	Task
Specialization	Responsibilities
Job	Job enlargement

Job enrichment

Departmentation

Function organization

Product or service organization

Customer or location organization

Authority

Delegation

Unity of command

Chain of command

Organization chart

Accountability

Span of management or span of control

Centralization

Decentralization

Line-and-staff organization

Line activities

Staff activities

Functional authority

Superordinate goal

Matrix organization

Concept 21

Managers divide up the work of an organization so as to define the tasks to be performed in the most effective manner for accomplishing the goals of the organization.

When a number of people join together, for whatever purpose, a basic decision must be made about who does what. In a formal organization, this decision is primarily made by management. Over the centuries, in fact since the time of the building of the pyramids in Egypt, managers have learned that such a **division of labor** is made more effective when it is based upon specialization of effort. In most recent years, managers have also observed that such specialization must be modified, or enhanced, by broadening the scope and increasing the depth of the resulting task assignments.

Specialization

Historical records make it clear that builders of the pyramids chose certain people to cut stones, others to transport them, and still others to put them in place. This practice was out of favor for centuries, however, because of the evolution of the concept of a "journeyman" who could perform multiple tasks. A cabinetmaker, for example, was expected to be able to cut, shape, join, and finish a chest of drawers without the help of another person. As the factory system grew, however, and as hundreds and thousands of products came to be made, specialization became the accepted practice for organized group effort. **Specialization** is the assignment of a rather narrow, or limited, task or function to a single individual so that the individual may become proficient at performing it.

Adam Smith, a famous economist in the 1700s, observed that in the manufacturing of a pin, "18 distinct and separate operations were performed." He concluded that "division of labor" could enable each worker to become very proficient at a narrow specialty. Today, the starting point for the organization of work is still the concept that greatest efficiency will be derived by dividing the work into specialized tasks.

Job Content

The smallest division of labor assigned to one individual is normally called a **job**. A job consists of at least the following important elements:

- **Tasks** to be performed, such as, on an automobile assembly line, fitting the glass into a windshield frame; in an office, sorting, processing, and filing incoming sales orders; or in an engineering firm, designing a variety of parts for use in fabricating aircraft instrument panels
- **Responsibilities** associated with that set of tasks, such as, for the office employee, handling a given number of orders each day without making more than a specified number of errors
- *Access to resources* needed to perform these tasks and discharge its responsibilities, such as specified office machines, order forms, filing cabinets, a telephone, and a computer

The tasks and responsibilities of a job are often referred to, simply, as "job duties." From the point of view of the manager who is engaged in the organizing process, a job—or work unit—is the smallest building block in the eventual organization structure.

Job Enhancement

While specialization promotes efficiency, it also often leads to boredom. Highly specialized jobs are typically repetitive. They require only a limited number of skills from the workers engaged in them. Boredom and monotony induce carelessness, indifference toward organization goals, and—in some cases—outright sabotage. Increasingly, managers have been made aware of this problem and have sought to enhance the quality of the work itself. This is accomplished when the outcome of the job is meaningful and when its performance requires greater use of an employee's skills and knowledge. Two approaches, in particular, are used to enhance the quality of the work itself:

1. **Job enlargement** broadens the scope of the job. The windshield assembler's job may be enlarged to include installation of dash-panel fixtures and rear-view mirrors. Thus, a job that might once have taken only 5 minutes to perform now will take 15 minutes. The job is repeated only 32 times a day as compared with 96.

2. **Job enrichment** deepens the scope of the job. That is, it requires the worker to use more judgment, knowledge, or skill than before. The automobile assembly worker's job might be enriched by giving him or her (a) responsibility for inspecting the configuration of the frame before installing the windshield, (b) use of a more complicated device for installing panel fixtures, and (c) authority to exercise judgment in deciding whether or not to install mirrors that appear faulty.

Practical Implications

The Situation. Jill Downs, manager of the word processing department of the National Association of Trade Underwriters, is organizing the work of her department. She is at the first stage of the process: dividing the work into units that will become jobs for assignment. Having carefully analyzed the various components of a word processor's job in working on any kind of document, she has concluded that these components are

1. Obtain the text or dictation tape.
2. Turn on the transcriber.
3. Get a blank disk.
4. Establish a format.
5. Keyboard the document.
6. Proof each page on screen.
7. Set up an index on the disk.
8. Print the document.
9. Proofread, and correct errors on screen.
10. Print the corrected document.
11. File the disk.
12. Place the printed document in the out box.

Jill concludes that it would be nonproductive to divide up the work according to these components. Instead, she examines the possibility of dividing the work according to the kinds of documents prepared by the department, as follows:

A. Correspondence, personalized

B. Form letters

C. Technical reports

D. Project status reports

E. Summary reports

F. Statistical tables

Jill identifies the preparation of each of these documents as a specialized work unit or job, and organizes her department according to these six jobs. Since there is a greater work load for some documents than other, she has more employees assigned to some jobs, such as form letters and statistical tables, than to other jobs, such as correspondence and summary reports.

Six months after organizing her department this way, Jill is confronted by complaints from the employees who work on the highly repetitive jobs such as preparing form letters and statistical tables. Not only that, the productivity of these employees has never reached the standards set for those jobs.

Question. How might Jill redesign the jobs in her department to improve the productivity of those who are assigned to them?

Answer. The present division of work may call for too much specialization, as evidenced by the complaints and the low productivity. Jill might try one of the three different solutions listed below, or she might use aspects of all three.

1. Combine job B (form letters) with job F (statistical tables). The resultant enlargement would add the challenge of achieving the necessary precision to the work of employees who are bored by the routine and repetitiveness of preparing form letters, while perhaps also providing some relief to those persons typing statistical tables. Other job enlargement could be attained by combining jobs C, D, and E.

2. Enrich job B by combining it with job A, which seems to require greater versatility and judgment. Job enrichment for all jobs could also be attained by such techniques as (a) asking employees to check their own

work (or that of others) for accuracy, (b) allowing employees to select or design the forms they use, and (c) inviting employees to participate in establishing and monitoring their own work standards.

3. Establish only two jobs: (a) basic word processing and (b) advanced word processing. The first might include present jobs A, B, and F; the second C, D, and E. Within these two jobs, allow and encourage *rotation* of assignments at the discretion of the employees.

Concept 22

Managers collect similar tasks and group them into departments according to a variety of organizational structures that indicate relationships as well as functions.

Once the work of an organization has been divided into jobs, the next step is to group these jobs together according to some sort of plan that provides a system of coordination. This grouping process is called **departmentation**. It can be accomplished in a number of ways.

Departmentation by Function

The most common approach to departmentation is to collect similar tasks and place each within its own function. This is called **function organization** and is illustrated in Figure 5.2, which shows how jobs in a bank may be grouped according to function. In a great many companies, tasks are grouped into production or operations, marketing, and finance and accounting departments. Departmentation can continue

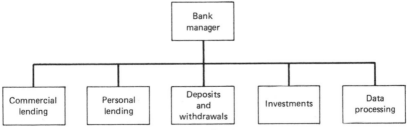

Figure 5.2. Example of departmentation by function.

with subfunctions. A human resources department, for example, can be divided into employment, compensation, health and safety, training, and records functions.

In large corporations, this subgrouping of departments continues to as many as 7 or more levels. At one time, General Motors Corporation had 12 levels in its hierarchy.

The major advantages of departmentation by function are that it (1) continues the concept of specialization and (2) provides a convenient way to oversee and coordinate similar tasks. Its major drawback is that it does not provide specialized attention for different product lines or customers.

Departmentation by Product or Service

In addition to creating departments by function, it is also a common practice to group tasks according to the product or service those functions are involved in producing or serving. This is **product** or **service organization**. A manufacturer of machinery, for example, may have a farm-equipment department, an agricultural-machinery department, and a construction-equipment department. In a great many cases like this, the company also creates functional subgroups so that, for instance, each of the three product departments will also have subdepartments for production and for marketing, as suggested by the product departmentation shown in Figure 5.3.

The major advantage of this format is that each of the product departments—and their subdepartments—can (1) become expert in performing the tasks associated with their particular product or service and (2) react quickly to environmental changes affecting those products or services. The major drawback of this format is that there is often a duplication of subdepartments from product department to product department.

Departmentation by Customer or Location

Following the same kind of rationale as with product departmentation, you can also have **customer** or **location organization**. Departments can be created according to (1) the different customers served by an organization or (2) the different geographical locations in which an organization is located or operates. Thus, a consulting company may have in-

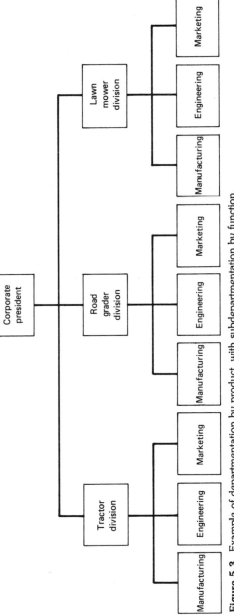

Figure 5.3. Example of departmentation by product, with subdepartmentation by function.

dustrial, commercial, and government departments. A national insurance company may have northeastern, southern, central, and western departments. As with product organizations, departmentation by customer or location may also be followed by subgroupings of functions. Or customer or geographic departments, themselves, may be subdepartments of a functional or product organizational format, as illustrated in Figure 5.4.

The advantages and disadvantages of these formats are similar to those associated with product or service departmentation.

Implied Relationships

Inevitably, as departmentation proceeds, certain groupings will appear at the same level of an organization's hierarchal structure and others will appear above or below them. When those departments are charted, a relationship is implied:

- Those on the same level are on an equal footing, with cooperation among them expected.
- Those above can be presumed to be able to call on the services of the departments below them.
- Those below can be presumed to be responsive to the needs of the departments above them.

Practical Implications

The Situation. During a gubernatorial campaign in a large midwestern state, the candidate appointed a campaign manager, Jim B., who was charged with coordinating all the tasks involved in preparation for election day. The manager sorted out the major tasks to be performed: (A) fund raising and allocation, (B) advertising, (C) scheduling of events, (D) recruitment and supervision of volunteers at designated county offices, (E) telephone-center operations at headquarters and also at the county offices, and (F) publicity at headquarters and at the country offices.

Question. What sort of departmentation would best lend itself to coordination by the campaign manager?

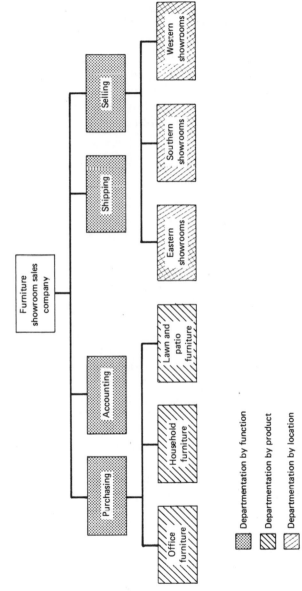

Figure 5.4. Different methods of departmentation combined in the same company.

Answer. Jim chose a combination of departmentation by function and by location, which appears to be well suited to the candidate's objective to get elected governor.

At the top, for the headquarters organization, Jim chose function departmentation: A, B, C, D, E, and F. He added another headquarters department: (G) coordination of county offices.

Jim then created subdepartments under G for location in each of the state's 37 counties. Further, he created subdepartments under each location for those functions that might benefit most from local attention: (D) recruitment and supervision of volunteers, (E) telephone-center operations, and (F) publicity.

Concept 23

The authority for carrying out tasks, or groups of tasks, is distributed from the top to the bottom of an organization through a chain of command.

In creating jobs and departments, the emphasis has been upon dividing up the work into tasks, duties, and responsibilities. A vital aspect, however, of the organizing process has been deferred to this point: the process by which authority to command the necessary resources, including the services of others, is distributed along with these responsibilities.

Authority is defined as having two aspects: (1) the right to take action (such as spending funds, operating machinery, or sending out a news release) in performance of one's job and (2) the right to require subordinates to perform duties to which they are assigned. The person at the top of the organization (the company president, for example) is presumed to have complete authority. Once an organization has been divided into departments, however, the top person must then pass on to subordinates not only tasks and responsibilities but also the authority to implement them.

Delegation

The process of distributing authority along with responsibilities is called **delegation**. Two principles have evolved that govern this process: unity of command and chain of command.

Unity of command means that no person should have more than one boss. When a subordinate reports to two superiors, conflict and confusion inevitably arise. Whose orders and instructions have highest priority? If the orders are in conflict, which one should be presumed to be correct? Unity of command is intended to eliminate these problems. As departmentation becomes more complex and extends to many levels, unity of command is often hard to preserve.

Chain of command (also called the "scalar chain") refers to an unbroken hierarchy of authority that links superiors and subordinates from the top to the bottom of an organization. Each department is "commanded" by an individual, who receives commands from above and has authority to issue commands to subordinates in charge of departments lower in the hierarchy. This chain provides an orderly way for the organization to function. It prevents employees down the line from going over their boss's head with requests or complaints. Similarly, it prevents managers up the line from circumventing intermediate departments to issue orders directly to departments that are subordinate to the intermediate departments. The chain of command has its drawbacks. The process can be awkward and very time-consuming as things proceed through channels. In addition, the formality of the chain can be used to insulate superiors from what is actually happening down the line.

Organization charts are designed to show the chain of command and to reflect the relationships between departments. It should be emphasized that organizations are rarely static. They undergo constant change in departmentation and in authority relationships. Organization charts, therefore, are only "snapshots" of how an organization looks at a particular point in time.

Authority, Responsibility, and Accountability

The process of delegation must always include three elements:

1. Tasks or duties to be performed
2. Responsibilities associated with these duties
3. Authority to command the resources needed to perform the tasks and discharge the responsibilities

The authority delegated must always be appropriate to the responsibility assigned. The authority should be neither too great nor too small: it should be balanced.

There is a further aspect to this concept: *Responsibility and authority can — and should — be delegated, but* **accountability** *can never be.* That is, managers may delegate a responsibility to their subordinates, but if something goes wrong, it is the managers who did the delegating who should be held accountable to their superiors, not the subordinates.

Practical Implications

The Situation.   Sam McLean, president of Leisure Fabrics Company, was puzzled about a problem that had just arrived on his desk. Helmuth Lessing, manager of the cutting and dyeing plant, has complained that Jessica Smythe, the purchasing manager (PM), who reports to the president, had bought and shipped to the plant unsuitable fabrics.

> HELMUTH: I specifically told the PM that fabric from that source fouled up our processes and should not be purchased.
>
> SAM: "Why didn't you tell me about it?"
>
> HELMUTH: I thought it would cut red tape if I spoke to her directly. Furthermore, my dye supervisor called the supplier and told them never to ship that stuff to us again.
>
> SAM: Well, this supplier is particularly sensitive to us under our present purchase contract. Your actions have placed us in an embarrassing situation. In the future, let the purchasing manager decide whom we'll buy from, and never call a supplier direct. That's the PM's responsibility.
>
> HELMUTH: I didn't call the supplier. The dye supervisor did.

Question.   In terms of the principles of delegated authority, what needs to be more fully clarified or corrected by the president?

Answer.   First of all, the *unity-of-command* principle is not fully observed in this company: The plant manager takes orders from the president, but he is also expected to take direction from the purchasing manager with regard to raw materials for his operation.

Second, the plant manager is accused of circumventing the *chain of command* in going directly to the purchasing manager—and to the supplier.

Third, the plant manager denies *accountability* for the actions of a person who reports to him.

The president may resolve the first two issues by clearly establishing that, in matters of raw-materials purchase, the purchasing manager is acting directly on the president's behalf and that the plant manager must act as if orders from the PM were, in fact, orders from the president. That would preserve unity of command. The president must then remove the ambiguity about chain of command, so far as it affects communications. The simplest solution would be that, again—*in matters of raw-materials purchase*—the plant manager must follow the chain of command: this would require that the president *also* respect the chain of command *in these matters*—neither talking directly with the plant manager about raw-materials purchases nor asking that the PM bring these matters directly to the president.

As to accountability for his subordinate's action, the plant manager should be completely disabused of the thought that he can pass the buck downward.

Concept 24

Authority, or control, over an organization's activities and resources may also be centralized or decentralized.

When designing an organization structure, there is always the question of how many departments a manager can oversee and coordinate. Technically, this is referred to as the **span of management** or **span of control**. The term "span" refers to activities or departments, not people. When the spans are narrow, the tendency is to create tall structures, with many levels in the hierarchy. When spans are broad and managers coordinate the activities of many departments, the structures are relatively flat, with shallow hierarchies.

At one time, it was thought that six activities was the ideal span of control for a manager. Today, the decision regarding span is influenced by the following considerations:

- *The degree of professionalism of subordinates.* That is, how well can they be expected to function independently without close supervision?

- *The degree of training and competence of subordinates.* The more skilled and better trained they are, the greater the span may be.

- *Task simplicity.* The more routine the tasks to be supervised, the greater the span of control.

- *Physical dispersion.* The farther apart the activities are located, the narrower the span should be.

- *Existence of standards and procedures.* The fewer standards and procedures there are, the greater the need for managerial control and coordination.

Centralization

When authority is held closely at the top of an organization, it creates a structure characterized by **centralization**. The effect of this reluctance to delegate is (1) to place a continuing burden of control on upper-level managers and (2) greatly to inhibit the initiative of subordinates. When Laura L., a retail store manager, for example, insists on verifying all checks presented to the cashier, checking the receipt of all incoming merchandise, and closely supervising shelf inventories, then she will discover two things. First, she will have little time left to handle her more important planning activities. Second, the subordinates in charge of daily receipts, incoming shipments, and inventory management will become lax in their work, expecting the store manager to discover anything that might go wrong and to make any suggestions for improvement of their operations.

Centralization is most appropriate where very close control of finances or processes is vital to the success of the organization. It is an expensive form of organization to support, since more managers are required, and it is sluggish in its reaction to changes in the environment, since communications travel so slowly up and down the hierarchy.

Decentralization

When authority is delegated freely throughout the organization, **decentralization** has occurred. This organizational format yields fewer levels in the hierarchy. As a result, the organization is less costly to operate, and it can respond more quickly to changes in the environment. If a customer's preferences change, or a competitor's pricing is switched, or new technology is available, these changes are communicated quickly up the line so that action can be considered without undue delay.

The drawback of decentralization is the possibility of loss of control. When managers down the line are given greater authority—and hence, greater freedom—they may make decisions and take action that is not in line with the intentions of a company's goals or policies. Not infrequently, misdirection occurs and damage to the organization takes place before the misdirection is detected and corrected. Accordingly, decentralization is most appropriate (1) where a high degree of initiative and responsiveness to the environment is required and (2) where the absence of close control is not likely to be damaging.

Practical Implications

The Situation. A manufacturer of photographic equipment had, for years, employed Stephen Schneider, a vice president and scientist, to oversee its extensive research activities. Under Stephen's leadership, a formal organization structure, with five levels of management, had been created. He had *three key people* reporting to him: director of research, manager of administrative services, and manager of patent registrations. Reporting to the director of research were *two division heads* — one for the basic research and another for applied research. Under each of these division heads were *managers for five fields of investigation:* physics, organic synthesis, chemical processes, reaction mechanisms, and analytics. In turn, these field managers each had *two or three supervisors of specialty areas* reporting to them. It was also Stephen's practice to review all projects at several phases of their progress before granting authority and funds for a project to advance to the next phase.

With this arrangement, the company had a long and distinguished history of effective research. Thousands of patents had been granted. Of late, however, competing Japanese and German companies had been continually making breakthroughs. Their research teams had been detecting improvements in technology sooner and moving more quickly into product development. When Stephen retired, a new vice president for research was appointed. The mandate of this new vice president was to restructure the research activities so that they would be more responsive to the environment and more effective overall.

Question. What fundamental approaches should the new vice president for research pursue to improve the effectiveness of the research activities?

Answer

1. The number of levels in the research hierarchy should be reduced.

2. Spans of control should be increased. The vice president's span is only three; the director of research has only two; the division heads, five; and the field supervisors, two or three.

3. Authority should be less centralized. The practice of involving the top person in all reviews is obviously acting as a deterrent to initiative as well as slowing down response time for the entire research process.

4. A more decentralized organization with fewer levels of management and broader spans of control might be worked out this way:

- Reporting to the vice president would be seven departments: physics, organic synthesis, chemical processes, reaction mechanisms, analytics, administrative services, and patent registration. The company would, at this level, do away with the distinction between basic and applied research. Heading each of the research areas would be a director.
- Reporting to each of the five research directors would be five

or more supervisors of specialties, plus a coordinator of product development.

- With only three levels in the hierarchy, the five directors would have authority to review and approve project advancement. The vice president would be involved only with general funding of each research department.

Concept 25

Most large organizations also extend authority to support and advisory staffs and thereby create useful, but often conflicting, relationships with departments that are in the direct chain of command.

As organizations and specialties within them grow, there is an increasing need for horizontal coordination. This is especially true when advisory and support departments have been created. The chain of command does not anticipate this need. As a consequence, several solutions have been evolved, including (1) **line-and-staff organization**, (2) the concept of partial or modified authority, and (3) the matrix organization.

Line-and-Staff Organizations

The chain of command considers all functions performed in direct fulfillment of an organization's primary mission to be **line activities**. If the mission of the Apex Valve Company, for example, is to manufacture and distribute plumbing fittings through industrial wholesalers, then its line organization will certainly include a manufacturing department and a marketing department.

When other departments are created to provide advice or support services to the line organization, their work consists of **staff activities**. The Apex Valve Company may, for instance, add a legal staff, a personnel department, and a purchasing department. These staff departments are expected to offer specialized advice, service, or both to the line departments. On an organization chart, staff departments are often shown off to the side of the direct chain of command. When line departments and staff departments are combined in an organization, the structure is called "line and staff," as illustrated in Figure 5.5.

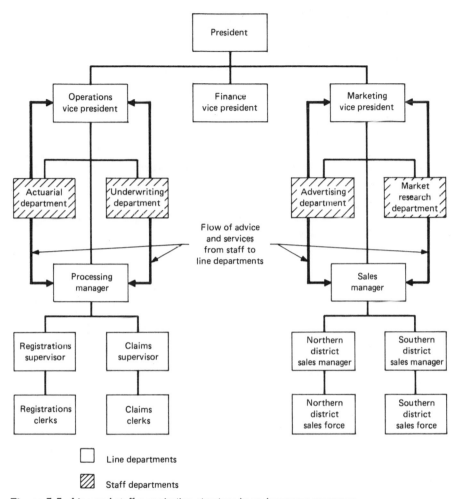

Figure 5.5. Line-and-staff organization structure in an insurance company.

Modified Authority

It is critical that the authority of a staff department, relative to that of the line departments, be made as clear as possible. To aid in this clarity, four kinds of staff authority have been created. The extent of staff authority progresses from a condition of practically no authority to full authority over matters within the realm of its specialty.

1. *Traditional authority.* Essentially, no authority, except for the privilege of giving advice, even if not asked for it.

2. *Must-consult-beforehand authority.* Requires a line department to

seek consultation before taking action. A production manager, for example, who wants to hire a mechanic may be required to speak to the personnel manager beforehand so as to get a good idea of hiring rates and the like.

3. *Must-obtain-concurrence-beforehand authority.* Requires that the line manager obtain, in effect, approval for an action before taking it. The production manager may want to discharge an employee, but would be required to get an agreement from the personnel manager first.

4. *Functional authority.* With **functional authority**, a staff department has full authority to prescribe policies and procedures for matters that fall within the staff's specialty. The purchasing department, which is essentially a service staff, may specify the exact procedures a line department must follow when buying materials and supplies.

Conflict between Line and Staff

In their interest in perfecting the application of their function, staff departments inevitably encroach on line prerogatives. Line departments, typically, resist such encroachment. Even when a staff department's authority is carefully proscribed, line departments have a tendency to circumvent procedures that they regard as nuisances. The result is often conflict between line and staff.

Serious, disruptive conflicts are difficult to resolve. They usually require the mediation or intervention of a third party, specifically the manager to whom the line and staff departments report. The best preventive measures are (1) the presence of more clearly defined roles, together with (2) an acceptance of the need to direct actions toward the higher-level goals of the organization—**superordinate goals**.

Matrix Organizations

A relatively new organizational form has emerged to solve the unique problems faced by research organizations, engineering firms, government subcontractors, and any firms that regularly engage in one-of-a-kind projects of limited duration. This unique form, called a **matrix organization**, allows a project manager to call on the time and skills of personnel—for a limited period of time—with various functional specialties. When the project is completed, the specialized personnel return to their home units to await assignment to another project. Because

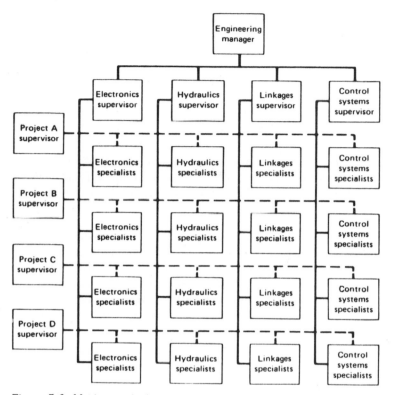

Figure 5.6. Matrix organization.

project managers exercise their authority horizontally across the basic organization, while the specialists receive permanent supervision from the bosses above them vertically on the chart (Figure 5.6), this form of organization has been designated a matrix, with the subordinates occupying cells in the matrix.

The drawbacks of the matrix organization are that (1) it violates the principle of unity of command, because the specialists report to two bosses, and (2) the commitment of the specialists to their temporary assignments may not be as strong as to their home units.

Practical Implications

The Situation.   When Bill Murf founded Murf's Mobile Home Sales, everybody who came to work for him was expected to do everything. Gradually, however, Murf organized his business into three major functions: lot display and maintenance, sales, and financing. After Murf focused his business on these three main activities, it kept right on growing. The time came, however, when Murf needed a personnel manager — someone to take care of recruiting personnel for all departments, watching over payrolls, and keeping employment records that were required by government.

Initially, Muriel Smart, the new personnel manager, was greeted with some suspicion by the three department heads. But when they realized that she was going to take a lot of tiresome details off their backs, she was welcomed. As time passed and Murf's Mobile Home Sales continued to grow, the responsibilities of the personnel manager grew along with it — but not her authority. The matter came to a head when these three incidents occurred:

- Joe Murphy, the lot manager, suspended a janitor for drinking on the job. Joe notified the personnel manager, but only after the suspension had taken place. "You were right in your action," said the personnel manager, "but suspension is such a sensitive matter that, next time, it would be less risky if you would check with me first. It's your decision to make, of course, but I may be able to provide valuable inputs before you take action."

- The sales manager gave a pay raise to a salesperson despite the objections of the personnel manager, who said that this salesperson's salary would be completely out of line with what other salespeople were paid, and it would surely cause dissent.

- The finance manager hired an accountant without any guidance from the personnel manager, notifying her only after the commitment had been made. "I could have shown you five other, equally competent people to choose from," she said. "We are an equal employment opportunity employer, and we should have advertised that job and seen a representative group of candidates."

Question.   How might the personnel manager's staff authority be clarified to avoid similar problems in the future?

Answer

1. Line managers should retain the ultimate authority for suspending or discharging an employee for cause. On the other hand, this kind of action ought to be placed under the restraint of a consultation-required authority by the personnel manager, for the reason she expressed.

2. Line managers will always do battle with personnel managers over pay scales. The personnel — or compensation — manager is usually held

responsible for maintaining an equitable scale, however. At the least, this kind of action should fall into the concurrence-required category of staff authority.

3. Since this action enters an area in which legal compliance is essential, it should be governed by the personnel manager's functional authority. The finance manager *must* be required to follow the employment procedure established by the personnel manager, even though the finance manager may make the ultimate choice from among the candidates.

Comprehension-Check Case for Chapter 5

The Case of the Shrinking Lumber Company

For easy reference, the text of the comprehension-check case is numbered to correspond to the assignment questions that follow.

The Peg-Top Lumber Company had undergone massive expansion in recent years. It had begun as a small, northwestern sawmill in the early 1900s. Then, it had begun to acquire forestlands and to build ever-larger mills. By the 1970s, it was one of the largest timber-products companies in the world. Then, as building of both homes and commercial structures slowed down dramatically in the 1970s and early 1980s, the firm had to tighten its belt. Not only at headquarters, but also in its sales offices and in its plywood and fabricated-products plants, Peg-Top was undergoing radical revisions of its organization structure.

1. At the company's Wisconsin plywood plant, the processes had been greatly automated, but the jobs of plant employees had remained essentially as they were in the 1950s. The human resources manager proposed a fresh start in defining jobs in the stripping room. In the past, there had been a number of very specialized manual jobs: soaker, puddler, stripper A, stripper B, stripper C, diverter, etc. Now, the process was carried out in large vats through which the incoming logs were moved progressively along conveyor chains manipulated by an operator in a control tower. Supporting the operator were two unskilled laborers, who, at the operator's direction, would engage or disengage logs that might be blocking the flow through the vats.

The work of the operator required far more knowledge, skill, and responsibility than any of the former jobs. The work of the laborers, however, was on a level of skill with the least of the original jobs, and was dirty and dangerous, to boot.

2. At its peak, Peg-Top had prided itself on the efficiency of its headquarters office. Massive files there held records of thousands of customer-

product specifications. Now, however, shipments were made from the plants to regional warehouses, which served customers within designated territories. Furthermore, all home-office records had been converted to a computerized data bank and could be made available on an instant's notice to the field. In Peg-Top's reorganization scheme, regional sales offices were created for six parts of the country, with each office having immediate computer access to the central data bank.

3. Ron Banks, the president of Peg-Top, wished to maintain consistency of action all the way down the line. He insisted that his instructions be passed on progressively so that each level of management was clearly and exactly informed of the new policies and procedures.

The president did delegate the responsibility for sales to a marketing vice president, to whom all regional sales offices reported. Because sales revenues were so critical to financial funding, however, the president directed the regional sales managers to report their daily sales directly to the controller. Because the marketing vice president was frequently in the field at the day's end, more often than not the controller, Joyce Mills, felt that she had to give instructions to the regional managers about where their focus should be the following day. Sometimes Joyce's instructions were contrary to those originally given by the marketing vice president.

4. The net effect of the changes in Peg-Top's organizational structure was to reduce the number of levels of management. The jobs of many middle-level managers were permanently eliminated. The remaining managers took up the slack, with the result that each now supervised more activities than in the past.

5. At the Wisconsin plant, a quality-control department had been set up to check the process at critical stages and to inspect final product coming off the line. On several occasions the manager of quality control had attempted to halt the line while it was running, but the plant manager always overruled this decision. As a result, the amount of faulty end product that could not be shipped was having a damaging impact on profits.

In order to resolve problems like this, Peg-Top's president appointed a task force. Joyce Mills was put in charge of the task force. Specialists from the engineering, quality control, production, purchasing, and sales departments were detached temporarily from their regular duties and assigned to the task force for the duration of the investigation.

Assignment Questions

1 (a)   The changes in the definition of jobs in the stripping room represents a:

_____   *a.* change in departmentation.

_____   *b.* move toward centralization.

_____   *c.* more specialized division of labor.

_____   *d.* less specialized division of labor.

1 (b)   Under the new setup in the stripping room, the operator's job has grown through:

_____ *a.* job enlargement.

_____ *b.* job enrichment.

_____ *c.* job enhancement.

_____ *d.* all of the above.

1 (c)   What might be done to improve the quality of the work of the laborers' job?

_____ *a.* Broaden the scope of their duties.

_____ *b.* Give them more responsibility.

_____ *c.* Provide safer and cleaner working conditions.

_____ *d.* All of the above.

2 (a)   Assigning all the tasks, duties, and responsibilities for collecting and maintaining customer-product specification records at headquarters represents departmentation by:

_____ *a.* function.

_____ *b.* product.

_____ *c.* location.

_____ *d.* matrix.

2 (b)   Establishment of six regional sales offices represents departmentation by:

_____ *a.* function.

_____ *b.* service.

_____ *c.* location.

_____ *d.* line and staff.

2 (c)   Establishment of these six regional sales offices so as to react instantly to needs in the field indicates a corporate move toward:

_____ *a.* centralization.

_____ *b.* decentralization.

_____ *c.* departmentation.

_____ *d.* matrix structures.

3 (a)   Even under the new organization structure, the president wants his instructions to follow the:

_____ *a.* line-and-staff path.

_____ *b.* functional-authority principle.

_____ *c.* departmentation lines.

_____ *d.* chain of command.

3 (b)   In asking the regional sales managers to report daily sales figures directly to the controller, the president was violating the principle of _____; and the controller, in giving instructions directly to the sales managers, was violating the principle of _____.

_____ *a.* unity of command; chain of command

_____ *b.* chain of command; unity of command

_____ *c.* job enrichment; functional authority

_____ *d.* centralization; decentralization

4 (a)   The reduction in the number of levels in Peg-Top's organizational hierarchy represents:

_____ *a.* less delegated authority.
_____ *b.* tighter control from the top.
_____ *c.* centralization.
_____ *d.* decentralization.

4 (b)   The reduction in the number of middle managers led to_____
_____ spans of management (or control) and _____ organization structures.

_____ *a.* broader; flatter
_____ *b.* narrower; taller
_____ *c.* broader; centralized
_____ *d.* narrower; decentralized

5 (a)   In order to be able to halt the production line when a quality problem arises, regardless of how the production manager feels about it, the quality-control manager needs:

_____ *a.* authority of consultation.
_____ *b.* authority of concurrence.
_____ *c.* functional authority.
_____ *d.* None of the above will enable the quality-control manager to halt the line.

5 (b)   The task force that the president created to solve problems like the one of quality control appears most like _____ organization structure.

_____ *a.* functional
_____ *b.* service
_____ *c.* line-and-staff
_____ *d.* matrix

6

Staffing: Placing the Right People in the Right Jobs

The staffing process puts life into an organization. It provides the people who will use muscle and minds to carry out a company's mission. As such, it is considered by many authorities to be the pivotal act of management. This requires planning and foresight to assure that neither too many nor too few people are recruited. The success of the staffing activity, however, depends upon carefully specifying exactly what each position requires from a candidate, along with its proper compensation. With these as a foundation, a search is made to develop a pool of candidates from among whom the most appropriate individuals can be selected and placed in the organization. The process does not stop there. Staffing entails continual administration of an employee's passage through, or out of, the organization. This monitoring is enhanced by programs for the training and development of all employees along with regular appraisals of their performance.

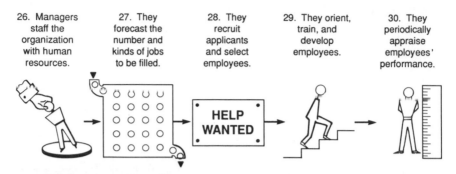

| 26. Managers staff the organization with human resources. | 27. They forecast the number and kinds of jobs to be filled. | 28. They recruit applicants and select employees. | 29. They orient, train, and develop employees. | 30. They periodically appraise employees' performance. |

Figure 6.1. Concepts 26–30.

Key Concepts Regarding the Staffing Process

Figure 6.1 illustrates the five key concepts that relate to the staffing process. These key concepts are:

26. The staffing of an organization is the pivotal process that puts in place the individuals who will carry out the organization's missions and plans. This process is greatly regulated by law and is further influenced by the presence of labor union activity.

27. Human resources planning forecasts the numbers and kinds of positions that need to be filled, specifies the exact requirements of each job or position, and prepares the compensation system by which individuals will be paid.

28. Managers recruit employees from convenient sources, select the most appropriate and available personnel, and administer their placement and subsequent movement through the organization.

29. Managers supervise and coordinate the orientation, training, and development of an organization's employees.

30. Managers periodically conduct formal appraisals of employees' performance in order to ensure conformance to the organization's standards.

Key Terms

To get the most from the key concepts, you must understand the following terms:

Human resources management	Equal Employment Opportunity Commission (EEOC)
Affirmative action	
Occupational Safety and Health Commission	Promotion
	Separation
National Labor Relations Roard (NLRB)	Orientation
Collective bargaining	Vestibule training
Labor Contract	Apprenticeship program
Job analysis	Job Instruction Training (JIT)
Job description	Coaching
Job specification	Interactive method
Job evaluation plan	Performance appraisal system
Employee benefits program	Objective standard
Recruiting	Subjective judgment
Applicaton blank	Trait approach
Employment in terview	Forced-choice method
Test reliability	Behviorally anchored (BARS)
Test validity	Forced-choice method
Transfer	Halo effect

Concept 26

The staffing of an organization is the pivotal process that puts in place the individuals who will carry out the organization's missions and plans. This process is greatly regulated by law and is further influenced by the presence of labor union activity.

The encompassing term for management's staffing function is **human resources management**. It includes planning and specifying the human resources (or personnel) needs of an organization, as well as the recruitment, selection, placement, compensation, training, development, and evaluation of these personnel. The staffing process itself may be classified into three related activities:

1. *Acquiring human resources.* Includes planning and forecasting of personnel requirements, job analysis and specification, recruitment, selection, and orientation.

2. *Maintaining human resources.* Includes routine administration of

pay; internal movements such as promotions and transfers; and supervision of safety, health, and employee benefit programs.

3. *Developing human resources.* Includes training employees in new skills, implementing management and professional development programs, and appraising employees' performance.

Legal Aspects of Human Resources Management

Over the last 80 years or so, the law of the United States has increasingly guaranteed certain rights and privileges to employees. These rights and privileges, in turn, place restrictions on management as it carries out the staffing function. Such legislation falls into three general categories:

1. *Assurance of equal employment opportunities.* The intention of this legislation is to guarantee the right of all persons to be employed and to advance in that employment on the basis of merit, ability, and potential without any form of discrimination because of race, color, religion, sex, age, or national origin. The main body of these laws is illustrated in Figure 6.2. These laws are enforced by the **Equal Employment Opportunity Commission (EEOC).**

EQUAL PAY ACT OF 1963 Requires "equal pay for equal work" and states that members of one sex may not be compensated at a rate lower than that paid to members of the opposite sex who are performing the same work.

TITLE VII OF THE CIVIL RIGHTS ACT as amended by the Equal Employment Opportunity Act of 1972. An all-encompassing federal law. Deals with job bias. Prohibits discriminatory actions based upon race, color, religion, sex, or national origin. The Equal Employment Opportunity Commission was established to enforce this law.

AGE DISCRIMINATION IN EMPLOYMENT ACT. Amended in 1978 to prohibit job discrimination based upon age for persons between 40 and 70.

VOCATIONAL REHABILITATION ACT OF 1973. Requires affirmative action programs for the handicapped in businesses with federal contracts or subcontracts.

VIETNAM-ERA VETERANS' READJUSTMENT ASSISTANCE ACT OF 1974. Requires affirmative action programs for Vietnam-era veterans in businesses with federal contracts or subcontracts.

PREGNANCY DISCRIMINATION ACT OF 1978. Prohibits job discrimination against pregnant employees, and is an amendment to Title VII.

Figure 6.2. Legislation that establishes equal employment opportunities.

A unique aspect of this legislation is the requirement that firms with federal contracts of $50,000 or more institute and maintain an **affirmative action** program—a program designed to increase opportunities for women, minorities, and people in certain other protected categories (such as the handicapped) so that they may become more fairly represented in the work force. Specifically, this means that firms must demonstrate significant efforts to recruit, train, and promote women and minorities so that their presence in the work force at all levels will be somewhat in proportion to their presence in the local population.

2. *Assurance of safe and healthful working conditions.* The significant legislation here is the Occupational Safety and Health Act of 1970. It requires—with great specificity—that employers develop and implement comprehensive safety and health plans. Such plans include inspection of work facilities, removal of hazards, presentation of educational programs, and filing of detailed safety and health reports with the federal government. This law is enforced by the **Occupational Safety and Health Commission**.

3. *Assurance of fair compensation standards and of employees' rights to bargain collectively with management.* The most significant of these laws are listed in Figure 6.3. The Fair Labor Standards Act established the 40-hour week as a basis of compensation. The other laws establish conditions under which labor unions that represent employees may negotiate with management so as to establish relationships that are rewarding to both parties. The principal enforcement agency is the **National Labor Relations Board (NLRB)**.

NATIONAL LABOR RELATIONS ACT OF 1935 (The Wagner Act). Legalized collective bargaining and required employers to bargain with the elected representatives of their employees.

FAIR LABOR STANDARDS ACT OF 1938 (Wages & Hours Law). Outlawed the use of child labor and set a minimum wage and maximum basic hours of work for employees of firms engaged in interstate commerce.

TAFT-HARTLEY ACT OF 1947. Intended to balance the power of unions and management by prohibiting a number of unfair labor practices, including the so-called closed shop, which prohibited management from hiring non-union workers.

LANDRUM-GRIFFIN ACT OF 1959. Requires regularly scheduled elections of union officers by secret ballot, and regulates the handling of union funds.

Figure 6.3. Legislation affecting relations between management and labor unions.

Human Resources Management and
Labor Unions

About half of all employees in the United States are affiliated with labor unions that represent their interests to their employers. In practice, this means that a great many companies must modify their human resources programs in accordance with terms established through **collective bargaining** with a trade union. In other words, where employees are represented by a labor union, management cannot make unilateral decisions about pay, hours, or working conditions. These become the subject of collective bargaining with the union. The **labor contract** that emerges from these negotiations establishes the agreed-upon conditions, and both management and employees must conform to them for the duration of the contract.

Practical Implications

The Situation.   MicroMaster Fabricators is a construction firm that has just undertaken a major government contract. In the past, it has employed few women or minorities as engineers, draftspeople, or in upper-level managerial positions. On the other hand, it does employ a great number of minorities—but not women—in lower-level laboring jobs. Most of these lower-level jobs are included under MicroMaster's contract with its labor union. Soon after the government contract was signed, the EEOC sent in an agent to discuss the company's plans for affirmative action. Mac Field, the company's human resources manager, said that he would like to see some women and minorities in the professional and managerial grades, but qualified candidates were simply not available. As to employing women in the lower-level jobs, Field was sure that the labor union would resist any actions that upset its prevailing seniority rules.

Question.   What might the human resources manager do under these circumstances to comply with the requirement to develop a genuine affirmative action plan?

Answer.   Complying with the requirements of an effective affirmative action plan is not easy, but there are several positive steps that might be taken:

1. Perform a human resources utilization analysis, to identify jobs in which minorities and women are underemployed.

2. Based upon the analysis, prepare a set of target goals and a timetable for attaining them.

3. Establish an equal employment opportunity policy to guide all recruitment, selection, placement, compensation, and training activities.

4. Appoint a qualified individual to oversee the implementation of the policy.

5. Solicit assistance from the labor union and from agencies and educational institutions in the local community to help recruit and train minority personnel and women for the targeted positions.

6. Set up an audit system to periodically check progress against the affirmative action goals. For comparison, a study of federal contractors between 1974 and 1980 demonstrated that affirmative action programs showed gains of 33 percent for black males, 77 percent for black females, and 30 percent for white females. Gains for noncontracting organizations duringthe same period were 28, 47, and 17 percent, respectively.

Concept 27

Human resources planning forecasts the numbers and kinds of positions that need to be filled, specifies the exact requirements of each job or position, and prepares the compensation system by which individuals will be paid.

How many and what kinds of jobs need to be performed to achieve a company's goals? That's the basic question that human resources planning must answer. Once this staffing base has been established, the impact of the organization's growth or decline on the employment structure can be forecast. As a matter of fact, the staffing of most organizations is always in a state of change.

As an organization grows, the jobs to be filled will change in kind and grow in number. When a company's business is declining, the number of jobs to be filled will also decline, and the kinds of openings may change also. People leave an organization unit (such as a department) often, for any of a number of reasons, and new people often join the work force, as shown in Figure 6.4. It is a management responsibility to

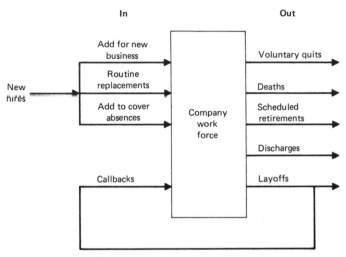

Figure 6.4. Human resources flow into and out of a company's work force.

provide the specifications for each position and the numbers of people needed to fill each position. This is accomplished through job analysis.

Job Analysis

The process of deciding exactly which jobs need to be performed is similar to what occurs under a division of labor. The main difference is that, under job analysis, it is assumed that most jobs already exist in some form, even though new ones may be created in the future. **Job analysis** is the process of examining a job to determine its components and what it will require of the person who fills it. To ascertain a job's duties and responsibilities, an analyst asks these questions:

What is done?

When is it done?

Why is it done?

Where is it done?

How is it done?

Who does it?

What does a person *need to know* to be able to do it?

What *essential skills* must the person possess to be able to perform the job in a satisfactory manner?

Two essential documents are prepared from the information gathered in a job analysis:

A **job description**, which is a written statement describing the objectives of a job, the work to be performed, the skills required, the responsibilities involved, the relationships to other jobs, and the working conditions. A sample job description is shown in Figure 6.5.

A **job specification**, which is a written description of the special qualifications required of the person who fills a particular job, including skills, education, and previous experience. It is used to guide the recruitment of candidates and the selection of individuals to fill a particular job opening.

Compensation

Today's employees rightfully believe that their pay should be fair and equitable. The latter is expressed in the principle of "equal pay for equal work" embodied in the equal employment opportunity laws. Accordingly, most firms design a system of compensation that follows that principle and also provides an incentive for attracting and retaining productive employees.

Many compensation systems are based upon a **job evaluation plan**. Such plans provide a systematic method for ranking jobs according to their difficulty and their contribution to the organization's objectives. The relative rankings that emerge from job evaluation are often designated as "job grades" (or "position grades"). A compensation plan is then developed to provide a related wage and salary scale, often with rate ranges from a starting wage or salary to a top-of-the-rate pay limit within each grade.

Employees may be paid wages for hourly work or salaries when work is performed on a weekly, monthly, or annual basis. Under some compensation plans, employees may earn a wage incentive or a salary bonus based upon their productivity or sales attainment. A growing number of companies supplement their regular compensation system with profit-sharing plans.

Almost all companies add an **employee benefits program** to the basic compensation plan. This includes such things as paid health and life insurance, holidays, and vacations. Such programs often amount to 30 percent or better of a company's annual payroll.

POSITION: Shipping Clerk
DEPARTMENT: Shipping and Receiving
LOCATION: Building C Warehouse

JOB SUMMARY. Under general supervision of warehouse manager, processes shipments to customers in accordance with shipment authorization forms forwarded by the sales department. Together with other clerks and packers, removes goods from shelves by hand or by powered equipment and packs them in containers for shipment by truck, rail, air, or parcel service. Prepares and processes appropriate paperwork and maintains related files.

EDUCATION.   High school graduate.

EXPERIENCE.   None required.

DUTIES PERFORMED

1. The following represent 70 percent of working time:
   a. Removing stock from shelves and racks, and packing into proper shipping containers
   b. Weighing and labeling cartons for shipment by carrier designated on the shipping order
   c. Assisting in loading carriers
2. The following represents 15 percent of working time:
   a. Preparing and processing authorization forms (e.g., packing lists, shipping orders, and bills of lading)
   b. Maintaining shipment records by tally sheets or keypunch
   c. Doing miscellaneous typing of forms and labels
   d. Maintaining appropriate files
3. The following represents the balance of working time:
   a. Driving company truck to post office or for an occasional local delivery
   b. Assisting in taking inventory
   c. Acting as checker for other shipping or receiving clerks
   d. Keeping workplace clean and orderly

SUPERVISION RECEIVED.   Except for general instructions and special problems, works independently.

RELATIONSHIPS.   Works in close contact with packers, material handlers, and other clerks. Has contact with truck drivers when loading. Has occasional contact with sales-order department personnel.

EQUIPMENT.   Operates mechanized stock picker, powered conveyor belts, carton-sealing machinery, keypunch terminals, and typewriter.

WORKING CONDITIONS.   Clean, well-lit, and heated. Requires normal standing, walking, climbing, and lifting. Subject to drafts when shipping doors are open.

Figure 6.5. Sample job description.

Practical Implications

The Situation.   Charley Breen answered an ad for a "clerical assistant," placed by a large trucking firm. He was interviewed by the personnel manager, judged to have the proper qualifications for the job, and hired. Charley was assigned to assist the firm's office manager in a variety of duties. Almost from the start, however, Charley's boss was dissatisfied with Charley's work. The complaints were, "In the first place, Charley doesn't know enough about accounting, and furthermore he hasn't had the experience needed to do the job." The personnel manager retorted that Charley was about the best person who could be found for a clerical assistant's job that paid so little compared with what junior accountants were paid by the firm. "Well," said Charley's boss, "do whatever you have to do to get me the right kind of assistant."

Question.   What might the personnel manager do to get the "right kind" of person for this particular position, as well as to avoid such problems in the future?

Answer.   First of all, an accurate job description should be developed through a systematic job analysis of what a clerical assistant's job entails when working for the office manager. The title, alone, carries no real meaning. Based upon a comprehensive job description, a job specification can be used to recruit candidates with the designated educational and experience requirements. Finally, pay for the job (1) should be set in proportion to the value of that job to others in the firm and (2) should be reasonably competitive with going pay rates for truly comparable jobs in the community.

***

Concept 28

Managers recruit employees from convenient sources, select the most appropriate available personnel, and administer their placement and subsequent movement through the organization.

***

The staffing process begins for sure with **recruiting**. This is the stage in which a number of applicants are attracted to a particular job opening. It is important that the group be large enough to offer a good chance of obtaining one or more satisfactory candidates from among them. Many sources of applicants can be tapped, and these sources vary according to ease of use, cost, and the quality of applicants obtained. They include:

- *Referrals from current employees.* This is often the best and least costly source. Employees know the company's needs and practices and are not likely to recommend people who will be unsatisfactory coworkers.

- *Newspaper advertisements.* This is a simple and commonly used method. Its drawback is that it provides little or no screening of applicants: there may be large numbers of applicants but few good candidates among them.

- *Private employment agencies.* These firms provide screening, and they often know how to find good candidates with special skills. They charge either the candidate or the company a fee, which can be quite large. "Executive-search" firms (headhunters) specialize in recruiting upper-level management and professional candidates who are in short supply.

- *Public employment agencies.* Most states maintain this service, especially for jobs requiring basic skills. There is no charge for this service, and training may be provided under certain circumstances.

- *Educational institutions.* Universities, colleges, vocational schools, and high schools are also good sources. Many companies regularly send recruiters to colleges, for example, to recruit candidates for professional and entry-level management positions.

Selecting the Most Qualified Individual

Selection of the best person from among many good candidates is a difficult task. Accordingly, several devices and techniques have been created to assist in this decision.

Application Blanks. Candidates are required to provide specified information about themselves on **application blanks** before they are invited to an interview. The problems with the application blank are that (1) the candidate may provide misleading or incorrect information, and (2) the information that may be requested is greatly limited by federal and state laws. In general, requests for educational and experiential backgrounds are approved. Almost all else may be considered "discriminatory" and, thus, illegal, as enlarged upon in Figure 6.6.

Employment Interviews. Interviewing provides an opportunity for a face-to-face exchange so that the candidate may be evaluated on a

---

- *Race or color.* Don't ask. Don't comment.*
- *Religion.* Don't ask. Don't say, "This is a Catholic (or Jewish, or Protestant) organization."
- *National origin.* Don't ask. Don't comment.
- *Sex.* Don't ask. Don't comment. Don't indicate a prejudgment of physical capabilities.
- *Age.* Don't ask, "How old are you?" Don't ask for birth date. You may, however, ask if the applicant is between the ages of 18 and 70.
- *Marital status.* Don't ask about marital status or ages of children, or where a spouse works.
- *Disability.* You may ask if the person has a present disability that will interfere with the job to be performed, but not about past disabilities or illnesses.
- *Address.* You may ask for the applicant's address and how long the person has lived there. You may ask if the applicant is a citizen of the United States and, if not, whether the person has the legal right to remain permanently in the country. It is generally unlawful to press for answers beyond this point.
- *Criminal record.* You may ask if the person has ever been convicted of a crime and, if so, when and where it took place. You may *not* ask if the person has ever been arrested, nor can you deny employment on the basis of a criminal record, unless it can be proved that such a record would damage the employer's business.
- *Physical capabilities.* Don't ask how tall or strong an applicant is. This may indicate a sexist prejudice. You may, however, explain the physical aspects of the job, such as any lifting or pulling that is involved, and you may show how the job is performed.
- *Education.* Questions are largely unrestricted.
- *Experience.* Questions are largely unrestricted.

*This list is not complete, and there are many nuances that require legal interpretation according to the circumstances. The main point is that an employer must be able to demonstrate that all questions are relevant to the job for which the individual is applying.

Figure 6.6. Representative list of restricted subjects for either an application blank or an employment interview.

broader basis than what appears on the application blank. The problems with **employment interviews** are that (1) they are subjective, (2) prudent candidates will show only their best sides, and (3) interviews are subject to the same legal restrictions as application blanks. Generally speaking, better results are obtained when two or more people interview each of the better candidates so as to get more than one opinion.

Testing.   Testing of any sort has become highly suspect and difficult to administer within EEOC guidelines. Generally speaking, tests of skill and ability (such as typing, mechanical dexterity, and arithmetic) are likely to be acceptable. Personality and interest tests are all right for certain jobs, such as salespersons or managers. Aptitude tests and any that measure potential (especially so-called IQ tests) are likely to invite charges of discrimination.

In any event, screening tests must pass two hurdles: reliability and validity. **Test reliability** means that if the test were given over and over again, each testee would repeat his or her score. **Test validity** means that the test results must be indisputably related to job performance. In other words, it must be shown that those who score well will succeed on the particular job for which they are tested and that those who score poorly will not.

Reference Checks.   Checking references is useful in verifying that job candidates do, in fact, have the education and experience they claim. Beyond that, few legal inquiries can be made. Even fewer valid responses are likely to be obtained, because of fears of charges of discrimination.

Placement and Movement Within an Organization

Once the decision is made to hire (or place) an individual, it is important that this person be properly introduced to the job. This entails an orientation that makes the person feel comfortable in new surroundings. (More about this later under concept 29.) An employee's initial placement, however, is often only the beginning of his or her movement through the organization. Accordingly, management—usually the human resources manager or administrator—traces and records a number of possible job changes. These include:

Transfers are usually lateral moves that involve neither a promotion nor a pay change. They take place either because of changes in the operating demands of the organization or to provide an upwardly mobile individual with a variety of experiences.

Promotions involve an increase in both responsibility and compensation. The recruitment and selection process is often repeated as a part of the promotion procedure and is subject to the same EEOC restrictions as initial employment.

Separations may be temporary, as with a layoff caused by a company's lack of business, or permanent, as in a termination. They may be voluntary, as when an employee resigns, or involuntary, as when an employee is discharged for cause or when a company closes down an operation permanently.

When employees are represented by a labor union, promotions and terminations may be subject to contractual provisions, especially seniority. That is, the most senior person gets preference for a promotion and the least senior person goes first in a layoff.

Practical Implications

The Situation. Jill Marston, a project leader in the test-model department of an aircraft assembly plant located in the northwestern United States, was hiring a machinist. The personnel department had been able to supply more than 10 possible candidates. Now, the project leader had narrowed down the list of candidates to 3. Each of them appeared to be very good—based upon the information on their application blanks. Ms. Marston was preparing to interview them in order to elicit the most useful information about their experience and to judge how well their personalities would suit the tightly knit character of her work group.

Question. What questions might Ms. Marston ask that would help her to judge the qualities of each candidate without overstepping legal bounds?

Answer. Questions should focus on helping to make judgments about (1) technical competence and (2) personal characteristics that would make the candidate amenable to working conditions in the test-model group.

Assessments of *technical competence* might follow this line of questioning:

- Where did you get your most valuable experience? Suppose you tell me about your working experience, starting with your first job.
- How do you feel that your experience would help you in performing the job I've just described?
- Which particular skills do you consider your best ones?
- What sort of machining assignments do you find most difficult? Why?

Personality assessments can follow this line of questioning:

- Whom did you report to on your last job? Can you describe that supervisor?
- What is it about this kind of work that appeals to you most? Least?
- How would you describe your health? What kind of attendance record have you maintained during the last year?
- In your last job, how closely did you have to work with others? What kind of person did you find most enjoyable to work with? Least?
- Why did you leave your job at XYZ Company?

Concept 29

Managers supervise and coordinate the orientation, training, and development of an organization's employees.

Regardless of how well chosen employees are for the jobs they are placed in, their knowledge and skills for these assignments should be considered only as a foundation upon which to build continuing improvement. Employees newly hired or assigned to a different department within a company need a comprehensive orientation to their new workplace. Experienced employees benefit from training that helps them to improve skills and knowledge relevant to their present jobs. A great many employees will be candidates for training that will enable them to accept assignments and promotions in areas other than their current specialization. Individuals in the management ranks, from supervisor to company president, will benefit from continuing programs of management development.

Induction and Orientation

When a new employee is hired — or when an employee is transferred or promoted into a different department — an induction, or **orientation**, session should be provided. Such an orientation program can take place in two phases: (1) a talk explaining basic rules and practices of the new department and (2) a physical tour of the new workplace.

An orientation *talk* normally includes the following:

- Pay rates, pay periods, how employees are paid, the date when the first pay will be received, and pay deductions
- Hours of work, reporting and quitting time, lunch periods, and washup time
- Overtime, overtime pay, shift pay, and other premium pay
- How to report sick
- What to do when late
- Basic safety and health rules, potential hazards, and how to report accidents
- The employee's options under company benefit plans, such as group life and health insurance

An orientation *tour* may include the following:

- Tour of department, plant, or company
- Locations of lockers and washrooms
- Location of first-aid room
- Introduction to coworkers
- Assignment to work station

Employee Training Programs

The content of most jobs is under constant change. There are always new demands for greater skills and knowledge, as well as pressure to modify attitudes — toward work quality, coworkers, technology, or customers. With operatives — so-called rank-and-file employees, whether blue- or white-collar — the great majority of all training takes place on the job. Often, the supervisor or an experienced coworker is the instructor. Off-the-job training is usually reserved for broad-gauge subjects, like safety, blueprint reading, and computer literacy.

Occasionally, employees undergo **vestibule training**. They learn by practicing a skill on sample materials outside the plant or office under close supervision before they enter the organization to work on real assignments.

Some workers still receive their training under **apprenticeship programs**. This training may last from 2 to 6 years. It combines on-the-job skills training with off-the-job classroom instruction in the fundamentals of the particular craft, such as toolmaking.

Job Instruction Training (JIT) provides the basic structure for most employee training programs. Developed during World War II, it leads a trainee through four steps, each under the close supervision of an instructor, who is usually a coworker or supervisor.

Step 1. Prepare the trainee to learn. Put the trainee at ease. Explain the importance of the task and how it fits into the other jobs being performed.

Step 2. Demonstrate how the job is performed. Do so by showing as well as telling. Point out key stages of the job, as well as where a particular knack will make it easy and where a mistake will cause problems.

Step 3. Try the trainee out under close supervision. Allow the trainee to perform the easy parts of the job first, while the trainer takes care of the difficult parts, as shown in Figure 6.7. Gradually, let the trainee perform the whole job from start to finish.

Step 4. Put the trainee on his or her own. Check back periodically to answer questions and to give instruction on variations that may occur.

Management Development Programs

When it comes to providing training for managers and executives, the emphasis switches from instruction to coaching and interactive methods. **Coaching** takes place on the job when, for example, a department manager advises a supervisor about how to handle a problem of employee discipline.

The **interactive method** is used off the job, and can take many forms. It may depend mainly upon an exchange of views between participants and conference leader at a seminar or workshop. Or it may be a carefully structured opportunity for a manager to gain experience by interacting with other individuals under conditions that simulate real-life situations. As defined here, the interactive approach is essentially a way of acquiring knowledge and skills by sharing experiences and by testing out the new knowledge and skills through debate and in simulated situations. This method depends largely upon discussion by participants, case-study analysis, and role play.

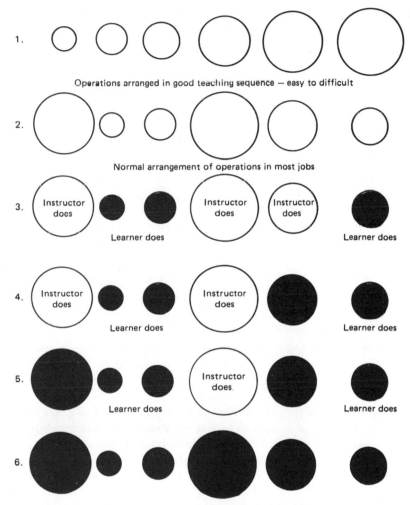

1. Operations arranged in good teaching sequence — easy to difficult

2. Normal arrangement of operations in most jobs

3. Instructor does | Learner does | Instructor does | Instructor does | Learner does

4. Instructor does | Learner does | Instructor does | Learner does

5. Learner does | Instructor does | Learner does

6.

Figure 6.7. Job training arranged in sequence of task difficulties.

Practical Implications

The Situation. Mark Green has finished his orientation as a sales correspondent in the sales-order department of a midwestern distributor of industrial goods. He learns that much of his dictation will be handled by the company's central word processing department, rather than by a personal secretary or stenographer. Mark's supervisor, Anne Holt, wants him to know how to give dictation using the word-processing system. The steps to be followed in operating the system are as follows.

1. Assemble whatever documents you need to refer to, and organize your thoughts before starting the process.
2. Turn on the machine and identify yourself.
3. Specify the format of the document you wish prepared: letter, memo, report; single- or double-spaced; standard or special format
4. Dictate the body of the document.
5. Provide your name and title.
6. Provide the names of copy recipients.
7. Indicate enclosures or attachments.
8. When dictation is complete, say "End of dictation."

From experience, Mark's supervisor knows that there are several key points that can make or break the use of the word processing system.

Question.   How can Anne make sure that Mark learns how to use the word processing system as quickly as possible and with the minimum of error?

Answer.   She should follow the four-step JIT process, being sure to point out the spots where a special knack is needed or an error will cause a problem. Here's how she might approach this training session with Mark:

Step 1.   She should put Mark at ease by saying something like this: "How much do you know about the use of a word processing system? Have you ever used it for dictation? If you have, there may be some similarities and some differences between the way you've done it before and the procedures we follow here. Don't be afraid to interrupt me and to ask questions."

Step 2.   During the demonstration step, she should alert Mark to the various make-or-break parts of the job. For example: "To turn on the machine, you must push both the 'on' and the 'connect' button at the same time. Otherwise you won't make a connection. Do it like this. When the green light goes on, you know that you're on the air. Only then should you identify yourself.

"The next step is to specify the kind of document, spacing, and format. If the format is not a standard one, you must describe it at this point. Otherwise, the operator will be unable to proceed. Let me show you how this is done.

"Now you can proceed to dictate the body of your document. Be sure to enunciate clearly and to spell out all technical words. If in doubt, spell them out." And so on.

Step 3. Mark's supervisor should now let Mark go through the procedure himself. She may handle the formatting instructions since this is probably the most difficult part of the procedure. She should stand by while Mark runs through the entire procedure several times, correcting him as necessary and answering his questions as they arise. She may repeat the key points that were emphasized in her demonstration.

Step 4. Then Anne should tell Mark that he will be on his own for the next 2 hours, but that, if he encounters difficulty, he should contact her for help. She should return after the 2-hour period to see how Mark is making out and to solve any problems he has been unable to handle.

Concept 30

Managers periodically conduct formal appraisals of employees' performance in order to ensure conformance to the organization's standards.

"How am I doing?" That's the unspoken question in the minds of many employees. And that's healthy, and it warrants a response from management as often as it is voiced. Unfortunately, this question is rarely raised by employees whose performance is not up to an expected standard. Accordingly, most progressive organizations maintain a formal **performance appraisal system**. Its purpose is to provide—in a systematic way—each employee with a periodic evaluation by management of his or her performance.

In the best situation, this evaluation will be largely based upon specific standards such as those for output, errors, absences, and other measurable actions. In the more normal situation, the appraisal will be based upon a combination of such objective standards and the appraiser's subjective evaluations. An **objective standard** is one against which an employee's performance can be compared numerically: for example, expected output is 100 units processed a day, while actual performance is lower (say, 90) or higher (say, 105). Objective standards are preferred, since such an evaluation does not depend upon judgment and can be verified by the employee. **Subjective judgments** are those that rely upon an opinion by the supervisor. Typically, these include appraisals of initiative, dependability, and cooperation. Such judgments are, obviously, subject to bias, whether intended by the supervisor or not.

Goals of Appraisals

Above and beyond satisfying the natural curiosity of an individual to know how he or she stands in an organization, performance appraisals have three important objectives:

1. To encourage good behavior and to correct and discourage below-standard performance. Good performers expect a reward, even if it is only praise. Poor performers must recognize and accept that continued substandard behavior will, at the very least, stand in the way of advancement, or at the worst, lead to termination.

2. To provide a foundation for later judgments that may concern an employee's career — pay raises, promotions, transfers, or separation. Most companies try to separate the performance appraisal from compensation considerations, at least at the time that the appraisal is made.

3. To provide a basis for the employee's immediate training and future development. An effective appraisal will uncover an employee's weaknesses and highlight his or her strengths. The former may be corrected by a specific training program; the latter may be developed by broadening assignments.

Appraisal Format and Methods

The most common format used to guide and record a performance appraisal is the so-called **trait approach**. In essence, the rater is supplied with a number of traits for which the employee's performance is to be judged as, say, "unsatisfactory," "satisfactory," or "excellent." Because the appraiser must classify the employee's performance for each trait under one of these headings, the format is often called the **forced-choice method**. The obvious weakness is that different raters will have differing interpretations of what a particular classification (like "unsatisfactory" or "excellent") stands for. To correct this shortcoming, many companies extend the format with **behaviorally anchored rating scales (BARS)**. That is, for example, a description of what constitutes "excellent" behavior is provided for each trait to be rated. This helps to ensure greater consistency among raters and also to reduce bias. A further modification places different weights, or values, on each trait—and on each classification within a trait. This enables the appraiser to calculate an overall numerical score for each employee's performance. A format that incorporates all the above modifications is illustrated in Figure 6.8.

Problems with Performance Appraisals

Performance appraisal systems, at their best, have serious drawbacks. For example:

- Raters tend to shift their own standards. A highly cooperative but poor performer may receive higher ratings than a superior but seemingly indifferent employee.

- Raters may allow personal biases to distort their judgment. Women may be judged more favorably than men, whites more favorably than blacks, and so on.

- Rating criteria, or standards, differ among raters. Like teachers, some are hard graders, while others are soft. Some organizations, the military in particular, employ **forced distribution**. It works this way. If there are, for example, five classifications from "unsatisfactory" to "excellent," the rater is directed to place 10 percent in the unsatisfactory class, 20 percent as below average, 40 percent as average, 20 percent as above average, and 10 percent as excellent.

- Raters are all subject to the **halo effect**. This is the common tendency for an appraiser to be influenced by a single incident or by a single, either very good or very bad, characteristic. As a consequence, an employee's overall rating may be unrealistically high or unreasonably low. Appraisers are usually cautioned to be aware of such influences as:
  1. *Recency.* Remembering what happened last week
  2. *Overemphasis.* Giving too much weight to one outstandingly good or poor factor
  3. *Unforgivingness.* Not allowing an employee's present performance to outshine a poor past record
  4. *Grouping.* Tarring all employees in a substandard work group with the same brush

DEPT._____
EMPLOYMENT IDENTIFICATION NO._____ TO_____
RATING PERIOD FROM _____ TO_____

Factor	Range				
1. *Quality of work* Performance in meeting quality standards.	4 Careless.	8 Just gets by.	12 Does a good job.	16 Rejects and errors are rare.	20 Exceptionally high quality.
2. *Job knowledge* Understanding in all phases of the work.	25 Expert in own job and several others.	20 Expert, but limited to own job.	15 Knows job fairly well.	10 Improvement needed: just gets by.	5 Inadequate knowledge
3. *Quantity of work* Output of satisfactory work.	8 Turns out required amount, but seldom more.	12 Frequently turns out more than required amount.	4 Slow; output is seldom required amount.	20 Exceptionally fast; output is high.	16 Usually does more than expected.
4. *Dependability* Works conscientiously according to instructions.	20 Dependable, no checking necessary.	16 Very little checking necessary.	12 Follows instructions.	8 Frequent checking needed.	4 Continuous checking and follow-up needed.
5. *Initiative* Thinks constructively and originates action.	9 Good decisions and actions, but requires some supervision.	12 Minimum of supervision required.	15 Thinks and acts constructively; no supervision required.	3 Requires constant supervision.	6 Fair decisions; a routine worker.

Note: To minimize halo effect, rating scales for some factors, such as job knowledge and dependability, are reversed. Other scales, such as dependability, are mixed in order. The particular form from which this sample was taken had a total of 12 factors, including adaptability, attitude, attendance, safety and housekeeping, potential, personality, and supervisory ability (if applicable.)

Figure 6.8. Employee performance rating form: sample factors.

Practical Implications

The Situation.   You were appointed a department supervisor 6 months ago, and you are now preparing to conduct your first performance appraisal interview with an employee, Millie Blaine. You have completed the company's rating form and are ready to invite the employee to come to your office so you can discuss your appraisal with her.

Question.   How should this performance appraisal interview be conducted so as to have the most beneficial outcome?

Answer.   Few matters can be more sensitive than this one. You'll want to avoid criticism of the employee as a person and focus your comments on performance. This helps to keep emotions in check and to exert a positive influence on the interview. There are a number of ways of handling this situation, but the seven steps listed below will help to lead to understanding and acceptance of your ratings.

Step 1.   When you issue the invitation, advise Millie to come to the meeting prepared to compare her own notes about her performance with yours.

Step 2.   Compare her performance with specific targets. Avoid generalizations. Be specific about what was expected (the standards) and how close the employee has come to meeting them.

Step 3.   Begin by giving credit for acceptable and above-average performance. There is often a tendency to take for granted those accomplishments that are all right.

Step 4.   Then, review aspects of Millie's performance that are below the performance standards. Emphasize the parts of her work in which improvement is needed. Explore with her why improvement is necessary and how it can be achieved.

Step 5.   Avoid giving the impression that you are sitting in judgment. If there is blame to be shared, acknowledge it. Don't talk in terms of mistakes, faults, or weaknesses. Never compare an employee with a third person. Stick to the facts.

Step 6.   Agree on targets to be met before the next appraisal. Relate them to what has not been accomplished during the past period. This will set the stage for an objective interview the next time.

Step 7.   Review with Millie what *you* can do to be of greater help. Improvement is, more often than not, a mutual activity. An employee who knows that you accept a share of responsibility for improvement will approach the task with greater confidence and enthusiasm.

Comprehension-Check Case
for Chapter 6

The Case of the Expanding World of
Kits 'n' Games

For easy reference, the text of the comprehension-check case is
numbered to correspond to the assignment questions that follow.

The World of Kits 'n' Games (WKNG) began as a part-time occupation of
Joe Burns, a government employee. Originally, he made hobby kits in his
basement and sold them by direct mail. In 1980, he opened Joe's Hobby
Shop, his first small retail store, in a downtown district. Joe's business
kept on growing, however, and eventually he quit his job, moved his shop
to a large shopping mall, and changed its name from Joe's Hobby Shop
to The World of Kits 'n' Games. The business kept on growing until
finally he incorporated and opened a chain of seven retail stores in the
greater metropolitan area. In addition, Joe bought out a small toy factory
and began making his kits on a large scale. As his business grew, Joe
found that he had to deal with a number of personnel problems that in
the past he used to ignore. Here are some of them:

1. After his firm acquired a government contract for $150,000, Joe re-
ceived a visit from an agent of the EEOC, who advised Joe that he would
have to take positive steps to employ more women and minorities. Soon after that visit, Joe arrived at his largest store one morning, only to be greeted
by pickets carrying signs that read, "World of Kits 'n' Games is unfair to
organized labor."

2. Geraldine Fitz, the general manager whom Joe had hired to run the
retail stores, complained that she would need additional help next year. Joe
asked, "How many?" Geraldine cited these figures:

Current employees	350
Additional employees needed to handle increased business	50
Employees needed to fill absences, at a rate of 2½ percent of 400	10
Employees needed to replace anticipated normal quits and discharges	70
Employees needed to replace anticipated retirements	20

The general manager also asked Joe for an OK to pay the chief clerk at
each store $50 more weekly than the other clerks, since the chief clerks had
more responsibility for checking inventories and cash receipts.

3. When Geraldine received an approval from Joe to hire the additional
employees, she posted notices in each store saying "Help wanted for retail

sales work." After 3 weeks of such postings, the general manager was disappointed because few people had applied and because those few applicants were not of the quality she had hoped for.

In addition, the chief clerk at one branch store quit, and Farley Mannix, the store manager, told Geraldine he had been startled when the candidate he wished to promote asked him to describe exactly what the job entailed. "I really can't accept that responsibility," said the candidate, "unless you can be specific about the job and what it expects from me."

4. Joe was often dismayed as he visited the retail stores to see how poorly informed some of the clerks were about the company's product line. New employees, especially, seemed not even to know that WKNG had its own factory. The general manager was disappointed, too, about many things that the store managers did or did not do. "We've got to do something to improve their performance," she said.

5. The need for better management of human resources was made clear to Joe and Geraldine by an unpleasant incident that cropped up at one of the retail stores. It involved Mary Zeller, a retail clerk who had been employed for 3 years. Her performance had been generally unsatisfactory, but Michael Murray, the store manager, had kept her on, hoping that she would improve. She did not, and one morning, after Mary ignored a customer who was asking for help, the store manager fired Mary on the spot. The incident didn't end there. Mary filed charges against the store manager and WKNG, saying that she had never been told that her performance was anything but satisfactory. The discharge, she said, was purely discriminatory. The store manager didn't like women, she said. When Michael was queried about the case, his excuse was, "Everyone in the store knows that Mary was the poorest clerk we had. If she didn't know that, too, she must have been deaf and blind."

Assignment Questions

1 (a)   What specific "positive" step does the EEOC want Joe to take in order to employ more women and minorities?

_____   *a.* Profit sharing
_____   *b.* Head-hunting
_____   *c.* Affirmative action
_____   *d.* Equal employment

1 (b)   The pickets at WKNG's stores are probably seeking representation by a labor union so that employees may enter into _____ with the company.

_____   *a.* collective bargaining
_____   *b.* equal employment
_____   *c.* affirmative action
_____   *d.* independent action

2 (a)   How many employees must the general manager hire during the next

year so that she will end the year with 400 employees?

_____ *a.* 50
_____ *b.* 80
_____ *c.* 100
_____ *d.* 150

2 (b) Before agreeing to a $50 raise for chief clerks, the general manager should develop a compensation plan that is related to the worth of each job to the company. Job _____ is the normal technique for determining this relative worth.

_____ *a.* analysis
_____ *b.* description
_____ *c.* evaluation
_____ *d.* specification

3 (a)   After preparing a job description and job specification for retail store clerks, the next step the general manager should take in her staffing program is to accumulate a pool of qualified candidates through an aggressive _____ _____ program.

_____ *a.* recruiting
_____ *b.* testing
_____ *c.* selection
_____ *d.* placement

3 (b)   Which document might most clearly answer the query from the person who was chosen for the chief clerk's job and who asked for a fuller description of its duties?

_____ *a.* Application blank
_____ *b.* Psychological test
_____ *c.* Job description
_____ *d.* Job specification

4 (a)   What sort of training program seems to be missing for new employees at WKNG's retail stores?

_____ *a.* Orientation
_____ *b.* Apprenticeship
_____ *c.* Job Instruction Training
_____ *d.* Vestibule training

4 (b)   What name is usually given to a training program designed to improve the performance of store managers?

_____ *a.* Coaching
_____ *b.* Interactive training
_____ *c.* Job Instruction Training
_____ *d.* Management development

5 (a)   What kind of program might help to eliminate incidents, such as the one involving Mary when she claimed that she had never been told that her work was unsatisfactory?

_____ *a.* Affirmative action
_____ *b.* Orientation
_____ *c.* Performance appraisal
_____ *d.* Job evaluation

5 (b)   Which federal agency would most likely investigate Mary's charge of discrimination against her as a female employee?

_____ *a.* Environmental Protection Agency

_____ *b.* Fair Trade Commission

_____ *c.* Equal Employment Opportunity Commission

_____ *d.* Occupational Safety and Health Commission

7

Directing: Providing Communications, Motivation, and Leadership

Directing is the managerial function that requires the greatest interpersonal skills of its practitioners. Plans and organizational structures staffed with people are essentially inert. They come alive only through the powers of communications, motivation, and leadership. These are the powers by which managers can release the inherent energies and talents of the organization. Some managers were seemingly born with these interpersonal skills. Most managers, however, acquire them through study and observation, and develop them through experience and application.

Key Concepts Regarding the Directing Function

Figure 7.1 represents graphically the five key concepts that relate to the directing function. They are:

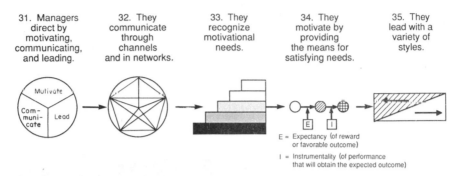

| 31. Managers direct by motivating, communicating, and leading. | 32. They communicate through channels and in networks. | 33. They recognize motivational needs. | 34. They motivate by providing the means for satisfying needs. | 35. They lead with a variety of styles. |

E = Expectancy (of reward or favorable outcome)

I = Instrumentality (of performance that will obtain the expected outcome)

Figure 7.1. Concepts 31–35.

31. Directing is the managerial function that energizes an organization. It requires skill in communicating, sensitivity in motivating others, and a knack for providing leadership.

32. Managers must use both the spoken and the written word effectively in order to impart information, instruction, and direction to the work force.

33. In order to understand what motivates others, a manager must become sensitive to the inner needs and personal goals that impel their behavior.

34. To provide motivation is to provide a means for each employee to seek and attain goals that provide satisfaction for his or her individual needs.

35. Managerial leadership grows from combining an inherent knack with a learned skill for exercising benevolent power and influence upon others, in pursuit of organizational goals.

Key Terms

If you are to make full use of the five key concepts, it is essential to understand the following terms.

Self-fulfilling prophecy	Communications channels
Communications	Communications networks
Feedback	Grapevine
Noise	Motivation

Maslow's hierarchy of needs

Herzberg's two-factor theory

Alderfer's existence-relatedness-growth (ERG) theory

McClelland's achievement motivation theory

Expectancy theory

Expectancy

Instrumentality

Valance

Equity theory

Behavior modification

Positive reinforcement

Punishment

Escape conditioning

Nonreinforcement

Leadership

Expert power

Referent power

Continuum of leadership styles

Managerial Grid©

Situational leadership

Path-goal leadership theory

Concept 31

Directing is the managerial function that energizes an organization. It requires skill in communicating, sensitivity in motivating others, and a knack for providing leadership.

You will recall that the management process consists of five functions, pursued in circular fashion. The directing function can be likened to the starting mechanism of an automobile. It turns on the engine, or "people power," of an organization. Directing starts the organization moving and keeps it moving on the right path toward its goals. Without direction, the management process is interrupted, and the organization stalls.

Three Major Components

The directing function has three interlocking components, and managers must provide them all and in the right proportions:

1. Communications. This is the voice of the management staff, individually and collectively, that tells the organization to get moving. The communications may be oral or written—or may even be implied by body language. The messages sent to others in the organization include information and ideas, instructions, and orders or commands. The purpose of such messages is to provide direction, so that people will know what to do, as well as when, where, and how to do it.

2. Motivation. Generally speaking, employees in an organization follow instructions and orders only for a very selfish reason: to satisfy a compelling personal need. The individual's need may be for money and security, or for friendship and respect, or to prove how good he or she can be at the work. A manager's task is to detect the personal needs of their employees, and to find a way by which the job itself can satisfy them.

3. Leadership. This intangible quality enables managers to exert a benevolent power over others in the organization. In most organizations, this power is only partly a reflection of the manager's status and authority. Leadership stems in much larger part from a manager's personal capability for persuasion and influence. Effective leaders are able to (a) anticipate the threats and opportunities that face a group and (b) provide insights that influence the group to follow the leader's sense of the right courses of action.

Self-Fulfilling Prophecies

Much of the outcome of the directing function will be a reflection of what a particular manager thinks about other human beings. Historically, managers in general have progressed through three stages in their analysis of what brings out the best effort from people at work.

Money. The traditional concept (upon which Frederick W. Taylor based his wage incentive plans) was that financial rewards provided the best incentive. In effect, this approach held, the harder people worked, the better the pay they would receive. Unfortunately, this concept ignored other important motivating factors, such as job security and the desire for respect and consideration.

Fair Treatment. This theory, advanced by the human relations school of management and pioneered by Elton Mayo, reasoned that employees would work harder if they received considerate treatment from their supervisors — in addition to financial rewards. This approach had its own shortcomings, in that managers retained all the authority for what should be done and for when, where, and how it should be done.

Sharing of Responsibility. This approach is based upon the concept of treating people as valuable resources. It acknowledges that employees can make major contributions to planning how best to perform their work. As a consequence of sharing with management decisions about their own work, employees come to find their work more meaningful. And they work harder to meet goals they have helped to choose for themselves. This approach is regarded as being more in tune with the reality of human resources today and with people's basic motivation to excel at what they do.

As you can see, this last theory of sharing is at odds with the traditional concept of money as the prime motivator. A noted observer, Douglas McGregor, predicted that managers would choose a method of directing based upon the degree to which they believed in either the traditional or the sharing theory of motivation. McGregor described the traditional concept as "Theory X" and the sharing concept as "Theory Y," as discussed in Chapter 3.

When *Theory X* prevails, human beings are regarded as (1) disliking work, (2) needing close supervision, (3) avoiding responsibility, and (4) preferring security and financial rewards above everything else.

When *Theory Y* prevails, human beings are regarded as (1) accepting work as a normal, fruitful human condition; (2) being capable of providing their own supervision; (3) being eager to learn; (4) having the ability to solve job-related problems; and (5) being motivated not only by money and security but mainly by the need for self-respect and personal improvement.

McGregor further predicted that a managers' belief about other people (either Theory X or Theory Y) would become **self-fulfilling prophecy**. That is, if managers believe in Theory X, most employees will react to them accordingly. Conversely, those managers who believe in Theory Y will find that their employees respond according to Theory Y.

Practical Insights

The Situation. Greg Wilson, regional manager of a chain of clothing stores, made a point of telling store managers that all cash on hand must be deposited in the nearest bank vault before the store was closed each night. He emphasized his point by saying, "The company doesn't want to risk a burglary just because you leave cash lying around in your store safe overnight." Most store managers found this order reasonably easy to comply with. Other managers, whose stores were located either in inner-city districts considered unsafe at night or far from the nearest bank vaults, did not always follow the regional manager's instructions.

As might have been expected, an inner-city store was burglarized one night and more than $2000 in cash removed. Wilson confronted the store manager involved and said, "You're fired! You knew the rule about removing cash to a vault each night, and you deliberately disobeyed it."

The store manager retorted, "That rule was unreasonable in my case, and you should have known it. There have been any number of holdups in my neighborhood when individuals were trying to make nighttime deposits to the bank vault. I've tried to tell you that, but you didn't listen. Besides, I know that the store is covered by insurance for this loss. You can't fire me for this, anyway. There's nothing in the written policy about it. I'll carry my case to the company president if I have to."

Question.   If you were the company president, what would you do?

Answer.   The company president would probably not support Greg Wilson's decision to fire the store manager. The offense was a serious one, of course, whether or not the instructions were in writing. But there were mitigating circumstances that the regional manager should have anticipated and tried to find a solution for beforehand.

Question.   How would you evaluate the directing capability of the regional manager?

Answer.   The company president might easily fault the directing activities of the regional manager. First, any rule serious enough to warrant a discharge should have been communicated in writing. Second, Wilson should have made it clear to store managers what the consequences of the rule violation would be. It is obvious that job security is an important personal need of the store manager in this case; a possibility of discharge would have been a strong motivating factor. Third, the regional manager, alerted to the threat of robbery on the street, should have provided leadership by suggesting an effective way for the store manager to avoid it, such as requesting that a police officer accompany the store manager on the way to the bank vault.

Good communications, motivation, and leadership would probably have prevented the burglary from occurring in that store, and perhaps also in many other stores where there were conditions that made it difficult to conform to the rule.

Question.   Which of McGregor's theories (X or Y) do you think the regional manager believes in?

Answer.   Greg Wilson appears to subscribe to the beliefs of Theory X. Had he used a Theory Y approach, he would have presented the disposition of cash at night as a problem to be solved with the help of the store managers. He would not have had to assume a threatening position. Instead, he would have challenged them to be ingenious in developing ways to comply with a reasonable request: that cash be protected from burglary.

Concept 32

Managers must use both the spoken and the written word effectively in order to impart information, instruction, and direction to the work force.

Managerial communications serve two vital purposes. They translate abstract goals and plans into language that triggers employee action. And they provide the glue that holds an organization to a common direction. **Communications** are the means by which management transmits and receives information. The process of communication may consist of an exchange of knowledge, or it may be essentially unilateral, as when a manager gives instructions that must be followed or orders that must be obeyed.

Interpersonal Communications

Even when the intention of a communications message is essentially one-way, the process itself requires a two-way exchange. This is illustrated in Figure 7.2, which shows the communications process as a closed loop. The manager (1) decides what information or action needs to be transmitted, (2) formulates it into a message, and (3) transmits the message through an appropriate channel—speaking, writing, or displaying with body language. (4) The message is received by the other person through (5) listening, reading, or observing. The receiver must (6) interpret the message and its meaning and (7) proceed with the action intended by the manager; or if necessary, the receiver must (8) seek clarification, verification, or both from the manager by means of feedback. **Feedback** in communications is achieved by restating the message or by asking questions to induce clarification. The communications process is not complete without such feedback.

The communications process is often disturbed by distractions, referred to as **noise.** Noise can be overt and physical. It can also be subtle, as when the receiver is distracted by other thoughts that demand atten-

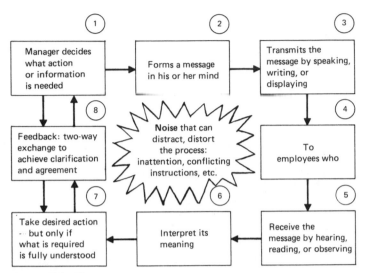

Figure 7.2. The communications process.

tion. Because of the common presence of the latter kind of noise, the art of listening is regarded as a major key to good communications. The receiver must listen attentively, of course. So, too, must the manager listen to the feedback from the receiver.

Organizational Communications

Interpersonal communications are, essentially, one-on-one and mostly face-to-face. When communications are viewed on a large scale, however, two other factors must be considered.

Communications channels within an organization occur (1) *downward,* as when a department head posts a notice on a bulletin board, (2) *upward,* as when an employee registers a grievance with the supervisor, or (3) *sideways,* as when one department transmits information to another department. The chain of command (see Chapter 5) specifies that communications should flow downward and upward through the organizational hierarchy. This often causes problems with horizontal communications, which may be delayed when the chain of command must be followed strictly. Accordingly, many organizations prescribe the kinds of information that should, or may, flow horizontally across the organization.

Communications networks describe the ways in which information is transmitted or exchanged within a small group. Several networks are illustrated in Figure 7.3. These can be characterized in two ways:

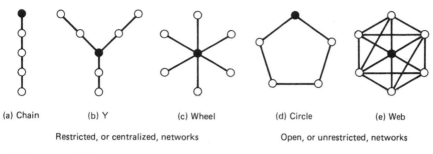

(a) Chain (b) Y (c) Wheel (d) Circle (e) Web

Restricted, or centralized, networks   Open, or unrestricted, networks

● Manager   ○ Employee

Figure 7.3. Communications networks.

1. Restricted, or centralized networks (*a*, *b*, and *c* in Figure 7.3) have supervisors retain control so that most information is channeled through them. For simple tasks, and those needing precise exchanges of information, the restricted network is fast and effective.

2. Open, decentralized, or web networks (*d* and *e* in the figure) allow free exchange throughout the work group. The supervisor acts to facilitate, rather than control, information exchange. For complex tasks requiring many inputs, an open network is more effective.

The **grapevine**, or rumor mill, is an informal, uncontrollable network of information exchange. The greater an organization's dependency upon restricted or formal channels, the more likely the grapevine is to flourish. Unfortunately, the grapevine carries as much misinformation as truth. The best antidote is frequent, open communications between management and employees, especially on subjects that employees consider important to their job security.

Practical Implications

The Situation. Mike, supervisor of packaging operations in a food-processing plant, is speaking to Mary, a labeling-machine operator. She has just made a serious error by not changing a roll of labels to match a change in product coming down the packaging line.

MIKE: How could you possibly let that happen! I've told you and told you to be careful.

MARY: I thought that I'd get a signal from the packer when a product change would occur. He never said anything to me.

MIKE: That's not what I meant. When I said "packer," I meant the packing machine, which flashes a red light when the product changes.

MARY: I guess I misunderstood you. Anyway, the day you told me about that I was half-crazy worrying about my mother, who was in the hospital for an operation. And, as a matter of fact, I didn't realize that mislabeling could cause a serious problem.

Question. What sort of conditions may have contributed to Mike's message not getting through clearly to Mary?

Answer. There were several barriers to clear communications:

- *Different perceptions.* Mary did not perceive the problem of mislabeling in the same way that Mike did.
- *Different language.* The technical term for this is "semantics." It means that the term "packer" can mean one thing to those familiar with the operation and another to those who are new to, or outside, the operation.
- *Emotional blocks.* Mary probably had a hard time listening when her mind was distracted by worry about her mother.

Question. What might Mike have done to ensure that the message would get through?

Answer. Mike might have overcome the barriers and avoided misunderstanding by (1) repeating his instructions and (2) asking Mary for feedback to make sure that she completely understood the procedure and its implications.

Concept 33

In order to understand what motivates others, a manager must become sensitive to the inner needs and personal goals that impel their behavior.

Before discussing motivation, we must first acknowledge that people are highly complex and greatly different, one from another. Therefore, "motivation" is defined and explained below in general terms that may or may not apply to a particular individual.

Motivation has been described as an inner state of mind and body — wishes, desires, needs, and drives — that activates individuals and causes them to act. It can be thought of as an "inner spring" that seeks release and, as a result, causes a certain type of behavior. When we say a person "is motivated," the resultant behavior is characterized by effort, persistence, and direction.

Experts have examined motivation from a managerial viewpoint and have developed two sets of theories about it: (1) content theory and (2) process theory. Content theory is examined here, and process theory is discussed under concept 34 in this chapter.

Content Theories of Motivation

There are several explanations of what motivation is, but only three of the major ones will be reviewed here.

1. Maslow's Hierarchy of Needs. As first discussed in Chapter 3 (Figure 3.3), Abraham Maslow conceived of a theory which is called **Maslow's hierarchy of needs**. In this theory, a person's inner spring is thought of as a series of needs, arranged in a hierarchy from the most basic to the most esoteric. The basic, or lower-level needs, he considered to be related to physiological needs to stay alive and to be secure from harm. The other needs in Maslow's hierarchy are psychological. They move upward from the need to socialize, to the need for respect from others, and finally, to the need to perform up to one's potential.

Maslow warned that an individual may develop different priorities for these needs according to circumstances at a particular time. Thus, the money needed to pay the landlord may be uppermost at the end of the month, whereas the need to find a place where you can do meaningful work may be most important when changing jobs.

Maslow's hierarchy has another important aspect for managers. It presumes that once a need has been satisfied, it will no longer serve as a motivator. Instead, the next lower unsatisfied need will be most powerful. If the needs below have also been satisfied, the next higher unsatisfied need will be the one that motivates.

2. Herzberg's Two-Factor Theory. This theory, too, was first discussed in Chapter 3, and it relates to Maslow's theory, as shown in Figure 3.4. Frederick Herzberg, in the theory popularly called **Herzberg's Two-Factor Theory**, contends that the first three needs of Maslow's hierarchy are fairly well satisfied by most jobs. It is the two uppermost needs — for respect and meaningful work — that tend to remain unsatisfied. And, importantly, it is at the upper levels that a supervisor or manager can have the greatest impact in motivating employees.

Pause here for a partial summary of the import of both of these content theories: Motivation is a condition within an individual. A person "is motivated" when he or she strives to satisfy a compelling inner condition. Managers "motivate," or "provide motivation," when they provide a means, or establish conditions, by which employees can satisfy their inner needs. Note, too, that McGregor's Theory X and Theory Y (refer back to Figure 3.4) show that managers' viewpoints affect the kinds of motivational methods they employ.

3. Alderfer's ERG Theory. Clayton Alderfer revised and condensed Maslow's concept into three basic needs, and the result is called **Alderfer's existence-relatedness-growth (ERG) theory**. This theory adds the following factors to Maslow's concept:

- *Existence.* Includes all material and physical desires.
- *Relatedness.* Includes all needs that involve relations with people we care about.
- *Growth.* Includes efforts to improve oneself and one's environment.

Maslow predicted that humans move up the scale of needs by means of "progressive satisfaction." When a person cannot move upward in needs satisfaction, however, Alderfer says that the person suffers "frustration regression" and moves backward, to seek satisfaction from material and physical things. Most human behavior, according to this theory, is somewhat unpredictable because of a continual cycling between existence and growth needs.

Content Theory of *Managerial* Motivation

One content theory, **McClelland's achievement motivation theory**, seems to apply most particularly to managerial motivation and performance. David McClelland, working forward from Maslow and others, believes that three additional content needs must also be considered. He feels that this is especially true in connection with managers in the western world. The needs that McClelland discusses are as follows:

- *Affiliation need.* The recognizable need of so many people to socialize with and gain the approval of others. McClelland found that this need was not particularly strong among managers.
- *Power need.* Can be negative, as when a person seeks to dominate others simply to show superiority. Or it can be positive, as it is with so many managers, when the need is satisfied by obtaining the power

needed to influence the direction of an organization so that it attains its goals.

- *Achievement need.* The need to succeed. McClelland found this need to be very high in managers. It is demonstrated by (1) willing acceptance of responsibility, (2) a desire for immediate and concrete feedback on performance, and (3) a wish to perform well, and is tempered by (4) a tendency to set modest goals — so that the achievement may, in fact, occur.

Practical Implications

The Situation. Tom, the sales vice president for a realty firm, promoted Sally, the firm's best salesperson, to the position of sales supervisor. Sally has not worked out very well in this position. Her subordinates say that she is impatient with them and is hard to reach for advice and consultation. Sally also is dissatisfied. As a salesperson, she drew commissions for her sales immediately as they were closed. As a sales supervisor, however, her success depends upon the work of her subordinates. Furthermore, her bonus is now determined only at the end of each year. Sally has always been described as "highly motivated." She owns an expensive town house, drives a Mercedes, and lives up to the hilt of her income. Tom is puzzled by the seeming inconsistency between Sally's past and her present performance.

A consulting psychologist who was called in to study the situation concluded that the position of sales supervisor did not provide the right kind of motivation for Sally to work hard enough to succeed at it.

Question. Based on the information supplied here, why did the psychologist come to this conclusion?

Answer. This is how the four content theories of motivation might be interpreted by the consultant to fit this situation:

1. *Maslow.* Sally appears to be strongly motivated by both a need to succeed at her work (and she has done that already) and by lower-level needs to sustain her lifestyle. The new job adds little to her success at work and has the potential of taking some satisfaction away from her lifestyle needs.

2. *Herzberg.* While the new job offers a challenge and an opportunity to excel, it also includes some dissatisfiers regarding her salary and bonus.

3. *Alderfer.* Sally shows more of an interest in material (existence)

needs than in relatedness. She may also feel that the new position does not truly reflect personal growth for her. If so, she will become frustrated and regress to the level of valuing money more than either relatedness or growth.

4. *McClelland.*   Sally's relationships with her subordinates indicate a low affiliation need, which might be all right. Little is said to indicate what her power needs are, but her need for achievement seems very high. This new job does not, however, seem to offer as attractive an opportunity for achievement as that of salesperson. Further, Sally seems not to want to accept the broader responsibility for the work of others; and the feedback on her performance is greatly delayed as compared with her previous job.

In summary, there are fewer and weaker motivating factors in Sally's present job than in her previous one. Alderfer's theory will probably prevail, and Sally will feel much happier if she returns to her previous job as a salesperson.

Concept 34

To provide motivation is to provide a means for each employee to seek and attain goals that provide satisfaction for his or her individual needs.

Authorities draw a fine, but distinct, line between *what* motivates a person (the content) and *how* a person becomes motivated (the process). This is important to managers. They must not only make judgments about a person's motivation, but must also provide the conditions that convert this motivation into desired behavior.

Expectancy Theory

Victor Vroom considers motivation as a reflection of an individual's choice among several alternate behaviors. That is, an employee may choose to work very hard in order to get a raise. Or the same individual may work just hard enough to hold onto the job and gain acceptance and approval from coworkers. Or the person may find the job so distasteful that he or she will perform so poorly as to be discharged.

Vroom calls this the "expectancy theory of motivation," or simply **ex-**

pectancy theory. Its logic is that (1) individuals will exert effort at work (2) to achieve performance that (3) will result in outcomes that they prefer. This process is illustrated in Figure 7.4.

The manager intervenes in this process at each stage of the process. Take the example of supervisor Ann and employee Bob.

Stage 1. Ann specifics the effort she expects from Bob.

Stage 2. Ann tells Bob that if he works in the way that is specified, he will reach the level of performance judged to be satisfactory.

Stage 3. Ann further promises Bob that if he reaches that level of performance he will get a raise.

Now look at the process from Bob's point of view.

Stage 1. To consider making the effort prescribed, Bob must believe that the effort will actually lead to the specified level of performance. This belief, at stage 1, is Bob's **expectancy**.

Stage 2. Bob must also believe that Ann's promise will hold true — that if he reaches the specified performance level, he will, in fact, get the promised raise. This belief in the connection between stage 2 and 3 is called the **instrumentality**. Bob has to have not only the expectancy but a belief in the instrumentality.

Stage 3. Finally, Bob must value the promised outcome. If the raise is only $5 per week, it may have a low value (or **valence**) for Bob, and he may never exert the effort. It may be that a raise of $10 a week would have a high enough valence to motivate him.

Ann's task, then, has three elements. She must:

Stage 1. Specify the effort required of Bob.

Stage 2. Assure Bob that this effort will enable him to reach the required level of performance.

Stage 3. Offer a reward, or other outcome, to Bob that he will value sufficiently so as to be motivated.

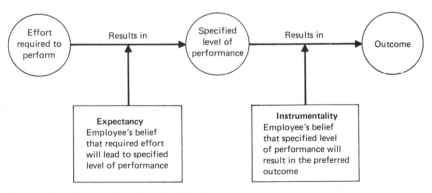

Figure 7.4. Expectancy theory of motivation.

If Bob's feelings and beliefs are such that he rejects any of these propositions, he will not be motivated and will not proceed as Ann desires him to.

Equity Theory

Equity theory is somewhat related to expectancy theory. It holds that individuals, inherently, want to provide an equal balance between what they put into a job and what they get out of it. In other words, when they believe that what they are asked to do is fair, they will contribute an equally fair effort. If, on the other hand, employees think that they are being asked to do too much in relation to their rewards, they will slack off in their efforts to attain equity.

Management's problem here is to design both jobs and compensation systems that strike a balance in the perceptions of their employees. This requires (1) sensitive estimates of motivational needs and (2) objective reviews of job demands and the tangible and intangible rewards associated with them. Said another way, many jobs must be adjusted so that they either demand less or pay more, so as to restore equity.

Behavior Modification

B. F. Skinner and others believe that behavior is learned through experience. This is an important concept, since it implies (1) that motivation causes certain behavior, but (2) that under certain kinds of reinforcements, the behavior will persist after the motivation is removed. The technique is called **behavior modification**. In its simplest form, this concept holds that a cat who has jumped on a hot stove to satisfy curiosity will be motivated by self-preservation to get off quickly. The "punishment" has been so severe, however, that the cat will not jump on a stove — hot or cold — again. The cat has learned through harsh experience that stove tops are dangerous and should be avoided. In a different but analogous approach, Skinner taught chickens to peck buttons to satisfy their hunger. Each time a chicken pecked a certain button, it was rewarded with a kernel of corn. After a while, however, Skinner no longer rewarded the chicken for pecking the right button. Nevertheless, the chicken would continue to peck that button.

In the language of behavior modification, the chicken's "correct" behavior had been rewarded by **positive reinforcement**, and that correct behavior could then be expected to continue. The cat had received negative reinforcement, or **punishment**, and it had learned to desist from

certain undesirable behavior, such as jumping on stove tops. Human beings, observed Skinner, learn in much the same way. When appropriate
behavior is rewarded with positive reinforcement, they are motivated to
repeat that performance. When improper behavior receives negative
reinforcement, employees are motivated to avoid such behavior. They
are said to have received **escape conditioning**.

There is also a third way to condition employee behavior. If an employee who constantly complains about an assignment is ignored—and
is not rewarded with a more acceptable assignment—the employee may
eventually stop complaining. Using the absence of either reward or
punishment to change behavior is called **nonreinforcement**.

Practical Implications

The Situation.   Roscoe L. is a night desk clerk at a large resort motel.
The motel manager, Dan D., made this proposal to Roscoe, "In addition to your regular check-in, checkout duties, I'd like you to verify
and post to the proper room accounts all room-service charges that
occur after 9 p.m. You should have plenty of time to do this since the
desk is so slow after that hour. Of course, your salary will be raised by
$75 a week for taking on this additional responsibility." The extra
pay looked good to Roscoe, and he believed that the manager would
keep his part of the bargain. Nevertheless, Roscoe was doubtful
about his ability to handle the necessary bookkeeping work properly,
and said so.

Question.   What might the motel manager do to increase Roscoe's expectancy that he could perform this work satisfactorily?

Answer.   Roscoe believed in the *instrumentality* and placed a high *valence* on the outcome. The problem, however, was Roscoe's weak *expectancy* that his effort would lead to his attaining the specified performance. The motel manager might increase Roscoe's expectancy by (1)
providing special training for a few days under the guidance of the motel accountant and (2) volunteering to be available each evening for advice and coaching until Roscoe got the hang of the new assignment.

An alternate would be for the manager to apply equity theory and ask
only that Roscoe verify the room charges (without posting them), for
which the additional pay might be $40, rather than $75.

Concept 35

Managerial leadership grows from combining an inherent knack with a learned skill for exercising benevolent power and influence upon others, in pursuit of organizational goals.

Leadership is not synonymous with management. Management involves the five functions of planning, organizing, staffing, directing, and controlling. Leadership is only one component of the directing function, albeit a vitally important one.

Leadership is the aspect of management which enables a manager to persuade others to seek and pursue specified goals enthusiastically. Within formal organizations, leadership is an expression of a manager's personal power. This power stems only in part from the legitimate authority that allows a manager to coerce others through the threats of punishment and the distribution of rewards. In larger part, a manager's effective leadership power is based upon other factors. The most important of these are expert power and referent power.

Expert power is associated with a manager's expertise, special skills, and general knowledge. These qualities gain the respect and cooperation of peers and subordinates. This form of leadership power may be acquired and developed.

Referent power is less easy to identify. It is associated with intangible personal qualities that attract followers who admire these qualities and wish to be associated with them. This kind of leadership power—sometimes called "charisma"—is more likely to be inherent than acquired and developed.

Leadership Traits

For years, investigators have been trying, without success, to identify the personal qualities that give some people more leadership charisma than others. Instead, there is some reason to believe that certain traits are characteristic of unsuccessful leaders. These *nonleadership* traits may be summarized as follows:

1. Insensitivity to others; abrasiveness; an intimidating manner

2. Coldness, aloofness, arrogance

3. Betrayal of trusts and confidences

4. Excessive ambition; playing politics

5. Oversupervising; failure to delegate

6. Inability to build a cohesive team

7. Choosing weak and ineffective subordinates

8. Difficulty in thinking strategically

9. Inflexibility in adapting to different bosses

10. Excessive dependence upon a mentor

As a consequence of weaknesses in identifying distinguishing leadership traits among managers, research has moved in several different and more productive directions.

Basic Concepts of Leadership

Two theories, in particular, attempt to explain how successful leaders behave.

Continuum of Leadership Styles. Robert Tannenbaum and Warren Schmidt believe in a **continuum of leadership styles**. They think that successful leaders operate along a continuous scale from (1) a point at the lower end that is completely boss-centered to (2) a point at the upper end that is completely employee-centered, as shown in Figure 7.5. This assumes a flexibility that allows a leader to take a Theory X attitude toward some employees and situations, and a Theory Y attitude toward others. The boss-centered style is designated as "autocratic," the

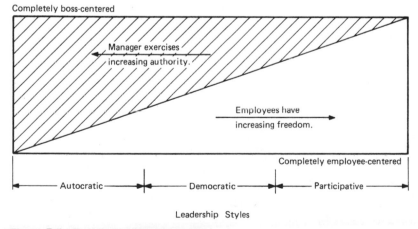

Leadership Styles

Figure 7.5. Continuum of leadership styles.

employee-centered as "participative." Midway between the two is a "democratic" leadership style.

Two-Dimensional Leadership.   This theory is based upon the notion that managers combine two styles simultaneously, but in differing proportions. One style is *job- or task-centered*. The other style is *employee-centered*. The most popular application of this theory is shown in the **Managerial Grid©** developed by R. Blake and J. Mouton (Figure 7.6). They plot the two dimensions on a chart, the vertical axis of which represents increasing concern for people, and the horizontal axis, an increasing concern for production. These axes are numbered along scales from 1 to 9. Thus, a manager who is rated at 1,1 is considered to be completely ineffective. A manager at 9,1 is thought to give too much priority to people and not enough to getting the job done. Conversely, a manager at 1,9 is thought to be inconsiderate and too demanding of production. Managers at the midpoints (5,5) show balance. The ideal ranking to strive for, however, is 9,9, which indicates maximum regard for people, combined with maximum focus on the need to produce.

Advanced Concepts of Leadership

Many authorities believe that the basic theories of leadership do not fully explain the complexities involved. Accordingly, two other theories (with several variations) have evolved in attempts to shed light on the subject.

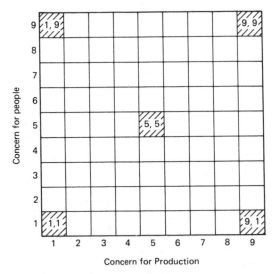

Figure 7.6. Concept of the Managerial Grid©.

Situational Leadership. Pioneered by Fred Fiedler, the **situational leadership** theory implies that the choice of the right style of leadership is dependent upon the distribution of three factors that are present in a particular situation. These three factors are:

1. *Leader-member relations.* How much confidence employees have in their supervisors; also the degree of mutual loyalty.
2. *Task structure.* The degree to which employees' jobs are routine and repetitive, as opposed to unstructured and complex.
3. *Position power.* The degree to which the manager has legitimate authority, along with the power to reward and punish.

Fiedler then borrowed from the concepts of two-dimensional leadership to describe two distinct leadership styles. He prescribes that these should be used independently, and not in tandem, as implied by the Managerial Grid©. His names for the two styles are "task-oriented" and "relations-oriented." His research pointed to the following usage:

- Task-oriented leadership will be most effective (1) in situations in which all three of the above factors are favorable and, conversely, (2) in situations in which these factors are relatively unfavorable.
- Relations-oriented leadership will be most effective (1) in situations in which the three factors are only moderately favorable and (2) in situations in which only some factors are favorable.

Path-Goal Leadership Theory. Drawn heavily from the expectancy theory of motivation, the main thesis of **path-goal leadership theory** is that the leader, or manager, is the key person who can bring about improved employee motivation, satisfaction, and performance.

The path-goal theory, unlike Fiedler's theory, proposes that four styles of leadership may be applied by the same leader. In effect, the leader helps to establish and smooth the path along which subordinates can move in achieving their goals. These styles are:

Directive. The manager points the way, with no participation from the subordinates.

Supportive. The manager demonstrates interest in, and provides help to, subordinates as they move toward their goals.

Participative. The manager asks for, receives, and uses suggestions from employees.

Achievement-oriented. The manager sets challenging goals for subordinates, shows confidence in their abilities, and allows them to choose their own paths.

Cautionary Note

It would appear that managers must provide leadership as a part of their directing function. The appropriate style of leadership, however, will depend upon (1) factors in the situation itself (as Fiedler and others have demonstrated), (2) factors in the employees who are supervised (the nature and force of their motivational needs and job expectancies), and (3) personal and referent factors in the manager, as well as the manager's capability of genuinely applying a variety of styles. Accordingly, the capacity of managers for sensitivity, common sense, and flexibility is crucial to effective leadership. These are rare and valuable qualities, which require a great deal of nurturing and development.

Practical Implications

The Situation.   Paula, supervisor of a data processing center, has several programmers and several computer operators reporting to her. By nature, Paula is considerate of other people. She finds the programmers' work to be highly complex and variable. On the other hand, the work of the computer operators is routine and structured, and it demands great accuracy. Paula gets along well with both groups. There is some question, however, about the extent of Paula's authority, since her employees sometimes receive conflicting instructions from the director of management information services.

Question.   Which of Fiedler's styles of leadership is likely to be most appropriate for the programmers?

Answer.   For the programmers, a relations-oriented style would appear to be most effective. Paula has only moderately favorable position power but favorable relationships, and the programmers' task is unstructured. These mixed conditions favor Paula's natural style.

Question.   Which style for the computer operators?

Answer.   For the computer operators, a task-oriented style appears to be most appropriate. The task is highly structured, the group has good relationships with Paula, and her position power is moderately favorable.

Question. Should Paula adopt a different style for each group?

Answer. The path-goal theory would advise Paula to be participative or achievement-oriented with the programmers and directive or supportive with the computer operators. As a practical matter, Paula might find it difficult to be too task-oriented, and might employ that style only for the most demanding situations.

Comprehension-Check Case for Chapter 7

The Case of the Take-Charge CEO

For easy reference the text of the comprehension-check case is numbered to correspond to the assignment questions that follow.

The Saturn Computer Company, like many another high-tech firm in Silicon Valley, started off like a rocket. Like many others, it also began to fizzle as the competition from the big corporations on the east coast became severe. When Saturn first started up, it seemed to be all fun and games. Top management came to work in T-shirts and blue jeans. It was hard to distinguish them from rank-and-file employees. But when the economic crunch came, things changed radically. The original, freestyle chairperson stayed on, but William S. Jones, a new chief executive officer (CEO), was brought in. Jones had come from an old-line, starched-collar corporation, and his ways were far more structured and traditional than those the company was used to. The general attitude among the executive staff was, "We'll see how long this guy lasts until the chairperson takes over the reins again."

1. One of the first internal crises arose after the new CEO called the first staff meeting, for 8:30 in the morning. On the day of the meeting, the staff were still straggling in at 9 o'clock. Jones, wearing a jacket and necktie, glared at the latecomers: "I'll say this once, and I won't repeat it. All official business of this company will start at the designated hour. Those of you who cannot conform, be prepared to tender me your resignations by 5 o'clock this afternoon. For the time being, and until I know you better, I'll hold all of you suspect. You can forget about your past performance. From now on, it will be what you and I, together, do in the future that counts." By 5 p.m., only 2 of the 10-member staff had resigned.

2. Within the next month, several significant changes were made. Jones issued a number of policy directives affecting a great many of the established procedures. From the beginning, he repeatedly advised his vice presidents that all major matters must first be cleared with him before being relayed to staff. Later, Jones complained that there was a lack of coordina-

tion between the research, design, manufacturing, and marketing departments. Saturn was faced with tremendous competitive problems in all these
vital areas, and no unifying strategy was being developed. Some executives
still muttered, "How long will the chairperson tolerate these goings-on?"

3. Jones also ordered a complete review of the company's compensation
system, then issued a 15 percent reduction in all executive salaries, across
the board. This caused three more members of his immediate staff to re-
sign. The head of the research department, however, was heard to say, "I
hate what is going on around here, but the challenge of developing a computer to beat IBM is too big for me to quit right now." The production
manager, who had been expected to be among the dissidents, surprised
some people by remarking, "I'm not sure that I like Jones very much, but at
least he's setting targets that my department can hit. And when we meet
them, he's the first to acknowledge that we're doing well."

4. On the other hand, the purchasing manager expressed dissatisfaction
by saying, "Jones has asked me to cut our materials costs by 15 percent. He
holds out a carrot to me by offering me a juicy year-end bonus if I can do it,
but the job is simply impossible. As of now, I'm circulating my résumé up
and down the Valley."

The remaining executive staff were amused by Jones's treatment of Bo
Hopkins, the marketing vice president. Hopkins had the reputation of a
crybaby, who had gone to the previous CEO's office daily with complaints
about this department and that department. Jones's technique was to let
Hopkins cool his heels in the waiting room. And when he did meet with
Hopkins, Jones brushed aside the complaints and climbed all over Hopkins
about the weak level of sales performance. Before long, Hopkins began to
spend more time in the field and far less time around Jones's office.

5. As time passed, Saturn began to make a sound recovery under Jones's
administration. The staff grudgingly acknowledged that he knew the computer field inside out, and his judgment about business matters seemed
flawless. Gradually, too, Jones relaxed his hard-nosed attitude and began to
give the research and design departments more freedom. He did keep a
tight rein, however, on the manufacturing and purchasing departments.
But there was no longer any talk about whether or not Jones would stay on.
The consensus among his staff could be summed up as, "He's not the kind
of person I thought would make out here, but he has given us the kind of
leadership we needed to get back on track."

Assignment Questions

1 (a) In his first meeting with his staff, Jones used not only straight talk but:

_____   *a.* memorandums.

_____   *b.* body language.

_____   *c.* bad language.

_____   *d.* sweet talk.

1 (b) Based upon his first meeting with his staff, Jones would be considered

to have a _____ attitude toward them.

_____ *a.* conciliatory
_____ *b.* forgiving
_____ *c.* Theory X
_____ *d.* Theory Y

2 (a) Based upon the information furnished, Jones depends mainly upon a(n) _____ channel of communications.

_____ *a.* indirect
_____ *b.* horizontal
_____ *c.* upward
_____ *d.* downward

2 (b) Jones seems to have established a(n) _____ communications network for the company.

_____ *a.* open
_____ *b.* restricted
_____ *c.* coordinating
_____ *d.* grapevine

3 (a) For the head of the research department, Maslow's _____ need appears to have greater motivating power than does Alderfer's _____ need

_____ *a.* self-achievement; existence
_____ *b.* survival; relatedness
_____ *c.* social; growth
_____ *d.* survival; existence

3 (b) The production manager would appear to be highly motivated by McClelland's _____ need.

_____ *a.* affiliation
_____ *b.* power
_____ *c.* achievement
_____ *d.* survival

4 (a) The purchasing manager appears not to be motivated by Jones's bonus proposal because he has a _____ expectancy of his achieving satisfactory _____ .

_____ *a.* high; instrumentality
_____ *b.* low; instrumentality
_____ *c.* high; performance
_____ *d.* low; performance

4 (b) What technique did Jones use to discourage Hopkins, the marketing manager, from bringing complaints to him?

_____ *a.* Positive reinforcement
_____ *b.* Negative reinforcement
_____ *c.* Nonreinforcement
_____ *d.* Escape conditioning

5 (a) Much of Jones's eventual leadership strength came from his _____ power.

_____ *a.* expert
_____ *b.* referrent
_____ *c.* charismatic
_____ *d.* personality

5 (b)   It would appear that Jones gradually adopted a(n) _____ leadership style for the research department and a(n) _____ leadership
style for the manufacturing and purchasing departments.
  _____ *a.* task-oriented; relations-oriented
  _____ *b.* relations-oriented; task-oriented
  _____ *c.* autocratic; democratic
  _____ *d.* boss-centered; employee-centered

8

Controlling: Monitoring Progress and Exercising Control

Controlling is the function that brings the management cycle full circle. It is the steering mechanism that links all the preceding functions of organizing, staffing, and directing to the goals of planning. And, when indicated, it is the activity that triggers new plans and goals — ones that are more consistent with the resources of the organization and the environment in which it operates. The control process sets standards, and measures progress against them. Corrective action is taken when the gap between what was planned and what is actually happening becomes too large. Controls may be exerted before, after, or at any stage within the conversion process. Controls are most effective when applied selectively at critical, make-or-fail points.

In practice, the major controls are concerned with (1) operations, (2) finance, and (3) human resources.

| 36. Managers set standards to control performance. | 37. Controls are applied selectively at strategic points. | 38. Financial controls are implemented by revenue and expense budgets. | 39. Operating controls focus on materials, schedules, and quality. | 40. Human resources controls focus on vital employment and performance criteria. |

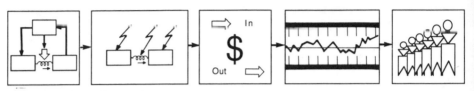

Figure 8.1. Concepts 36–40.

Key Concepts Regarding the Controlling Process

Figure 8.1 illustrates the five key concepts that relate to the controlling process. They are:

36. Management control is the systematic effort taken to set standards, compare progress with them, and take corrective action when necessary to bring performance into line with what was planned and expected.

37. Controls are most economic and effective when applied selectively at the crucial points most likely to determine the success or failure of an operation or activity.

38. Financial controls focus on the accumulation of funds needed to sustain an organization, and on proper disbursement of these funds so as to assure its survival and growth.

39. Operating controls monitor progress of, and results from, the activities associated with the conversion processes of an organization.

40. Human resources controls are concerned with inducing and maintaining satisfactory performance by an organization's work force.

Key Terms

To make full use of the concepts, you need to understand the following terms.

Control process

Preliminary, or preventive, controls

Concurrent, or steering, controls

Feedback, or postperformance, controls

Key-point (strategic) controls

Balance sheet

Income statement

Statement of cash flows (flow of funds)

Budget

Variable budget

Overhead budget

Flexible budget

Variance report

Economic order quantity (EOQ)

Perpetual inventory control

Material requirements planning (MRP)

Just-in-time (JIT) inventory control

Kanban

Production and operations management (POM)

Sequential scheduling

Parallel scheduling

Gantt chart

Network planning methods (PERT and CPM)

Inspection

Quality control (or assurance)

Statistical quality control (SQC)

Tolerance

Table of organization (TO)

Indirect labor ratio

Concept 36

Management control is the systematic effort taken to set standards, compare progress with them, and take corrective action when necessary to bring performance into line with what was planned and expected.

Controlling is the final function performed in the management process, as illustrated in Figure 1.3 in Chapter 1. It completes the cycle by seeing whether or not the goals that were planned have actually been met. If these goals have been attained, the process is allowed to continue undisturbed. If not, corrective action is taken to place the process back on track.

The **control process** requires four steps, as illustrated in Figure 8.2 and described below:

1. Establish Performance Standards. Standards are derived from the goals originally set while planning. They should be concrete and measurable. Thus, a goal of "improving departmental output by 10 percent" may be translated into a performance standard of "110 units of output per employee per shift."

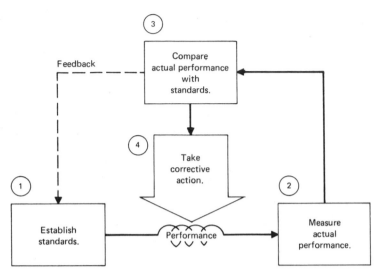

Figure 8.2. The control process.

2. Measure Actual Performance.   It is essential that a reliable, economic way be devised for measuring the performance that actually takes place. Thus, an employee's completion of a unit may be automatically recorded by a counting mechanism and transmitted to a computer system.

3. Compare Actual Performance with the Standard.   This is often done in the form of a computerized daily report that provides the department manager with a record of each employee's daily total printed alongside of the standard.

4. Take Corrective Action.   If the deviation from standard is judged to be within a specified "tolerance," the manager allows the operation to proceed unchanged. If, however, the deviation is judged to be significant, the manager must make changes to bring the performance into line with the standard.

Corrective Action

The changes needed to correct unsatisfactory performance can be directed at a great variety of targets. Incoming materials may be faulty. Employees may be improperly trained or poorly motivated. Equipment may require repair, or be incapable of performing quickly or accurately enough to meet the standards. The process may require redesign, or schedules may need greater coordination.

There is always the possibility that the original goals were too ambitious and must be lowered. Or the standards may have been set inaccurately.

Variances may not always be below standards; they may reveal performance that exceeds standards. If so, action may be indicated so as (1) to exploit unexpectedly favorable conditions or (2) to raise goals and standards that may have been set too low.

Practical Implications

The Situation. Metropolitan Airlines is dissatisfied with the performance of its cabin-maintenance crews. Not only are the cabins not fully cleaned between flights, but the crews clean, on average, only 40 airplanes per day instead of the specified 50.

Question. What can Letitia, the cabin-maintenance supervisor, do to get better control over this operation?

Answer. The cabin-maintenance supervisor can approach the problem from three different standpoints.

1. *Focus on performance.* She can attempt to better select, train, instruct, and motivate the crews.
2. *Focus on the standards.* This will require a review of two important elements, as follows:

   Output (production) standards. Are they attainable? How does Letitia know? Are they based upon historical records, time studies, and crews that are similar to the present ones in terms of size and experience? If not, the production standards may have to be lowered to an attainable level, say 45.

   Quality standards. Are they specific and measurable? What constitutes an "acceptable quality level"? All debris removed, windows washed, upholstery cleaned, seat pockets refilled, etc?
   Standards must always reflect costs (such as crew size), output requirements, and levels of acceptable quality.

3. *Focus on plans, policies, and procedures.* Is there enough time allowed between flights for the quality of cleaning desired? Which policies are being promoted by the airline: low costs, service, or cleanliness? Are the prescribed cleaning procedures and equipment the

most effective for the task? If not, what changes can be made to improve them?

Concept 37

Controls are most economic and effective when applied selectively at the crucial points most likely to determine the success or failure of an operation or activity.

In terms of timing, controls may be applied with good effect at any stage of the typical conversion process. Controls should be applied selectively, however. Too much control is not only expensive but also slows down the process and is demotivating for employees.

Locus of Control

Controls are conveniently described by their timing, purpose, or point of application.

Preliminary controls, or **preventive controls**, are applied before the conversion process begins. Raw materials, for example, are inspected and counted to make sure that the process will not be delayed. Funds are reviewed to make sure that enough cash will be on hand to pay bills as they occur. Machinery is checked to see that it is in good operating condition.

Concurrent controls, or **steering controls**, are applied as the conversion process takes place. Temperatures and pressures are checked for conformance to prescribed conditions. Parts are inspected as they move down an assembly line. Errors are checked in the word processor before documents are printed. Deviations from standards (or gaps) indicate to operators and managers, alike, whether or not corrective action must be taken.

Some concurrent control is of a "yes-no" or "go–no-go" form. Either the process can continue or it must be stopped and corrected before resuming; a product is either accepted or rejected.

Other concurrent controls are of a "steering" variety. Dependent upon the degree of deviation, the process is gradually brought back into line, without stopping. It is akin to steering a car along a winding road, with the driver constantly correcting the car's position in relation to the center strip.

Feedback controls and **postperformance controls** resemble one another in that all controls have a degree of feedback associated with them. That is, at the time when the comparison is made and a deviation detected, the information is fed back to the process, operator, or manager so that corrective action can be taken. On a larger scale, however, measurements and comparisons made after an operation has been concluded (postperformance) serve to guide future planning, goals, inputs, and process designs.

Key-Point (Strategic) Controls

Even when accomplished through automatic, or "cybernetic" systems, controls are expensive to install and maintain. Furthermore, when process operators or managers are faced with too many correction decisions to make, the system suffers from "overcontrol." Therefore, the rule is that controls should be strategically placed (1) where they are most likely to detect conditions before they are uncorrectable ("go" or "no-go") and (2) at those key points that will have a major impact on the success or failure of an operation. Hence the term **key-point (strategic) controls**.

Generally speaking, these key points occur in any of three broad areas of a company's operating spectrum:

- *Financial conditions.* Controls focus on capital acquisition and structure, revenues, expenditures, and cash management.
- *Operating conditions.* Controls focus on supplies and inventories, schedules, production and cost standards, and product and performance quality.
- *Human resources.* Controls are mainly concerned with employee head counts, payroll costs, absence and lateness, grievances, and performance.

Practical Implications

The Situation. A manufacturer of jogging, tennis, and other sporting footware found itself in a price war with its major competitors. To compensate for lower sales revenues, the company's management ordered a three-part cost-cutting program, targeted mainly at reducing raw materials costs by 10 percent, costs of production by 15 percent, and distribution costs by 5 percent.

Question. What sorts of controls might the company initiate to reach these goals?

Answer.   The company might introduce the following controls:

1. *Preliminary controls*.   Lower purchase-price targets (or budgets) for raw materials could be established by these controls, so that the purchasing department might strive for quantity discounts to meet them.

2. *Concurrent controls*.   These would establish (a) for the production department, increased output standards and lower cost standards, and (b) for the sales department, new and higher sales standards (or quotas) and tighter, lower advertising and shipping standards (or budgets). Controls for the production department might be monitored daily, and those for the sale department, weekly.

3. *Feedback controls*.   To indicate to top management whether or not the other controls were effective in the chosen areas or might better be applied elsewhere, as in design specifications—or with a different concept, such as the attainment of a higher level of sales so as to obtain economies of scale in both manufacturing and distribution—feedback controls would be useful.

Concept 38

Financial controls focus on the accumulation of funds needed to sustain an organization, and on proper disbursement of these funds so as to assure its survival and growth.

Financial controls go far beyond the province of financial officers and accountants. While these important professionals provide much of the basis for fiscal control, the implementation is achieved mainly by other executives, managers, and supervisors across the organization and down the line.

Capital Structure and Financial Statements

It is in the area of preliminary and postperformance controls that the financial officers of a company are most dominant. For example, they set goals and target standards for an organization's capital structure: extent of financing by long- and short-term debt or by ownership equity.

Financial officers also establish goals and standards for, and exercise control over, a company's fiscal performance. The chief postperformance feedback controls are three vital financial statements, discussed below.

Balance sheet.   The **balance sheet** is a periodic review of an organization's financial structure at a particular point in time, in terms of its assets, liabilities, and owners' equity.

A number of popular control "ratios" are derived from the balance sheet, such as debt-equity, current, and quick ratios.

Income Statement.   An **income statement** is a report of a company's performance over a period of time, showing its revenues, its expenses, and the difference between them (profit or loss) during the period.

A number of useful control ratios are derived from the income statement alone or in combination with the balance sheet. These include profit on sales, return on investment, asset turnover, and inventory turnover.

Statement of Cash Flows (or Flow of Funds).   The **statement of cash flows (flow of funds)** enables managers to plan for and control the actual flow of cash into and out of the organization, from and to all sources, over a period of time.

Budgets

These are the control devices that most managers, supervisors, and project leaders must become most familiar with. A **budget** is, literally, a financial standard for a particular operation, activity, program, or department. Its data is presented in numerical form, mainly in dollars — either to be obtained through sales or spent for a particular purpose — over a specified period of time. Budgets are derived from planning goals and forecasts, as shown in Figure 8.3. For most businesses, the sales (or revenues) budget (stated in dollars and numbers of units to be sold) becomes the fountainhead for all other budgets.

Typically, the budgeted revenues are apportioned into two major classes of expense budgets:

Variable budgets, in which expenses can be expected to vary according to sales or production volume.

Overhead budgets, which cover expenses that are relatively constant with regard to either sales or production.

Flexible Budgets

Since the forecast of sales revenues is so uncertain, many companies make use of flexible budgets, rather than budgets that are fixed for the particular period of time. A **flexible budget** is presented as a series of

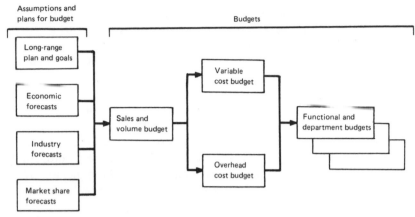

Figure 8.3. How budgets are derived.

budgets, each of which is dependent upon a different volume of sales or production, as shown in Table 8.1. The actual budget that applies will be selected according to the volume that prevails for the period.

Variance Reports

Budgets are presented to the manager or supervisor in charge of the particular activity before the control period begins. At the close of the budget period, a variance report is issued. The **variance report** provides data on budgeted and actual performance and shows the extent of each deviation where it has occurred. According to preestablished tolerance limits for these deviations, the manager is expected to take appropriate corrective or postperformance action, or both.

Practical Implications

The Situation.   When Buck Henry, town manager of a New England town, drew up the annual budgets for the town's various operating departments, he distributed their expenditure allotments equally throughout the 12 months. By midyear, the water-treatment plant was considerably under budget. At the same time, the roadway maintenance expenditures were far over budget. Buck was critical of the budgetary-control efforts of the roadway maintenance supervisor. As a solution, however, he proposed that the surplus in the water-treatment budget be transferred to the roadway budget for the balance of the year. Will

Table 8.1. Example of Flexible Budget

Account title	Monthly allowances based upon four operating levels in terms of tons produced			
	3500 tons	4000 tons	4500 tons	5000 tons
Direct labor	$7,000	$8,000	$9,000	$10,000
Indirect labor				
Material handling	600	600	900	1,200
Shop clerical	500	500	500	500
Supervision	1,200	1,200	1,200	1,200
Overtime premium	0	0	450	450
Shift premiums (2d and 3d)	0	0	0	100
Operating supplies	350	400	450	500
Maintenance and repairs	1,200	1,400	2,000	2,800
Gas, water, steam, compressed air	1,500	1,800	2,100	2,400
Electrical power	700	800	900	1,000
Total controllable costs	$13,050	$14,700	$17,500	$20,150
Insurance	$120	$120	$120	$120
Taxes	80	80	80	80
Depreciation of equipment	400	400	400	400
Building occupancy	800	850	900	950
Total allocated costs	$1,400	$1,450	$1,500	$1,550
Total allowable costs	$14,450	$16,150	$19,000	$21,700

Jameson, the roadway supervisor, claimed that he had a good defense for his overbudget performance, and Suzanne Kreider, the water-treatment supervisor, protested vigorously against the transfer of any funds from her budget.

Question. What defense might the roadway supervisor make?

Answer. Road maintenance for snow removal is particularly high during the first few months of the year. Expenses will drop during the spring but rise again during the summer months when roadways are repaired. A budget that calls for equal expenditures every month is not realistic.

Question. What good reason might the water-treatment supervisor have for not wanting to part with some of the remainder of her budget?

Answer. The water-treatment supervisor has a similar argument. Water usage in New England tends to be lower during the winter and early spring. It peaks up during late spring and summer, as people water their lawns, fill their swimming pools, and take more showers. Suzanne will need the money "saved" from her budget in the spring for the summer months.

Question. How might the town manager improve his budgeting process?

Answer. A budgeting plan that recognizes differing needs according to the extent of a department's anticipated activities per month would be far more effective. As a form of *flexible budgeting,* the roadway budget could be apportioned according to the inches of snowfall or the number of snowstorms. The variable-expense portion of the water-treatment budget could also be flexible, apportioned according to the number of gallons treated.

The Situation. The variance report for the contract administration department of a defense contracting division of a major government supplier is shown in Figure 8.4.

VARIANCE REPORT FOR EXPENDITURES			
Department: CONTRACT ADMINISTRATION Date: JUNE 198X			
Account Number: 023			
Expense Category	Year-to-Date		
	Actual	Budgeted	Over (Under)* Budget
DIRECT SERVICE PERSONNEL	23,850	23,850	0
CLERICAL PERSONNEL	8,000	6,000	2,000
SUPERVISION	5,625	5,625	0
DATA PROCESSING	4,640	5,700	(1,060)
LEGAL COSTS	4,500	6,750	(2,250)
TRAINING AND CONSULTING FEES	2,586	3,200	(614)
TRAVEL, LODGING, AND ASSOCIATED	10,193	9,600	593
SUPPLIES AND POSTAGE	1,497	1,600	(103)
ALLOCATED COSTS (HEAT, RENT, INSURANCE, AND SO ON),	4,718	4,650	68
TOTAL	65,609	66,975	(1,366)

*Figures in parentheses are under budget. For an expense budget, it is best to be on budget or under budget.

Figure 8.4. Variance report for expenditures.

Question. Which accounts seem under control and which are not in control?

Answer. Expenditures for clerical personnel are out of control by $2000 (or +33⅓ percent). This warrants serious corrective action. While expenditures for travel, etc., are over budget by $593, the figure is relatively small (+6 percent) and probably within tolerance limits. Allocated costs are less than 2 percent over budget and can probably be ignored. Data processing, legal, training and consulting, and supply costs are well under budget.

Question. Given the total variance for the department, how would you rate the control performance of the manager of this department?

Answer. Since the total variance is under budget by $1366, or 2 percent, control performance can be judged to be good. Perhaps the clerical budget will need upward adjustment, and the data processing and legal budgets downward, when postperformance control action is taken by the department that sets future budgets.

Concept 39

Operating controls monitor progress of, and results from, the activities associated with the conversion processes of an organization.

The conversion process is the middle stage between input resources and output results. It is during this critical stage that concurrent steering controls are most applicable. Three areas, in particular, receive considerable attention from control-minded managers: materials, production movements, and product and service quality.

Materials Controls

In manufacturing operations, the contribution of raw materials, purchased parts, and finished goods held in stock contributes significantly to total costs. Accordingly, several control devices have been developed.

Economic Order Quantity. This technique focuses on control of the ultimate costs of buying and holding inventories. The **economic order**

quantity (EOQ) formula optimizes two opposing considerations: the larger the quantity of goods purchased at one time, (1) the lower the price of purchase but (2) the greater the cost of holding the goods in inventory until they are used. Companies seek to control material costs by optimizing the order quantities.

Perpetual Inventory Control.   In order to prevent losses or overstocking, almost all companies count their inventories periodically, usually once a year. With the advent of the computer, however, more and more companies maintain **perpetual inventory control**. That is, their control system automatically notes all additions to and withdrawals from inventory as they occur, and the present levels of inventory are always known.

Materials Requirements Planning.   The technique of **materials requirements planning (MRP)** aims to combine optimum purchases with optimum scheduling practices. It (1) explodes a company's sales forecast into product-by-product production schedules and then (2) explodes these schedules into materials required to complete the schedules at the exact time the materials are needed.

Just-in-Time Inventory Control.   The **just-in-time inventory control (JIT)** borrowed from the Japanese **Kanban**, controls inventory costs by requiring a company's suppliers to maintain the anticipated inventories and to ship them to the production line "just in time."

Production Controls

The need to coordinate the complex activities of great numbers of workers and machines in the production of a variety of products or services has led to increasingly complex systems of production control. Parenthetically, as services have begun to occupy an increasingly large part of the economy, the term "operations" is used to supplement the term "production" in referring to the creation of services. Many texts now generalize the conversion activity by calling it **production and operations management**, or simply **POM**.

Production Scheduling

Production scheduling techniques range from the simple to the complex, including the following:

Simple, Step-by-Step, or Sequential Scheduling.   **Sequential scheduling** is, essentially, how assembly lines are planned and controlled. One operation is completed before another can begin. Thus, if there are 5 operations, taking 2, 5, 8, 3, and 6 minutes each, the time budgeted to complete the assembly will be a total of these times, or 24 minutes.

Parallel Scheduling. The **parallel scheduling** approach plans for two or more operations to take place at the same time. Thus, in the example above, if the second and third operations can be scheduled to take place at the same time, the total time to complete the assembly will be 19 minutes (2 + 8 + 3 + 6). A special production control chart (the **Gantt chart** developed by H. L. Gantt) is commonly used to prepare such schedules and monitor progress against them. (See also pages 87–91.)

Network Planning Methods (PERT and CPM). There are two similar techniques that come under the general heading of **network planning methods**: program evaluation and review technique and critical path method. PERT and CPM enable schedulers to examine hundreds and thousands of related operations and to condense them into a single, unified network of schedules. Using these techniques means that the total time needed to complete a project can be vastly shortened. Network planning methods are particularly suitable for large, complex, one-of-a-kind projects—such as building a bridge, a ship, or a prototype airplane, or launching a complex advertising campaign. (See also pages 87–91.)

Quality Control

It is at the operational stage that terms like "inspection" and "quality control" (QC) have their greatest application.

Inspection is the more negative concept, implying that a completed activity is either go or no-go. If it is no-go, the result of the activity, whether a processed document or an automobile part, is lost. It must be discarded, or at the least, reworked. Many authorities view inspection as a necessary evil, at best. They observe that "Quality cannot be inspected into a product or service: quality must be put there to begin with." That's what quality control tries to assure.

Quality control (or **quality assurance**) is the broader term, and it implies a positive approach. QC considers that preliminary—or preventive—controls are most effective, focusing on (1) assuring all the correct inputs and (2) preparing in advance for all the correct procedures and attitudes. Such an approach invites the participation of all parties in sharing both the planning and the responsibility for the most error-free operations. That is the ideal. In practice, a number of important quality-control measures are employed.

One, in particular, that is especially effective, is **statistical quality**

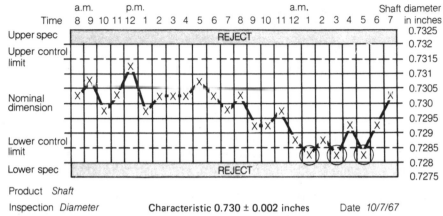

Figure 8.5. Statistical quality-control chart.

control (SQC), an approach based upon the statistics of probabilities. SQC enables an observer to predict in advance when a particular operation may go out of control. By sampling—at random intervals—raw-material supplies, operating conditions, or products as they are being produced, an operator is able to control the operation, or bring it back into line before it creates no-go products or services. Such controls are governed by preestablished high and low limits, called **tolerances**, as shown in Figure 8.5. When conditions fall within the tolerance limits, they are considered acceptable; when they fall outside, they become defects, errors, or rejects. The SQC system is designed to signal (feed back to) the machine, operator, or manager in advance so that adjustments can be made to keep the conditions within the control limits.

Practical Implications

The Situation. An operating division of a computer-accessories company encountered the following problems:

1. When working on a short-lived product, the division found itself with a very large purchased-parts inventory. The inventory had to be disposed of at a great loss.

2. Soon after, the company accepted a contract to produce a rather complicated controls system for a major computer manufacturer. It would be a one-time contract, and it involved a great many diverse operations. The deadline for completion was tight, and the company wasn't sure that it would fit in with its normal production scheduling system.

3. In the manufacture of its primary product, one of the shop machines had to make thousands of small Teflon parts in a plastic injection-molding machine. Repeatedly, the machine could not hold its initial control settings, and hundreds of parts were made with dimensions that fell outside the allowed tolerances before the defective parts were discovered by an inspector at the next stage of operations.

Question. For the first problem, what sort of inventory control might reduce the possibility of such a great loss in the future?

Answer. The use of an *economic order quantity* technique would probably show that the high cost of holding inventories of that particular part (with the subsequent loss) could not justify the savings of buying in large lots. It would probably point to small-lot purchases.

Question. In the second case, which kind of scheduling system and control might be most applicable to this situation?

Answer. *Network planning methods* (PERT and CPM) are made to order for jobs like these, that require close coordination of a great number of operations with a specified completion deadline.

Question. Regarding problem 3, which kind of quality-control technique might help to eliminate the occurrence of these defects?

Answer. A system of *statistical quality control* would direct the operator or inspector to periodically measure the parts as they emerged from the machine. These dimensions would be plotted on a chart like the one in Figure 8.5. As the dimensions approached either the lower or upper limits of the tolerance, the operator would adjust the machine setting to bring the parts dimensions back toward the centerline of the specification.

Concept 40

Human resources controls are concerned with inducing and maintaining satisfactory performance by an organization's work force.

To a great extent, most human resources controls reflect a traditional attitude toward the work force. That is, employees are regarded to some degree as machinery to be monitored. Accordingly, some of the more commonly applied measurements and controls are discussed below.

Table of Organization. The **table of organization (TO)** is a popular control in the military and for government agencies, although it is not limited to public or service organizations. Essentially, the TO specifies the number of people and the skills required to support a particular activity or function. In private industry, the concept is reflected in daily head counts. Under either terminology, the idea is that total employment should be limited to a stipulated figure, just as payroll costs should be.

Indirect Labor Ratio. The **indirect labor ratio** is particularly suitable for industrial applications in which line employment (direct labor) can be differentiated clearly from advisory and service staffs (indirect labor). The concept is that because indirect labor contributes little, if anything, to the product itself, its ratio to direct labor should be strictly limited.

Absence and Lateness. Since both absence and lateness greatly upset operational scheduling, most companies establish acceptable limits and monitor employees' conformance carefully.

Performance Appraisal. As discussed in Chapter 6, employee performance standards and appraisal provide the most important controls governing individual productivity and development.

Human Problems with Controls

Many human beings react negatively to controls. This tendency may manifest itself in several ways, such as:

- *Beating the system.* Department heads, for example, frequently pad the budget in order to counterbalance any potential cuts. Employees often play games, by sticking to the letter rather than the intent of an unpalatable rule. Railway workers, for example, may slow down the system by overly strict adherence to safety precautions.

- *Providing inaccurate or inadequate information.* Managers, as well as employees, don't like to report data that shows their operations to be out of control. As a consequence, information may be purposely delayed, reported in incomplete form, or falsified.

- *Projecting an illusion of control.* The "Everything's OK" syndrome is why so many control systems are now automated and computerized to eliminate human subjectivity.

- *Slowdowns or outright sabotage.* If standards are considered unreasonable, employees may express their resistance by creating subtle slowdowns or even by damaging machinery. Under similar circumstances, managers, too, may purposely create confusion or problems to make sure the system won't work.

Practical Implications

The Situation. When national legislation limited highway speeds to a maximum of 55 miles per hour, owners of the Highball Express Company greeted it with enthusiasm. The owners liked the lower speed limits because of the projected savings of more than 10 percent in fuel costs. Highball's truck drivers, however, were unhappy about the new limits, because they interfered with the practice of driving at high speeds in order to lay over longer between loads.

To make certain that the new speed limits were observed and the fuel savings would materialize, the company installed electronic speed and running-time monitors on its trucks. Previously, the driver's log was the only evidence of what actually happened on the road; the record of delays and elapsed time between loads could easily be manipulated to suit the driver's interests.

Inevitably, the drivers protested the new controls. They complained that the speed records were inaccurate; that the elapsed-time records didn't tell the real story of road conditions; and that delays between loads were caused, not by the truckers, but at the docks where loads were discharged or picked up.

Questions. If you were the managers of Highway Express, what would you do to influence truckers to accept the new control devices?

Answer. Drivers' resistance to the new control systems might be reduced by any of the following measures:

1. Provide drivers with information that justifies the control system in terms of the need for fuel-gallonage savings to offset increased fuel prices.

2. Counsel drivers on the need for new driving habits to conform with the new speed limits.

3. Adjust the standards for time allowed between loads. Instead of in-

citing the drivers to beat the system, Highball Express might acknowledge the former layover practice, and allow specified and reasonable times for this purpose.

4. Make certain that other controls used by Highball Express are also closely observed. This creates a "control climate," in which employees learn to understand that the company takes its rules and regulations seriously.

Comprehension-Check Case for Chapter 8

The Case of Spectacular Ski Company

For easy reference, the text of the comprehension-check case is numbered to correspond to the assignment questions that follow.

When, during the post-World War II years, skiing changed from a skill practiced mainly by experts to an immensely popular sport, a couple of ski enthusiasts in Vermont were ready with just the right kind of skis for beginners. Jon Sunler and Bill Walsh had devised a short ski that enabled beginners at their ski school to learn very quickly. Soon, other ski schools were asking Jon and Bill to make these short skis for them. "You're getting spectacular results with short skis," they said, "and we'd like to do the same." Thus, Spectacular Ski Company was launched on the traditional shoestring. And it became an instant success.

As the company grew and prospered, it took on other lines of sporting equipment: tennis rackets, bows and arrows, and fishing rods. This diversification tended to draw the owners' attention away from their core business—the making of skis and ski equipment. When the boom in skiing slackened during the 1980s, competition became increasingly strong. Other companies were making equipment of good quality and selling it for surprisingly low prices. Jon and Bill were so disturbed by these developments that they were determined to "get control of the ski-equipment business again."

1. Jon and Bill first directed their attention to their production shop. They discovered what they should have already known: the operation was dominated by skilled, older craftspeople who practically built each ski separately by hand. "We don't even know how much labor really goes into a pair of skis," said Jon. "We'll hire a time-study person to establish just how many labor-hours we can afford to put into a pair of our model AAA skis." After studying an "average" craftsperson, the time-study person calculated that it took 5 hours to make one ski, or 10 hours per pair. At the end of ten 8-hour working days, however, the company's accountant showed Jon that

1000 pairs of model AAA skis had been made, and the shop had logged in 12,000 hours of work time.

When Jon looked at these figures, he said, "Something's got to be done about this. The shop has been taking an average of 12 hours per pair."

2. Bill took a closer look at one of the major problems in the shop. It had to do with ash lumber that was purchased in sheets, stripped, and slit into lengths before being laminated and bonded with plastic. A good deal of the laminating process was not taking place properly because the ash had not been properly seasoned. This problem was usually caught by inspectors before the final binding. Bill's solution was to set up an inspection station in the receiving shed to approve or reject the ash before it was accepted from the supplier and moved into the shop for processing.

Bill also made a study to determine the places where the company's operations were most sensitive to failure — places where things had to be right if the operation was to succeed.

3. One of the critical areas Bill uncovered was in the company's advertising department. He found that Ernie Braverman, the advertising manager, kept the costs that varied with the amount of sales pretty much in line, but that fixed advertising expenses were far higher than the company could tolerate. Accordingly, Bill set up a new advertising budget that would control both kinds of budgets.

The packaging operations represented another critical control area. Spectacular's head accountant showed Bill that expenditures for that department remained the same month after month, even if there were radical changes in the number of skis packed and shipped. "This has got to stop," said Bill. So the accountant issued a set of budgets each month to the packaging department. The allowable expenditures for each budget varied according to the number of skis packed that month.

4. A third critical control area was found in the failure of the shop to produce the proper number of skis on time. As a result, shipments were often delayed, or the shop had to work expensive overtime to catch up. Jon called in a consultant, Gerry Ferguson, to look at this problem. She recommended a simple, parallel-type scheduling system that allowed several operations to take place at the same time, rather than waiting their turn in sequence.

After Bill had set up the inspection station in the receiving shed, he assigned the inspector, Steve Craven, to also inspect the ski-strap buckles as they arrived in caseload lots. Steve complained that it would take him days to complete an inspection if he were to look at each buckle, one at a time. Gerry suggested that not every buckle need be inspected. An examination of a few buckles, selected at random from each case, would probably indicate whether or not the rest of the buckles in a case were acceptable.

5. The consultant also asked to see Spectacular's payroll sheets for the previous 10 years. She pointed out that the number of people assigned to each department had kept on growing, even though the business had leveled off 5 years ago. She also showed that the number of staff and support

people in relation to the number of people employed in the production shop had been increasing. "You ought to set up some sort of system to control the growth of these numbers," she advised.

After Spectacular began to implement its various control and budgetary plans, it found that the accountant had difficulty getting accurate production figures from the shop, the advertising manager began to pad his budget, and one laminating-machine operator actually jammed the machine with an abrasive material so that it was shut down for a week for repairs.

Assignment Questions

1 (a)   The 10 hours that it took an average craftsperson to make one pair of skis was adopted by Jon as a control:

_____   *a.* trigger.
_____   *b.* tolerance.
_____   *c.* standard.
_____   *d.* specification.

1 (b)   Which step of the control process was Jon carrying out when he observed that the actual shop times for the past 10 days had been 2 hours more per pair than the average craftsperson had taken?

_____   *a.* Establish performance standards.
_____   *b.* Measure performance.
_____   *c.* Compare actual performance with the standard.
_____   *d.* Take corrective action.

2 (a)   By setting up an inspection station in the receiving shed, Bill was employing a _____ control.

_____   *a.* preliminary
_____   *b.* concurrent
_____   *c.* steering
_____   *d.* postperformance

2 (b)   Bill's search for places where company operations were most likely to fail or succeed was an attempt to find places to apply:

_____   *a.* performance controls.
_____   *b.* postperformance controls.
_____   *c.* optional controls.
_____   *d.* key-point controls.

3 (a)   The two kinds of budgets that Bill set up for the advertising department were _____ for costs that varied and _____ for costs that were fixed.

_____   *a.* variable budget; overhead budget
_____   *b.* overhead budget; variable budget
_____   *c.* direct budget; indirect budget
_____   *d.* fixed budget; flexible budget

3 (b)   The set of budgets for the packaging department were _____ budgets.

_____   *a.* variable
_____   *b.* fixed

_____ _c._ flexible
_____ _d._ overhead

4 (a) The consultant recommended a _____ scheduling system for the production of skis to assure their completion on time.
_____ _a._ network-planning-method
_____ _b._ sequential, step-by-step
_____ _c._ Gantt chart
_____ _d._ milestone chart

4 (b) The buckle-inspecting system set up in the receiving shed was an example of a _____ control, using a _____ technique.
_____ _a._ concurrent; 100 percent inspection
_____ _b._ preventive; 100 percent inspection
_____ _c._ feedback; nondestructive-testing
_____ _d._ preventive; statistical-quality-control

5 (a) The human resources control method that should be set up, as advised by the consultant, to control the growth of total employment is _____ ; the method needed to control the growth of staff and support personnel is

_____.
_____ _a._ organizational turnover ratio; overhead ratio
_____ _b._ table of organization; indirect labor ratio
_____ _c._ turnover ratio; staff-and-line ratio
_____ _d._ absence reporting; overhead check

5 (b) The occurrences reported after the new budgets and controls were implemented at Spectacular represent:
_____ _a._ attempts to beat the system.
_____ _b._ provision of misleading control information.
_____ _c._ sabotage.
_____ _d._ all of the above, as forms of human resistance to the imposition of controls.

PART III

Skills that Managers Develop and Apply

9

Problem Solving, Decision Making, and Innovation

Many authorities observe that the main justification for management is the need for some individual in an organization to take the responsibility for solving problems and making decisions. This may be an oversimplification. But certainly, no informed person challenges the claim that managers do, in fact, spend a great deal of their time and talent in reacting to—or, better still, anticipating—problems, tracking down their causes, finding solutions, and taking the actions needed to implement the solutions. This process is most effective when carried out systematically; information and logic should make major contributions to the process. It is true, however, that creativity and intuition also play significant roles, both in the search for solutions and in the crucial moments when decisions are made.

Key Concepts Regarding Managerial Problem Solving and Decision Making

Figure 9.1 shows the five key concepts that relate to managerial problem solving and decision making. They are:

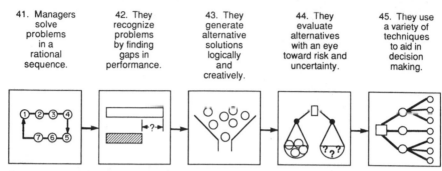

Figure 9.1. Concepts 41–45.

41. Problem solving is the process of identifying problems and their causes, developing and evaluating possible solutions, and taking decisive action based upon this analysis.

42. Effective managers learn to recognize, screen, and define problems at their early stages — and then to identify their underlying causes.

43. Potential solutions for the removal of underlying causes are generated — logically, intuitively, or both — by individual or group thought.

44. Potential solutions are evaluated within constraints imposed by the organization and by a manager's own attitude toward risk.

45. Decision making requires that managers choose between alternate courses of action; a number of mathematical tools can help to systematize the choice, which may be made based upon logic, intuition, or a combination of both.

Key Terms

To make full use of the key concepts, you should understand the following terms:

Problem	ABC analysis
Problem solving	Programmed solution, or programmed decision
Decision	Creative process
Rational analysis	Brainstorming
Gap analysis	Clean-slate approach
Potential problem	Nominal group technique (NGT)
Problem specification	Idea checklist
Pareto's Law	Evlauation criteria

Multiattribute utility (MAU)   Payoff tables
Cost-benefit analysis   Decision tree
"Satisficing"   Linear programming
Risk   Simulations
Risk averters   Game theory
Risk seekers

Concept 41

Problem solving is the process of identifying problems and their causes, developing and evaluating possible solutions, and taking decisive action based upon this analysis.

Research shows that first-line supervisors face on the order of 80 problems a day. Since each *solved* problem requires a decision, this would equate to something like 40 or 50 decisions each day, or about 10,000 decisions a year. We can be thankful that the great majority of these problems—and decisions—are minor ones. Nevertheless, the figures are staggering. Middle-level managers face fewer but more difficult problems. Top-level executives may face even fewer; however, their problems—and their decisions—not only are even more difficult but also have longer-lasting consequences. It should be noted that not all business problems are solved. Many are pushed under the rug; many simply fade away with time. Furthermore, not all problems are threatening; many lead to the discovery of opportunities.

A **problem** exists when there is a difference between an expected condition (such as a goal or standard) and the actual condition. There is a problem when a supervisor expects 25 employees to show up for work on Monday morning, and only 21 punch in. There is a problem when a customer wants 100 dozen cases shipped today, and there are only 10 dozen cases in your warehouse. There is a problem when your budget was based upon raw materials costing only $5 a pound, and your supplier announces an increase to $5.50.

Problem solving occurs when a manager makes a conscious effort to reduce the difference between the actual and the expected conditions. In the first problem cited above, the supervisor may call in temporary help, so that there will be 23 workers on hand. The inventory-control manager may arrange for a shipment of 50 cases from another warehouse, or the sales manager may persuade the customer to wait until the-units can be produced. The purchasing manager may find a supplier who will furnish the materials for $5.25 a pound.

A **decision** takes place when a choice is made between alternates. Besides temporary help, the supervisor may also consider overtime, or borrowing employees from another department. The inventory-control manager and sales manager may consider saying to the customer, "We'll ship 10 dozen today, 40 next week, and 50 the following week," or simply, "We are not in a position to accept an order requiring immediate delivery." The purchasing manager may consider trying to negotiate a lower price with the present supplier, or buying in larger quantities to get a discounted price. The point is that each decision should be made as the result of a choice between alternate actions leading to solutions.

The Problem-Solving Process

Problem solving and decision making are inseparable, as illustrated in Figure 9.2. The process of **rational analysis** moves through seven steps. Each step is dependent upon the previous steps, and all must be taken in sequence. The steps are as follows.

Step 1. Recognize the problem and state it clearly. This step, called "problem finding," is not so obvious as it may seem. This will be made clearer in the discussion of concept 42.

Step 2. Gather data and information relevant to the conditions associated with the problem. This prevents the manager from jumping to conclusions about causes or solutions until all the facts have been examined.

Step 3. Identify possible causes of the problem and select the most likely causes. This is done through a process of elimination, which will be explained under concept 42.

Step 4. Generate alternate solutions, or possible ways to remove or mitigate the likely causes. This step requires analysis and creativity. It will be discussed more fully under concept 43.

Step 5. Evaluate the alternate solutions. This step relies on objective, often mathematical, assessment of the pros and cons of each alternative. This step (the first of the two decision-making steps) will be explained more fully under concept 44.

Step 6. Choose from among the alternates: make a decision. The choice may be based upon logic, intuition, or both. In any event, it triggers the action that is to follow. Techniques for decision making are discussed under concept 45.

Step 7. Implement the decision and evaluate its outcome. This brings the process back full-circle to the problem itself. If the problem has been eliminated or reduced, the process has succeeded, at least to

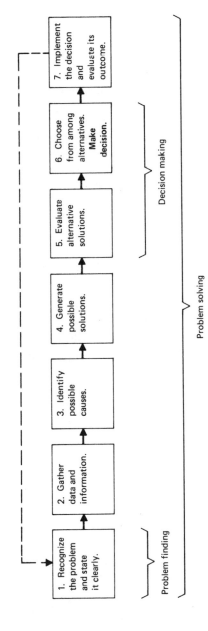

Figure 9.2. Problem-solving process using rational analysis.

some extent. If the problem remains unchanged or intensified, however, then the process must be reinitiated.

Practical Implications

The Situation.   Alicia Hawkins, the regional manager of a chain of video-rental centers, was troubled when she saw that sales revenues were dropping slowly at all 35 of her outlets. She knew that a problem existed, with no sign of its solving itself. She gave the matter some thought, then drew this conclusion: "Our product line is simply not broad enough or renewed frequently enough. We've got to invest considerably more in new videos so that we can replace them at a faster rate than at present." She carried out this decision, but the sales continued to fall.

Question.   What was the major weakness in the regional manager's problem-solving approach?

Answer.   She did not spend enough time on the second step: Gather relevant information. As a consequence, she jumped to a conclusion—a logical but wrong one. The major cause for the drop in sales revenues was the introduction of video rentals by the chain of convenience-store outlets located in her region. The stores were renting videos at "loss-leader" prices to attract store traffic. Alicia subsequently solved this problem by developing a competitive pricing package for her centers that more than matched the convenience-store prices. Since her chain had had a better and broader selection of videos in the first place, the investment in the new and expanded lines had been unnecessary. Furthermore, the convenience-chain prices were for an introductory period of 6 months only, and were dropped thereafter. A search for more information at the start would have led to discovery of the true cause of the problem, and would have saved the regional manager a headache and her company money.

Concept 42

Effective managers learn to recognize, screen, and define problems at their early stages—and then to identify their underlying causes.

Problems are detected by examination of variance and other control reports, by observation ("walking around the shop"), and by surveillance of the environment in which an operation or organization exists.

Gap Analysis

Step 1, definition of the problem—a difference between what was expected to happen (what *should be* happening) and the *actual* condition or state of affairs—describes the problem-finding mission. It is a search for gaps—spaces, intervals, discontinuities between "shoulds" and "actuals." This search has been dubbed **gap analysis.** A gap in the performance of a forms-processing department is shown in Figure 9.3.

The earlier a gap is discovered, the easier it is to fix. That's why it is so important to get control reports as quickly as possible. Gaps may occur in physical conditions, and in numbers and dollars. Gaps may appear in timing, such as delayed shipments and missed deadlines. Less quantitative gaps may be harder to spot, such as changes in attitudes and motivation. Attitude, or morale, surveys are often used to assist in the search for such psychological gaps.

By looking ahead to future conditions, gap analysis may help to detect **potential problems.** These are problems that will arise because of a predicted gap between what ordinarily should happen in the future and what the actual condition is forecast to be.

Problem Specification

Each gap needs to be defined carefully so as to specify exactly what the problem is. **Problem specification** is a description of the nature of the gap itself. For example, "There is a problem on the night shift whereby parts made by machine 3 are 0.002 inch smaller than the specified dimension of 1.000 inch." Note that the problem definition reports the problem only. It does not imply a cause, such as "because of a worn bearing on the main shaft of the machine." Nor does it suggest a solu-

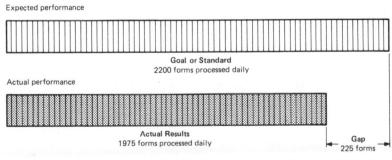

Figure **9.3.** How gap analysis "finds" problems.

tion, such as "which should be replaced as soon as possible." Causes and solutions should be avoided at this step.

Problem specification is, however, greatly aided by gathering all possible information about the problem's occurrence, which occurs in step 2 of the problem-solving process. Questions like those listed below should be asked at this time.

- When did it happen?
- Did it continue throughout the entire shift?
- Does it happen on other shifts?
- Do any products come out oversize, rather than undersize?

The more closely the condition can be pinned down, the easier it will be to locate the causes of the problem.

Identification of Causes

Step 3 in the problem-solving process is a search for the reasons that a gap has occurred. As the old saying goes, "Things don't just happen." The search for causes should be as extensive as possible: The greater the number of likely causes you can list, the better. The unlikely ones can be weeded out and set aside later in this step.

Searching for causes is accomplished by extending the line of questioning used in specifying the problem. The focus of the inquiry, however, shifts to conditions that may have changed. *Gaps occur because of change.* Changes may occur all along the line, involving any of the input resources as well as the process itself. Accordingly, investigation proceeds along broad lines like these:

- Are all conditions the same now as they were before this problem occurred?
- Is the raw material stock the same as before?
- Is the operator the same?
- Have instructions been revised? Tools changed?
- Is the lighting dimmer than before?
- Are inspections being made the same way as before?
- Have work attitudes been affected by labor unrest?

The occurrence of change identifies a cause. And for any problem, there may be—probably are—more than one cause.

The questions asked above imply that certain causes are likely. When the investigation shows no change in the suspect condition, that cause can be eliminated or set aside for the time being.

Problem Screening

Not all problems are important, or urgent. As indicated earlier, many are so obvious and their solution so simple that they are disposed of routinely. On the other hand, the chances are that there are more problems than there is time, money, and effort available to handle them. A good rule of thumb is that 20 percent of the problems that occur in any operation affect 80 percent of the results. Conversely, 80 percent of all problems affect only about 20 percent of the results. This phenomenom, known as **Pareto's Law**, advises that a manager should focus attention on the "vital few" problems and try to screen out as many as possible of the "trivial many" problems.

This principle is followed in inventory management. Sharpest control is exerted over the most expensive (class A) items, moderate control over medium-expense (class B) items, and practically no control over the lowest-expense (class C) items. Thus, the inventory manager screens problems according to Pareto's Law but calls the technique **ABC analysis**.

Practical Implications

The Situation.   Ted T., the manager of a large discount department store, is speaking to Nora F., the store's human resources manager.

> TED: We're running into a real problem here, Nora. Absences and tardiness are fouling up our whole operation. We never can staff a shift ahead of time. I'm scrambling with make-do all the time!
>
> NORA: Just how big of a problem is this? Does it occur every day?
>
> TED: Not every day. But it's still enough to be a bother. Mondays are the worst!
>
> NORA: Then, the problem occurs mostly on Monday mornings?
>
> TED: Yes.
>
> NORA: Let's look at the time cards to see what they show.
>
> TED: OK.
>
> NORA: Let's see. Of 30 employees, 5 were absent on Monday. The rest of the week, there were never more than 2 absent at any one time.
>
> TED: That's right. But look at the ones who are absent. It's almost always the same 5.

NORA: Hmm. And what jobs are they assigned to?

TED: They are all checkout clerks. That's why the problem is so annoying.

NORA: Oh, then the problem isn't absences in general, but absences among a few, and they are mainly assigned to checkout duty.

TED: That's right.

NORA: Now, about the lateness problem. Let's look at the time cards again. There are a few instances of lateness, but I don't see any great number of them. Nor is there a particular pattern. How much of a problem does lateness cause?

TED: It's more of an annoyance than a big problem. You just get the jobs for the day assigned, and someone comes in late and you have to make some readjustments.

Question. Based upon Nora's gathering of information, which problem deserves major attention: absences or lateness?

Answer. Nora's fact gathering indicated that the really serious problem involved absences, not lateness.

Question. How might the more serious problem be specified now?

Answer. Ted's statement of the problem was, typically, too general. He recognized the gap between what he expected from his employees and what was actually happening, but he was not nearly specific enough. Nora would probably define—or specify—the problem as: Absences among 5 particular checkout employees, mainly on Mondays, that interfere with the normal, efficient staffing of the checkout counters.

Concept 43

Potential solutions for the removal of underlying causes are generated—logically, intuitively, or both—by individual or group thought.

Step 4 of the problem-solving process is the cause-removal stage, in which possible solutions are generated.

Programmed Solutions

The solutions for many routine problems have been developed so often that they are called **programmed solutions**, or **programmed decisions**.

Organizational policies and procedures are, in effect, programmed solutions to frequently encountered problems. Even without policy guidelines, a great many problems have been solved so often that they do not need special analysis. Those problems that have no precedent, however, require nonprogrammed (or original) solutions and decisions. It is for the nonprogrammed solutions that the following procedures have been developed.

Generating Possible Solutions

The solution to a problem lies in its ability to remove — or lessen — the causes of the problem. For that reason, it is helpful to think of this process as "cause removal." For each of the likely causes identified and retained from step 3, there must be a plan, or solution, for removing it. These plans (ideas, remedies, cures, solutions) may be generated through logical analysis, or through free association — what we call "intuition." They may be generated by a single individual, such as a supervisor or a manager, or they may be created by some sort of group-think process. The objective is to attack the problem by providing as many solutions as possible that may remove the causes.

Rational Analysis.   The rational approach relies upon a systematic review of each cause with a view toward checking existing, "reasonable and logical" sources of solutions. This is where an examination of handbooks, reference texts, trade journals, newspapers, and government sources can be helpful. The idea is to look for reports of how similar problems were solved, and to adapt those solutions to the causes at hand.

Individual Creativity.   This approach relies upon the generating of solutions that may or may not be reasonable and logical. Above all, these solutions will be creative — either fully original or original in their suggested usage. Almost everyone can be creative to some degree. The **creative process** involves four stages: (1) preparation, (2) incubation, (3) insight, and (4) verification. Managers prepare to be creative, first, by becoming fully informed about the problem and its causes and, second, by exposing themselves to traditional and nontraditional sources of ideas. Incubation simply means allowing the mind to remain fallow — for an hour, or for a day or two. It is then that insights appear. In the verification stage, managers test the insights against the causes to see whether they are worthwhile or not.

Group Creativity.   Probably the most popular, and effective, group approach to idea generation is brainstorming. It encourages the creative process through free association of ideas, as they are exchanged openly in a small group. **Brainstorming**, conceived by advertising genius Alex Osborn, follows four basic rules.

1. No criticism is permitted during the session. This helps to reduce inhibitions.

2. A freewheeling approach—or free association—is welcomed. There is no pressure for ideas to be reasonable or logical; the wilder they are, the better.

3. Quantity takes precedence over quality. The concept is that the greater the number of ideas that emerge, the greater the assurance that some of them will be useful.

4. Combinations and variations are encouraged. Participants, unconcerned about redundancy, "hitchhike" on each other's ideas so as to stimulate a chain of inspiration.

Practical Implications

The Situation. When the Omex Corporation found that its existing windshield-wiper blade was being consistently outsold by a foreign import, it wrestled with the problem for months. Finally, the problem was described as one in which "a foreign blade is able to clear 0.05 millimeter of specified road grime from a windshield 10 seconds faster than Omex's."

The problem was given to the Omex design team to solve. After investigating a number of likely causes, they narrowed the main cause of the problem down to "an inferior linkage system between the blade and the wiper-drive motor." Omex's expert on linkages searched the various supply sources, such as *Thomas Register of American Manufacturers* and other references, with no particular success.

Question. How might the design team develop other possible solutions that are not readily available from traditional sources?

Answer. Brainstorming is a natural choice, but there are variations that might also be suitable, such as the following.

- The **clean-slate approach** says, in effect, "Let's discard everything we have now and start the design of the entire system from scratch."

- The **nominal group technique (NGT)** is similar to brainstorming except that (1) a specific cause is written on a blackboard visible to the entire group, and (2) possible solutions are written on cards and passed to the group leader, who (3) writes them on the blackboard, where (4) they are then evaluated by the group in open discussion.

- The **idea checklist** enhances either individual or group creativity by asking a mind-broadening series of questions, such as:

  1. Can it be put to other uses? Are there new ways to use an old technique? Can this one be modified?
  2. What can be adapted here? What else is similar? What can be copied?
  3. Can it be made smaller? Shorter? Lighter? Can something be omitted? Broken up?
  4. What can be substituted for it? Other ingredients, materials? Can it be done elsewhere?
  5. Can its components be rearranged? Will another pattern, layout, or sequence work better?

Concept 44

Potential solutions are evaluated within constraints imposed by the organization and by a manager's own attitude toward risk.

The four steps preceding step 5, evaluation of alternatives, are all preparations for decision making. It is in step 5 that a manager begins to sort out from among the possible solutions those that hold the most promise. This evaluation is influenced by a number of factors.

Criteria for Judgment

The basic need here is for an enlargement of the problem specification so that it includes not only a description of the gap, but also the exact nature of the satisfaction the final solution should provide. If, for example, you were buying a pair of shoes "that do not cause the discomfort your present ones do," you might also add that the new shoes, "should be no larger than size 9B, have a heel no higher than 2 inches, use buckles rather than laces, be black, and be attractive enough to wear to a white-collar job." These new dimensions are the **evaluation criteria** you have set for your decision choice for your new shoes.

Managers and organizations set such evaluation criteria routinely. In choosing to replace a faulty copying machine, they may specify that it fill the gap in performance created by the existing one, but that it also:

- Cost less than $5000.

- Accept both regular and legal-size paper.

- Have a speed of no less than 50 sheets per minute.

- Occupy no more than 6 square feet of floor space.

To these criteria may also be added typical organizational constraints, such as:

- The new copying machine must be purchased from a local supplier.

- The supplier must have reliable service available from 8 a.m. to midnight, 7 days a week.

- The company cannot buy brand T or brand W, because those brands do not configure to the rest of our equipment.

- The division head would prefer that the purchase be made from company A, since it is a good customer for our products.

The existence of a number of criteria (or objectives) helps to separate possible solutions that conform to the criteria from those that do not conform.

Weighting of Attributes

In a great many instances, a number of possible solutions will meet all, or most, of the criteria. In searching for the new copying machine, for example, 12 models offered by 5 vendors may qualify. This poses still another question for the evaluation process: *Which of these 12 models is the best buy?*

An answer can be approached mathematically by assigning weights to each of the criteria (or attributes.) This indicates the importance of each to ultimate satisfaction. The weighting may be carried further so that there is a range of scores within each attribute. For example, copy speed may have a weight of from 5 to 10 points, with 5 points for 50 per minute, 6 for 60 per minute, and so on. Using this **multiattribute utility**

(MAU) approach, the evaluation would produce a rating score for each of the 12 contending models.

Mathematical evaluation systems have obvious drawbacks:

1. Weighting systems are arbitrary and often complex.

2. Many attributes are hard to quantify. In **cost-benefit analysis,** for example, a public program for school lunches may have to assign weights to the value of an anticipated improvement in student health as compared with the value of reduced highway accidents in another program proposing the studding of highway centerline markers.

3. The parts played by subjective judgments, internal "political" pressures, and unidentified or unvoiced attributes go unrecognized. In an attempt to satisfy so many criteria and organizational pressures, most managers arrive at "realistic" evaluations that lead to a compromise, or **"satisficing,"** decision. Such decisions are found to be acceptable, if not optimum or maximizing.

Attitude toward Risk

One of the most powerful forces in evaluating solutions and making decision choices is the attitude the decision maker has toward risk. Consider these two truths:

- In every situation, the possibility of two extreme outcomes exists: complete success and absolute failure.

- In every situation, there are also two extreme sets of conditions: those we are certain about and those we are uncertain about.

Managers assign risk ratings to situations based upon their assessment of the certainty that exists. The greater the degree of certainty, the lower the risk. The greater the degree of uncertainty, the higher the risk. **Risk,** in this context, means the probability that the decision will be right or wrong — that it will result in an outcome of either success or failure, or somewhere between the two extremes.

According to their attitudes toward risk, managers may be classified in two extremes, with many managers falling somewhere in between.

Risk averters try to avoid situations in which there is a great deal of uncertainty. They prefer to solve problems for which alternate solutions can be highly quantified and in which subjective factors and dependence upon future forecasts can be held to a minimum.

Risk seekers tend to see problems as opportunities, and to be willing to take chances with uncertainty—provided the possible outcomes are attractive enough.

Practical Implications

The Situation. The Fabrico Home Products Company has been recruiting applicants for a position as salesperson to handle its enormous southwest territory. The company initially established the following criteria: (1) college degree, (2) experience in selling, (3) knowledge of the household-products industry, (4) willingness to travel, and (5) optimum salary range. The company has narrowed down its list of suitable applicants to six, all of whom satisfy the basic criteria.

Question. How might the company now make a further evaluation of the suitability of these six applicants?

Answer. Fabrico might now introduce some sort of *MAU system* for evaluating the suitability of the applicants (solutions to the southwestern region staffing problem), as follows:

1. *College education.* BA, 10 points; BS, 12 points; MBA, 15 points

2. *Selling experience.* 1 to 3 years, 20 points; 3 to 5 years, 30 points; more than 5 years, 35 points

3. *Industry knowledge.* 1 to 3 years in industry, 15 points; 3 to 10 years, 20 points; more than 10 years, 25 points

4. *Willingness to travel.* Some hesitation, 10 points; only moderate reluctance, 25 points; no restrictions, 50 points

5. *Salary requirements.* More than $35,000, 15 points; $30,000 to $35,000, 20 points; under $30,000, 25 points

A minimum acceptable score would be 70 points, and a maximum 150 points. Heaviest weight (greatest importance) is given to willingness to travel in such a large territory; lowest weight (least importance) to a college education, since all applicants already have met the basic criteria for that attribute.

Concept 45

Decision making requires that managers choose between alternate courses of action; a number of mathematical tools can help to systematize the choice, which may be made based upon logic, intuition, or a combination of both.

Mathematics and statistics have contributed a number of quantitative, or numerical, methods as an aid to decision making. These methods inject rigor and system into the decision process, but they do not eliminate the need for human judgment. Such judgment may be rational or intuitive. Mostly, a combination of rationality and intuition is used by managers in step 6 of the problem-solving process.

Dealing with Uncertainty

Many of the systematic methods help to clarify the decision maker's estimates of the degree of uncertainty, or risk, that prevails in a particular situation now—or in the future. These techniques force decision makers to "call their shots" with great precision. That is, they are asked to make firm statements (often in numbers) about the chances that designated things will happen in the future. For example, Tom Beacham, vice president for sales of an automobile manufacturing company, commits himself to predictions of the probabilities of next year's sales for a new model automobile. Tom's predictions are shown in Table 9.1. Note that the probabilities add up to 100 chances out of 100, or 100 percent, or 1.00. The knowledge that there are never more than 100 chances that can be divided up is at the heart of probability statistics. Every gambling casino operates on the basis of this knowledge.

Table 9.1. Probabilities of Next Year's Sales for the New Automobile

Number of automobiles	Probability of this number being sold		
	Out of 100	Percent	Decimal
100,000	10	10	0.10
200,000	25	25	0.25
300,000	40	40	0.40
400,000	15	15	0.15
500,000	10	10	0.10
	100	100	1.00

Payoff Tables. Managers use their estimates of future probabilities, like those in Table 9.1, in **payoff tables** to arrive at a numerical indication of how these estimates would pay off if they were to come true. One simple example is to use the probability data to calculate the most likely number of automobiles to be sold. This calculation is illustrated in Table 9.2, in which the numbers at the left are multiplied by the probabilities to find the probable numbers at the right. These are added to determine a probable total.

Other variations of payoff tables allow managers to calculate and compare the probabilities of profits for various investment opportunities. For example, the automobile company might develop a different set of probabilities for the sale of three different models. Using calculations similar to those in Table 9.2, Tom would arrive at different totals of "likely sales" for each model. The company then might chose to make the model with the likelihood of the highest sales.

Decision Trees

A **decision tree** is essentially a graphic portrait of the evaluation and choice steps of the problem-solving process. It shows how each alternative solution forks (or branches) into various possible outcomes. Suppose, for example, that supervisor Althea is faced with a decision about how to treat Peter, whose attendance has been very poor. Althea is considering three alternatives, as shown in Figure 9.4.

One alternative (A_1) is to enforce strict discipline by laying Peter off for 3 days. A second alternative (A_2) is to provide constructive encouragement. A third alternative (A_3) is to try a little of both.

Althea can presume that there are only three ways for Peter to react. He may respond only to strict discipline, he may respond only to encouragement, or he may respond favorably to both. The probably changes in Peter's performance from each kind of response is diagrammed, with a range of outcomes from very little improvement to great improvement. Thus, the improvement in Peter's performance will

Table 9.2. Most Likely Number of Automobiles to be Sold

Number of autos	×	Probability	=	Probable number
100,000		0.10		10,000
200,000		0.25		50,000
300,000		0.40		120,000
400,000		0.15		60,000
500,000		0.10		50,000
Most likely total number to be sold				290,000

Decision alternatives　　　　Employees' responses　　　　Probable change
　　　　　　　　　　　　　　　　　　　　　　　　　　in employees' performance

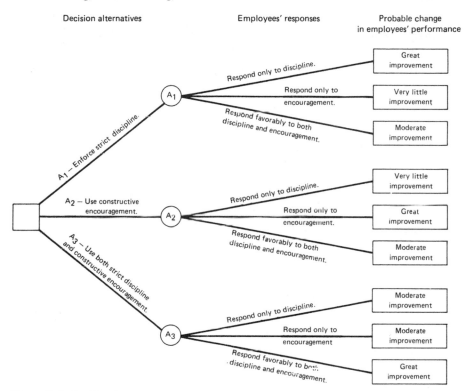

Figure 9.4. Decision tree.

differ according to each decision choice and to each possibility of how Peter might respond to it. The value of the decision tree is that it enables the manager to visualize the cumulative effect of a particular decision.

When each possible outcome in the decision tree is given a probability value, the tree can be converted into a payoff table (or matrix). That way, a numerical total can be computed for each choice. Suppose, for simplicity's sake, that the ultimate value of "great improvement" is 5, "moderate improvement" is 3, and "little improvement" is 1. A probable outcome for the A_1 decision will total 9; for A_2, 9; and for A_3, 11. This would lead Althea to choose A_3.

Other Decision-Making Techniques

Management scientists continue to explore ways of quantifying decision making, so as to reduce the need for subjective judgments. Some of these techniques are particularly helpful in selected applications. Among the more commonly used are:

Linear Programming. By using linear programming, managers can arrive at optimum solutions to problems requiring the allocation of a combination of limited resources. **Linear programming** is especially useful in finding the best mix of "economy," "regular," and "first-class" seats in an airline, or for locating a warehouse, or for choosing the most economical distribution system.

Simulations and Game Theory. By using computerized models, called **simulations**, that simulate actual and possible future conditions, managers are able to test their decision choices to see how they might work out now or in the future. **Game theory** uses probabilities and other statistical methods to enable managers to try out different competitive strategies (pricing, advertising, new-product introductions) to see what might happen in their economic marketplace.

Practical Implications

The Situation. Charlie O., manager of the estimating department of a construction company, is well versed in the quantitative techniques for problem solving and decision making. He feels uncertain, however, about when he should make decisions on his own and when he should ask others for help.

Question. When should Charlie handle problems independently, and when should he seek help?

Answer. Increasingly, in most organizations, it is a sign of maturity for a manager to share problem-solving and decision-making responsibilities with employees. It is not a sign of weakness, either, to ask help from others when your own knowledge or experience is limited. Table 9.3 provides some useful guidelines for Charlie.

Comprehension-Check Case for Chapter 9

The Case of the Puzzled Bank Manager

For easy reference, the text of the comprehension-check case is numbered to correspond to the assignment questions that follow.

Dan Williams, manager of the Metropolitan branch of the Coal County Fidelity Bank, has just experienced a puzzling month. Many things have

Table 9.3. Guidelines for Seeking Help in Problem Solving

Factors	Choice 1. You decide alone	Choice 2. You consult with one of your employees	Choice 3. You consult with a group of your employees
Whose problem is it?	Yours alone.	The employee's.	The groups (ours).
Amount of time.	Not available.	Have some time available.	Plenty of time available.
Expertise.	Fully expert.	Expert advice is needed to fill in gaps in your own knowledge.	Yes, as for choice 2.
Can others add to decision?	No.	Yes.	Yes.
Will you accept suggestions?	Not likely.	Yes, from someone you respect.	Yes, from an effective unit.
Will it help others to carry out the project if they are involved in the decision?	No; you will carry out the project.	Yes; helpful and essential.	Yes; necessary and essential.
Coordination of effort.	Not needed; you will handle it yourself.	Vertical; necessary with your superior or your employees.	Horizontal; needed and necessary among your employees.
Learning value.	No value to anyone else.	Value to one employee, potentially.	Value to whole group.

gone wrong at his branch, and not many things have been set right again. Five occurrences were particularly painful.

1. The automobile loan department reported five forfeitures. Five cars had to be repossessed because of nonpayment of loans, and each car was sold at a price lower than the outstanding balance of its loan. Dan called the automobile loan supervisor into his office and told her, "Lora, your department has become a problem spot. You are using bad judgment in approving loans. From now on, don't issue any loans for more than 75 percent of the car's *Blue Book* value."

"All right," said Lora, "I'll do as you say. But that policy will cause us to miss out on a lot of profitable loans." Sure enough, automobile loans for the month dropped from an average of 75 to 60.

2. Over in the teller department, Dan had been pleased with the bright young people that Felicia, the chief teller, had been able to hire from the inner-city high school. When Dan examined the bank's personnel count at the end of the month, however, he was shocked to see that the turnover rate for tellers had risen sharply from 1 per month to 3, or about 36 percent as an annual rate, as compared with Coal County Fidelity's overall rate of 15 percent.

Upset by these figures, Dan told Felicia, "You've got a turnover problem that shows you have to handle new tellers more carefully during their first few weeks here." She replied, "It's not how I'm handling them that is the trouble. We're not able to hire the best candidates—the ones with staying power—because our starting rate is a dollar an hour lower than other banks in the city. Our wages may be all right out in the county, but not here in town."

3. Take the matter of loan approvals on mortgages. Dan had been sure that the existing policy of requiring at least 25 percent down payment would assure no forfeitures. If the records were right, the policy wasn't catching all potentially bad loans: the collections department advised him that four home loans were presently up for foreclosure. The problem looked serious enough for Dan to call a meeting of the branch's mortgage approval committee. He advised the committee of the growth in potential foreclosures, and then asked that each member jot down on a 3- by 5-inch card what should be done to reduce the failure rate. Dan then wrote all the suggestions on a blackboard and invited the group to discuss the potential of each suggestion for solving the problem.

4. After the meeting with the mortgage committee, Dan made a list of criteria that should be met before issuing a mortgage. The list included items such as: (a) "Applicant must have a net worth of 50 percent of the mortgage value," (b) "Applicant's income from employment must exceed 5 times the monthly payment," and (c) "Appraised value of the home must be 25 percent higher than the mortgage." Dan then directed the committee to develop a system of rating each mortgage application according to the weights assigned to each of the items in the list.

When one member of the mortgage committee observed that Dan was setting up a system that would reject all but the safest mortgages, Dan replied, "I'd rather be safe than sorry."

5. The month ended on a sour note, when Coal County Fidelity's president advised Dan that deposits for the Metropolitan branch were far under budget for the year. "You'll have to provide better forecasts in the future," he said. As a consequence, Dan got together with his department heads in order to make a better forecast of next year's deposits. This is the payoff table that was developed as a result:

	Deposits	Probability, %
Most optimistic forecast	$2,000,000	20
Least optimistic forecast	1,000,000	30
Medium optimistic forecast	1,500,000	50

On the brighter side, Dan learned that a minicomputer would be purchased for the branch's exclusive use. Immediately, however, each department put in a request for priority time on the computer. When Dan totaled up the hours of usage requested by the various departments, he found that it came to half again more time than the computer could operate.

Assignment Questions

1 (a)   When Dan, the branch manager, immediately suggested a solution to the bad automobile loans, he skipped which important step in the problem-solving process?

_____ *a.* Recognizing the problem

_____ *b.* Gathering data and information

_____ *c.* Making a decision choice

_____ *d.* No important step

1 (b)   Since Dan's solution to the bad automobile loan problem didn't work out, it is clear that he did not:

_____ *a.* identify the cause of the problem.

_____ *b.* consider all possible solutions.

_____ *c.* follow rational analysis.

_____ *d.* do all of the above.

2 (a)   The discovery of the difference between the turnover rate this month at Metropolitan, the branch's average rate, and the average rate for Coal County Fidelity is the result of:

_____ *a.* problem screening.

_____ *b.* "satisficing."

_____ *c.* gap analysis.

_____ *d.* ABC analysis.

2 (b)   Dan and the chief teller disagree on the _____ of the teller turnover problem.

_____ *a.* cause

_____ *b.* specification

_____ *c.* screening

_____ *d.* They have no disagreement about this problem.

3 (a)   In assuming that the 25 percent requirement for mortgage approval would prevent foreclosures, Dan had depended upon a _____ solution to the problem.

_____ *a.* risk-seeking

_____ *b.* creative

_____ *c.* programmed

_____ *d.* nonprogrammed

3 (b)   The method Dan used to gather creative suggestions for possible solutions to the mortgage foreclosure problem is called:

_____ *a.* the clean-slate approach.

_____ *b.* rational analysis.

_____ *c.* the idea checklist.

_____ *d.* the nominal group technique.

4 (a)   The method Dan used with the mortgage committee for developing weights for the various criteria is called:

_____ *a.* ABC analysis.

_____ *b.* MAU analysis.

_____ *c.* linear programming.

_____ *d.* simulation.

4 (b)   From Dan's advice and comments to the mortgage committee, it would

appear that Dan is a(n):

_____ *a.* risk averter.

_____ *b.* risk seeker.

_____ *c.* "satisficer."

_____ *d.* equalizer.

5 (a)   An analysis of the payoff table that Metropolitan prepared for making next year's deposits forecasts would indicate that deposits of _____ would be most likely.

_____ *a.* $1,250,000

_____ *b.* $1,450,000

_____ *c.* $1,500,000

_____ *d.* $1,750,000

5 (b)   Which of the following decision-aid techniques would be most appropriate for apportioning the use of the new minicomputer among the branch's departments?

_____ *a.* Payoff tables

_____ *b.* Decision trees

_____ *c.* Simulation and gaming

_____ *d.* Linear programming

10

Information Management

With the onrush of the service industries and the emergence of the "knowledge" worker, the truth of the old adage "Knowledge is power" has become clearer than ever. Managers plan and coordinate the destinies of their companies through intelligent use of the information that pumps through an organization's arteries. Today, managers systematize the gathering and distribution of data and information through computerized networks. Increasingly, with the aid of computer-driven, statistics-oriented decision support systems, managers exert their influence from their own personal workstations.

Key Concepts Regarding Managerial Use of Information.

Figure 10.1 is a graphic representation of the five key concepts that relate to managerial use of information. The concepts are:

46. Information provides the substance for coordinating every aspect of the management process.

47. A management information system provides the network of information needed for planning, control, and decision making.

48. Computer systems provide the means for information gathering, processing, retrieval, and reporting.

49. Decision support systems enable managers to plan, monitor, and control performance from their own personal workstations.

| 46. Information provides the substance for coordination of the management process. | 47. A management information system provides the necessary information network. | 48. Computer systems accelerate and facilitate information processing | 49. Decision support systems assist and personalize managerial controls. | 50. Statistical analysis adds a valuable mathematical dimension to decision making. |

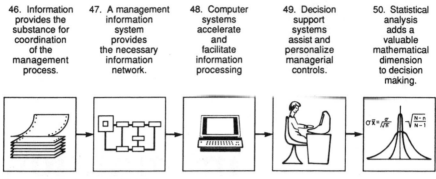

Figure 10.1. Concepts 46–50.

50. Statistical analysis adds a valuable mathematical dimension to management's interpretation and use of information.

Key Terms

To get the most from these concepts, you need to understand the following terms:

Data	Distributed data processing (DDP)
Information	Decision support system (DSS)
Internal source	Management by exception (MBE)
External source	Statistics
Secondary data	Sample
Primary data	Descriptive statistics
Database	Array
Management information system (MIS)	Central value
Data processing	Mean
Input functions	Median
Processing functions	Mode
Output functions	Dispersion
Mode of processing	Index numbers
Batch processing	Time series
Transactional processing	Inferential statistics
Real-time processing	

Concept 46

Information provides the substance for coordinating every aspect of the management process.

A business organization requires great inflows of information—about sales and markets, production and quality, inventories and purchases, cash levels and costs, and much, much more. An important distinction is necessary in defining information. **Data**, although commonly used interchangeably with "information," are facts, estimates, or opinions—often in numerical form—without particular significance or usefulness. **Information**, on the other hand, is data that has been processed so as to give it usefulness. Said another way, data is the raw material of information. The manager of a large retail store, for example, can be presented with thousands of individual sales slips at the end of a day. The slips, however, are only raw data. Analyzing them and summarizing them makes them far more informative. A brief report showing total sales, sales by departments, sales by product type, and sales by cash or credit is far more effective in helping with decisions than the individual sales slips.

Data Collection

Data is collected from, or generated by, two sources:

Internal Sources.   Data from **internal sources** are those generated from within one's own organization. They include, for example, tallies of the amount of goods or services produced, number of working hours spent on each unit of output, amount of materials used or wasted, and number of absences. These data are collected from operating departments and from staff departments, such as accounting and human resources.

External Sources.   Data generated outside one's own business or organization are said to be from **external sources**. Among the most important sources of such information are government agencies, trade and professional associations, and trade periodicals and newsletters. A number of private firms are also in the business of collecting and publishing useful information about either general economic or specific market conditions.

Classes of Data

Data collected and published by others are called **secondary data**. Such data are not compiled to help solve a specific problem of an individual company or institution. **Primary data** are gathered to meet the particular needs of a company and have not been published before in a usable form. This information can be collected from internal sources, or it can be collected from outside one's own company through privately sponsored surveys. Market research, such as surveying, is a common practice used to determine customers' preferences for a particular product, for example. Primary data are often expensive and time-consuming to collect.

Databases

The current trend in information collection is to assemble interrelated data into computer files for easy access, retrieval, and updating. Such a file, or system of files, is called a **database**, or less generally now, a "data bank." It is, in effect, an electronic library. A company may compile its own internal, exclusive database. It may also develop databases jointly with other companies that have mutual interests (such as a hotel trade association), from which all parties may draw information. Thousands of databases are now available that offer access to or retrieval from their files for a fee.

Practical Implications

The Situation.   A national company announced a contest to pick its best salespersons. When the contest closed, the company's executives were chagrined to find that they did not have the data available to declare winners. Headquarters regularly received sales reports from its regions, but the data had never been broken down by product lines.

Question.   What kind of database would the company have to compile to find the winners?

Answers.   The database would be one compiled from *primary data* collected from *internal sources*. (1) It would have to specify the exact way in which the data should be recorded and processed, so that (2) its retrieval would provide reports that showed how well each salesperson did in selling a particular product. Of course, the company should design the database to provide, in addition, a wide variety of other prespecified information.

Concept 47

A management information system provides the network of information needed for planning, control, and decision making.

The sheer volume of information generated by modern organizations is enormous. Even in a small business, it can flow like a deluge from dozens of sales slips, bills received from suppliers, invoices returned from customers, new products to consider making or buying, time sheets from employees, and on and on. In larger businesses or institutions, the amount and complexity of information that must be interpreted and acted upon often exceed the mind's grasp.

To sort out and help make sense of this welter of potentially valuable information, organizations increasingly rely upon management information systems. A **management information system (MIS)** is an organized set of processes that provides information to managers to help them discharge their responsibilities effectively. MIS procedures include collecting, analyzing, and reporting past, present, and projected information from within and outside the organization, as illustrated in Figure 10.2.

MIS Applications

Information available to managers through a management information system serves three vital functions:

1. It serves as a scorecard to report performance and results. Managers can find out at the end of any time period just how well they—and their organizations—have done.
2. It draws attention to problems. Through the process of gap analysis, a MIS enables managers to compare all sorts of actual conditions with what they were supposed to be. The technique of management

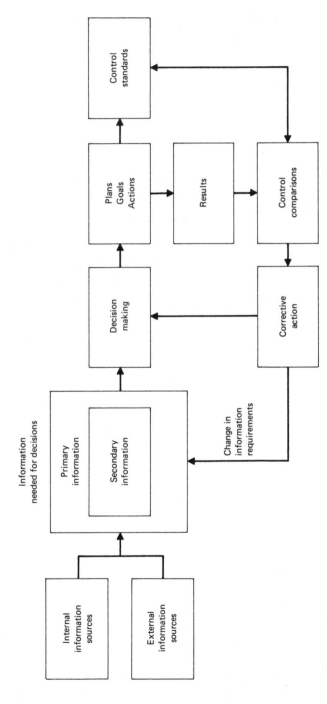

Figure 10.2. Components of a management information system.

by exception (explained in concept 49) is an example of this valuable MIS service.

3. It provides the basis for research and planning. An effective MIS gathers raw materials from all sources — internal and external — for further analysis. Data, so gathered, can be processed for research purposes or serve as the basis for planning future goals and strategies.

Criteria for Effective MIS

Information derived from a MIS should meet several criteria. It need not be fully computerized, or even electronic, but it should be:

- *Useful, above all.* The great drawback of many MISs is that they overwhelm managers with so much useless material that it is hard to find the vital information actually needed to make decisions.

- *Timely.* A great many decisions are made under time constraints. If a supervisor has to wait until Friday to get information that a production line should have been shut down on Tuesday, the MIS isn't doing its job.

- *Affordable.* Data collection and processing systems are expensive to design, acquire, and operate. Accordingly, a MIS should be scaled in size and cost to match its value to the organization.

Practical Implications

The Situation. Anthony C., supervisor of an assembly operation for a cabinet-making plant, set the following performance standards for his operations: 500 units per day, labor costs of $4000 per week, and an average weekly reject rate of 1.5 percent. These standards were based on information derived from the plant accounts and information about similar operations Anthony was able to get from his industry's trade association.

To set up his own little MIS, Anthony requested the following: daily output tallies from the shop clerk; weekly labor costs gathered from time cards (processed by the payroll section and recorded by the accounting department); and the weekly defects rate from the quality-control department.

Using the MIS diagram (Figure 10.3), Anthony plotted the data provided for 1 week: daily output of 480 units, or 20 below standard; labor

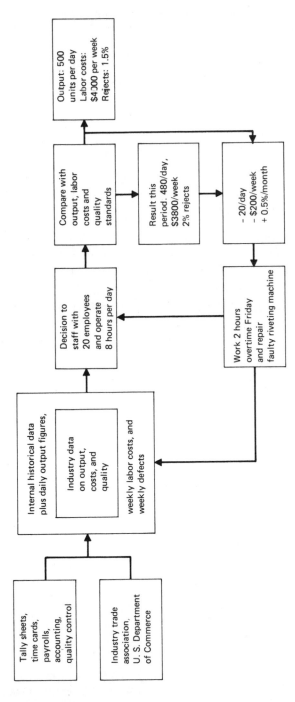

Figure 10.3.

costs of $3800, or $200 less than budgeted; and reject rate up to 2 percent, or 0.5 above standard, which is attributed to a faulty riveting machine.

Question.   What corrective action should Anthony take as the result of this information?

Answer.   On the basis of the control comparisons provided by his MIS, Anthony should take the following actions: (1) schedule his entire staff for 2 hours of overtime on Friday to raise output and (2) place a maintenance repair request to fix the faulty riveting machine.

Concept 48

Computer systems provide the means for information gathering, processing, retrieval, and reporting.

Without computers, most modern MISs would not be feasible. MISs in large organizations are almost entirely dependent upon the computer's enormous capacity for handling and storing data—and its ability to manipulate this data at incredible speeds. One has only to be caught in a supermarket when its cash register computers are "down" to know how great this dependency is.

Data Processing Functions

Data processing encompasses so many functions that it is often hard to distinguish one function from the other, or to determine when one ends and another begins. Essentially, however, **data processing** operations are classified three ways.

1. *Input functions.*   "Collecting" data, "preparing" data for entry in a format acceptable by the computer, and "entering" data—by keypunch, tape, credit-card reader, or optical scanning wand—are **input functions.**

2. *Processing functions.*   Once data has been put into the system, a number of different things can be done to it. These are the **processing functions.** Data can be "stored," or it can be "sorted," or arranged—alphabetically, numerically, according to dates, geography,

etc. Similarly, data can be "classified," or grouped according to classes such as unpaid invoices past due 10 to 30 days, 31 to 45 days, 45 to 60 days, etc. Data in the system can also be "updated" to add information—for example, about a customer's purchases on a credit card. A major function of the computer is "computation"; it will add, subtract, multiply, and divide. Finally, the process must be capable of "retrieving" data that was stored, either in its original entry form or as sorted, classified, and updated.

3. *Output functions.*   Generally speaking, data processing involves two kinds of **output functions**, and thus provides two kinds of output:

- *Responses to inquiries.*   These may be made, for example, when a salesperson calls a database (by voice or electronically) to check a customer's credit status before approving a purchase by credit card.
- *Reports.*   These are the familiar "printouts," such as variance reports, generated by the processing system on a regular, periodic basis; or reports may be generated in response to a specific inquiry.

Data Processing Modes

The **mode of processing** refers to the timing of updating-and-response processing with respect to the occurrence of a transaction. Data from a sale or a production run, for example, may be either collected at the end of the day or collected and processed immediately.

Batch processing is the most common mode. Data are accumulated and entered in batches at the end of a time period.

Transactional processing is an on-line mode that implies that the data is entered and processed as the transaction takes place. This way, the salesclerk in a department store enters the data at a "point-of-purchase" terminal at the cash register. The clerk may key in such data as the price, quantity, stock number, clerk identification, and sales tax. The data processing system then takes over automatically.

Real-time processing enables the processing itself to affect the transaction while it is taking place. For example, when a ticket request is made of an airlines reservation system, the master file for that flight is checked for availability. If a seat is available, it is temporarily held as "booked" while the reservation is being sold to the traveler. Once the seat sale is confirmed, the file is updated by the transaction.

Computer Networks

As computer usage has grown, so has the need for data processing to handle information from many sources, often widely separated physically. Such **distributed data processing (DDP)** enables a clerk in a purchasing office, for instance, to exchange processed data directly with a vendor's office. This interchange of data, often tapping the same databases, is now commonplace between a company's headquarters and salespeople in the field, between commercial banks and their branches, and between warehouses and retail stores.

Practical Implications

The Situation.   Mona B., the purchasing manager for a grocery chain, has found that the weekly reports from the company's regional warehouses often come in too late to enable her to order additional stock during peak periods.

Question.   What can she do to obtain the information she needs more quickly?

Answer.   The purchasing manager can take advantage of the "on-call" capabilities of most computer systems. That is, she need not wait for the periodic report, even though her company's MIS uses a batch processing system with daily entries but only weekly processing. It is a relatively simple matter to program the system to issue selected, summarizing reports on an on-call basis. Complete details may not be available until the week's end. Essential summary data, however, will be available—for example, stock levels for a preselected number of critical product lines. And this may be all Mona needs to know to make decisions about increasing her orders from vendors.

Concept 49

Decision support systems enable managers to plan, monitor, and control performance from their own personal workstations.

The area showing the greatest potential for managerial use of computers is the development of personal workstations as decision support systems. Since the advent of the micro, or personal, computer, thousands of executives have been equipped with computerized workstations. These allow the manager to retrieve, review, and manipulate data from a company's main computer, databases, or both

Decision Support Systems

A **decision support system (DSS)** is a computerized management information system designed to provide managers with data that enables the computer to answer "What if?" questions posed by managers as they develop and consider alternatives during planning, controlling, and decision-making activities. A manager may ask, for example, "What would happen if we raised prices by 5 percent?" Or, "What if we increased our advertising budget by 2, 3, 5, or 10 percent?"

The necessary data is computed and displayed in a "spread-sheet" format. That is, the distribution of the data (usually in numbers or dollars) is displayed in a checkerboardlike matrix. This can be done almost instantly for a wide range of variables. If, for example, the price of product X were to be raised by 5 percent, the spread sheet might show what happened to production, inventory, and distribution costs; to revenues from different territories in the company; and to the sale of other products in the company's line.

Exception Reports

Personal workstations also enable a manager to make greater use of the management-by-exception principle. **Management by exception (MBE)** is a form of variance reporting that not only (1) tells whether or not performance is within standard tolerances but also (2) indicates the degree of the variance and the particular level of management attention required. For example, the computer would identify for the manager four preset degrees of variance:

First degree.   Fully within standard tolerances; requires no managerial action.

Second degree.   Slightly outside standards; requires managerial attention, if not action.

Third degree.   Well outside standards; requires immediate managerial action.

Fourth degree. Extremely out of control; requires that the manager not only take immediate action but seek expert advice about the problem.

Practical Implications

The Situation. At the SuperCenter Shopping Mall, in suburban Miami, Mario M. is in charge of housekeeping, which includes a variety of tasks: washing storefront windows, mopping and polishing the center's floors, removing debris, and power-sweeping the parking lots. SuperCenter's management is proposing a major expansion, to be done in three stages, from its present 75 stores to 100, then to 125, and finally to 150. The center's financial officer wants Mario to make an estimate of the increases in housekeeping and payroll costs for each expansion level.

Mario thinks that there are a number of options that ought to be explored. He could (1) hire additional permanent help, (2) take up the extra work by working present crews overtime, (3) hire temporary help progressively as the expansions take place, (4) contract the extra work to private firms, or (5) try various combinations of all four options.

Questions. What would be the most effective way for Mario to arrive at the best option?

Answer. By inputting relevant data from the firm's files into a personal computer, Mario could create his own *decision support system.* Using standard spread-sheet programs, Mario could find the total costs of implementing each of his four principal options for each of the three expansion variables: 100, 125, and 150 stores. These totals would answer Mario's first "What if?" questions. He could then ask the computer to try out dozens of combinations of the four options for each level. For example: cover 50 percent of the added work with permanent personnel and contract out 50 percent. Most programs will automatically set up these "What if?" combinations at any number of preselected intervals, such as, for options 1 and 2, 5 percent for 1 and 95 percent for 2, 10 percent for 1 and 90 percent for 2, 15 percent for 1 and 85 percent for 2, etc. Or, it can take all four options and vary them automatically, too, as in (1) 85 percent, (2) 5 percent, (3) 5 percent, and (4) 5 percent; or (1) 0 percent, (2) 50 percent, (3) 5 percent, and (4) 45 percent.

Concept 50

Statistical analysis adds a valuable mathematical dimension to management's interpretation and use of information.

Computers, decision support systems, and statistics fit neatly together. **Statistics** has a twofold meaning: On the one hand, "statistics" refers to a collection of numerical data. On the other hand, in its more important sense, "statistics" embraces (1) methods of collecting data, (2) the art of summarizing and presenting data, and (3) the art and science of interpreting and drawing inferences from data.

Measurement and Sampling

The first part of statistics begins with measurement. Very often, the measurement is as simple as counting, as when a survey is taken to find out how many people between the ages of 20 and 30 are in a particular geographic market.

Statistical methods are most often used when large quantities of data must be interpreted. Many times, it is impossible to measure, or count, every item in a large group (called the "population" or "universe"). Instead, a **sample** is measured. A sample is a subgroup, chosen for measurement, which has characteristics similar to the entire group. Great care must be taken in choosing the subgroup so that it is truly representative, and not a biased sample.

Descriptive Statistics

The second aspect of statistics — **descriptive statistics** — is the classification and summarizing of measurements to make their meaning apparent. Suppose James N., manager of a telephone ordering service, wished to make a statistical analysis of the length of time it takes a clerk to handle a call. Here's what he would do:

1. Instead of timing every call, he'd time a representative sample of calls.
2. Next, he would place the measured times in an **array** — a group of numbers placed in order according to size, as shown in Table 10.1.
3. Next, he would "describe" this array in terms of its central value, its dispersion, or both.

Table 10.1. An Array of Sample Times Required by an Airlines Clerk to Process Reservation Requests by Telephone

Array	
Call number	Duration in seconds
8	63
3	64
2	65
9	66
13	68
11	79
5	92
1	111
12	116
15	129
14	130
7	132
4	280
6	360
10	364
Totals 15 calls	2119 seconds

The **central value** of the array is the number chosen, or calculated to be typical of the whole group. This may be the mean, the median, or the mode.

The **mean** (often called the "average") is calculated by adding up all the measurements and dividing by the number of measurements. (In Table 10.1, 2119 ÷ 15 = 141.3 seconds.)

The **median** is the point that divides an array in half: 50 percent of the measurements are greater than the median, and 50 percent are smaller. (In Table 10.1 the median is 111 seconds.)

The **mode** is the measurement that occurs most frequently in a set of numbers. For example, if a sample of 11 telephone times showed 70 seconds occurring 5 times, 90 seconds once, 110 seconds 3 times, and 140 seconds 3 times, the mode would be 70 seconds.

Using only one measure of central value may give a distorted picture. If several of the calls to the telephone ordering service were excessively long, for example, the mean would be misleading. The median would be needed to provide added information.

4. To describe the characteristics of the array even more clearly, the telephone manager could also calculate its dispersion. The **disper-**

sion of a group of numbers is an indication of how widely varied the numbers are. The wider the dispersion, or mean absolute deviation, the less descriptive is the central tendency. The narrower the range of dispersion, the more typical is the central tendency.

Index Numbers and Time Series

Two other descriptive statistics commonly used are index numbers and times series.

Index numbers provide a simple way of measuring and comparing changes over a period of time by expressing increases or decreases as additions to, or subtractions from, 100. The famous Dow-Jones stock index, for example, is based upon comparison with a base of 100. So, too, is the Consumer Price Index.

A **time series** is a collection of measures of the same variable, made repeatedly over a period of time. The measures in a time series are arranged chronologically. Thus, a report showing sales totals for each month during the past year is a times series, useful to a sales manager in forecasting monthly sales for next year.

Inferential Statistics

In many instances, the statistical description of what has occurred is only the beginning of analysis. To interpret the descriptions, managers use **inferential statistics** — a body of methods for drawing inferences, or conclusions, from one sample and applying them to another sample. When we speak of the sale of furniture being "correlated" to the number of new homes being built, for example, we are basing that conclusion on *correlation analysis,* one very useful technique of inferential statistics.

Practical Implications

The Situation.   Sharon, the traffic supervisor for an industrial distributor, was challenged by her boss, Henry, about the number of shipments logged each day by UPS.

> HENRY: Half the time, you're shipping only 100 packages a day. Other days, I see shipments of 150, 200, even 250 a day. I think you should be able to hold your average nearer the higher figures, say 200 a day.

> SHARON: Some shipments are smaller and easier to pack than others. I'm sure that the larger figures occur on days when our pounds-per-package are considerably lower than on days when we ship 100 cartons.

HENRY: It sounds like just another excuse to me.

SHARON: It isn't, and I can prove it.

Question. How can Sharon justify an "average day" for shipments that is lower than the 200 the boss would like?

Answer. Sharon should collect an array of daily shipments for the past year, then calculate the *mean,* the *median,* and the *mode.* The chances are very good that the mean or median, or both, will be closer to the 100-per-day figure. An examination of the *dispersion* of the figures may also show that the *range* of numbers is very wide, and that the high figures are out at the extremes and are not indicative of the *central value.*

Question. What can Sharon do to show her boss that the larger-shipment days are correlated with smaller packages?

Answer. By using *inferential statistics,* Sharon can demonstrate whether or not there is a correlation between pounds per package and number of cartons shipped. To do so, she would have to first compile an array that showed daily figures for both the number of packages shipped and the total weights. The total weight could then be converted to a pounds-per-package number for each day. The study would then attempt to correlate (1) the numbers of packages shipped daily with (2) the pounds per package for each day.

Comprehension-Check Case
for Chapter 10

The Case of Coleman Memorial Hospital

For easy reference, the text of the comprehension-check case is numbered to correspond to the assignment questions that follow.

Coleman Memorial Hospital is a small, 100-bed voluntary (or public) hospital located in a southern community. The hospital, built during a period when the community was growing rapidly, was named after a World War II veteran. Lately, the hospital administrator, Ms. Toner, has been faced with a number of financial problems. Many of them are attributed to the rising costs of hospital care, and to the pressure from insurance companies and the federal government to curtail costs. One by one, these are the problems Ms. Toner is wrestling with:

1. When Ms. Toner met with the hospital board to discuss the cost problems, she was pressed to compare Coleman's costs with those of other hospitals. Toner was able to dig up Coleman cost figures from her files, but was at a loss to provide comparative figures. She did volunteer, however, to check with the state hospital association, which had elaborate computerized data.

2. The board expressed dissatisfaction with the time it took Toner to assemble the figures they wanted to review. In response, she called in Mr. Ausburn, a computer systems consultant. The consultant proposed computerizing the hospital's files so that they would provide the basis for cost control and for preparing reports to the board. "This system will have to fit into a tight budget," Toner warned the consultant. "It will," he said.

3. "How will we get data into the computer system?" asked Toner. "For the time being," answered Ausburn, "I think you can use one of your office clerks to keypunch the necessary data at the end of each day." "How soon will we get the reports we need?" asked Toner. "You should have a report by each Saturday morning," was the reply.

4. "Will I have to become involved in the computer operations?" asked Toner. "Not if you don't want to — not now, at any rate," said the consultant. "But you may want to consider our setting up a system that will enable you to develop better annual plans for your board. Like figuring out the impact of bed occupancy on food service, or operating-room usage, or laboratory requirements." "That would be helpful," said Toner, "but for the time being, what I need are reports that show me whether or not we are over budget. I leave small variances to my department heads, but I want the important things brought to me for a decision. And if anything is seriously out of line, I've got to go to the board for an opinion immediately."

5. "One of our biggest problems," said Toner, "is our bed-occupancy rate. Since a local factory shut down 2 years ago, our occupancy rate seems to have been falling. I'm sure that practically everything we do around here is dependent upon our bed-occupancy rate, but I'd like to check it out. If I knew what the relationships really were, I could make the proper reductions in staff — say in the housekeeping and food-service crews."

Assignment Questions

1(a) Ms. Toner apparently had no trouble gathering cost data from _____sources, but she could not immediately provide the board with cost data from _____sources.

- _____ *a.* internal; external
- _____ *b.* external; internal
- _____ *c.* secondary; primary
- _____ *d.* reliable; unreliable

1(b)   The information that Toner intends to get from the hospital association is _____data; the association apparently maintains some sort of _____for that purpose.

_____   *a.* internal; service
_____   *b.* primary; library
_____   *c.* secondary; database
_____   *d.* primary; service

2(a)   What sort of computer system did the consultant propose that would enable Toner to get the planning and control information she needs?

_____   *a.* Cost-benefit system
_____   *b.* Management information system
_____   *c.* Distributed data processing
_____   *d.* Electronic data processing

2(b)   Whatever information system is to be installed at the hospital, Toner wants it to be useful, timely, and:

_____   *a.* state-of-the-art.
_____   *b.* top-of-the-line.
_____   *c.* dispensable.
_____   *d.* affordable.

3(a)   The hospital consultant recommended that the data for the _____function be keypunched by an office clerk.

_____   *a.* input
_____   *b.* processing
_____   *c.* output
_____   *d.* reporting

3(b)   The consultant also recommended that the processing mode be one of _____processing.

_____   *a.* batch
_____   *b.* on-line
_____   *c.* transactional
_____   *d.* real-time

4(a)   Toner did not want a _____, but she did seem to want the _____proposed by the consultant.

_____   *a.* decision support system; on-call system
_____   *b.* personal workstation; decision support system
_____   *c.* management information system; batch system
_____   *d.* on-call system; personal workstation

4(b)   The variance reporting system described by the hospital administrator is a _____system.

_____   *a.* flexible budgeting
_____   *b.* distributed data processing
_____   *c.* management-by-objectives
_____   *d.* management-by-exception

5(a)   If the hospital administrator were to arrange the records of daily bed-occupancy rates chronologically for the past 2 years, she would have constructed:

_____ _a._ an array.
_____ _b._ a time series.
_____ _c._ a descriptive statistic.
_____ _d._ all of the above.

5(b) To determine whether or not there was a correlation between bed-occupancy rates and labor-hours for housekeeping or food-service crews, the administrator would need _now_ to examine the information on the basis of:

_____ _a._ descriptive statistics.
_____ _b._ inferential statistics.
_____ _c._ measures of central values.
_____ _d._ index numbers.

11

Developing Interpersonal Skills

Though managers work together with other managers in an organization to form a management team, the greatest impact a manager has is as an individual. Accordingly, each manager must acquire a number of essential personal competencies. In exercising these skills, each manager must also develop his or her own unique management style. Among the most basic personal skills are time conservation, delegation, participation, and stress management.

Key Concepts Regarding Personal Skills and Styles

Figure 11.1 illustrates five key concepts that relate to personal skills and styles. They are:

51. While fundamental management principles should prevail, managers must also develop a number of important skills as well as their own personal styles.

52. Mastery over their own time and conservation of the time of their staffs remain elusive goals for most managers.

53. The practice of delegation is a powerful technique for conserving managerial time and for adding leverage to a manager's talents.

54. Participative skills enable managers to enlist the energies of an en-

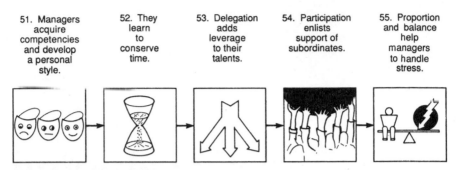

Figure 11.1. Concepts 51–55.

tire organization in the pursuit of mutually understood and accepted goals.

55. In order to avoid debilitating stress, managers must maintain a sense of proportion and balance in respect to both their capabilities and their responsibilities.

Key Terms

To make full use of the key concepts, you must understand the following terms:

Competency	Quality of work life (QWL)
Culture	Flextime
Processing time	Theory Z
Start-up time	Stress
Learning time	Stress reaction
Personal time analysis	Distress
Personal time budget	Stressor
Delegation	Type A behavior pattern
Participative management	

Concept 51

While fundamental management principles should prevail, managers must also develop a number of important skills as well as their own personal styles.

Being an effective manager requires more than an ability to follow generally accepted principles and to carry out the five primary functions of the management process. A number of specific personal skills are necessary. Additionally, prospective and incumbent managers must also consider the style of management most appropriate to their personalities.

Managerial Skills and Competencies

Many studies have been conducted to determine the nature of managerial competencies. In this sense, **competency** is the capacity to employ a particular skill. Hence, "competency" and "skill" are inseparable qualities here, but "competency" carries the broader meaning. Probably the best-supported list of necessary managerial competencies, developed through research carried out by AT&T, is as follows[1]:

Controlling the work

Problem solving

Planning the work

Informal oral communications

Providing performance feedback

Coaching a subordinate

Creating written communications and documentation

Creating and maintaining a motivative atmosphere

Time management

Attending meetings

Self-development

Providing career counseling for subordinates

Representing the company

Other studies have reinforced or supplemented the AT&T research with such competencies as: command of basic facts, sensitivity to events, emotional resilience, self-knowledge, delegating, innovating, ability to deal with the managers to whom one reports, and capacity to deal with people outside the unit or the company. Of particular note among the

---

[1]Adapted from a major AT&T research study of "master supervisors." Dale Barr, "More Needs Analaysis," *Training and Development Journal*, September 1980, p. 70.

items on most competency lists is the implication of the need for learning or developing highly personal skills, especially those of time management, delegation, participation, and stress management. These four
competencies will be discussed in this chapter.

A Range of Styles

Competencies can be acquired and developed. There is considerable
doubt, however, about how much people can change their own personalities. While some research has implied that leadership styles can be developed by training, many authorities believe otherwise. Instead, there
is wide agreement that the integrity and consistency of one's style are
most important.

It is helpful to consider some of the characteristics that contribute to
an individual's style of management. The following list suggests a range
between extremes of such qualities as:

Leadership	From autocratic to participative
Relationships	From cool to warm, from shallow to deep
Attitude toward risk	From risk-seeking to risk-averting
Problem solving	From intuitive to logical
Planning approach	From short-sighted or careless to visionary and precise
Decision making	From equivocating or impulsive to conclusive
Action orientation	From procrastination to initiating

If the second extremes presented above were generally thought to be
desirable for all managers, it is clear that few managers would measure
up to those criteria. Happily, management opportunities present such a
wide range of demands and situations that there is room for managers
whose personalities contain diverse mixes of these criteria. As a guideline, each manager must seek to find employment in which organizational conditions—or **culture**—best harmonize with his or her personality style. Rarely will there be a perfect fit. Nevertheless, a surprising
degree of natural selection takes place. That is, organizations tend to
seek out and develop certain styles of managers, and vice versa. Furthermore, human nature being what it is, there is also a great deal of
accommodating, adapting, and adjusting on the part of both organizations and managers.

Practical Implications

The Situation.   Grace K., a technical project leader who had a proven
record with a small Silicon Valley firm, switched jobs after her employer

shut down in an economic squeeze. Grace was hired for a similar position with a large government defense contractor. She soon ran into unanticipated difficulties. Her boss counseled her this way: "Grace, you're making too many decisions without running them through channels. And you're allowing your employees to get out of control. I admit that you keep your projects on target, but we can't allow a maverick operation around here."

Question. Can anything be done to resolve the problems arising from differences in style between Grace and her new employer?

Answer. The chances are that Grace will have to adapt her style so that it more nearly conforms to the culture of a bureaucratic organization. A certain amount of conformity is almost always demanded in any kind of organization. Part of Grace's needed personal development now is to learn how to make such accommodations. If, however, she can get exceptional results, she may be allowed a greater degree of freedom once she has demonstrated that competency.

Concept 52

Mastery over their own time and conservation of the time of their staffs remain elusive goals for most managers.

Time is a universal measure. It can be applied to each of an organization's many inputs. The time value of facilities and equipment is rent. The time value of money and materials is interest. The time value of labor is worker-hours. Similarly, an organization's output is valued in the number of units per minute, per hour, per week, per month, per year. Profits, too, are sized for a year's period of time. In almost all instances, time costs money.

Time is also an unforgiving measure of an organization's—and a manager's—effectiveness. It sets the restrictions on every activity and program. Two persistent questions are "How long will it take? and "Was it completed on time?"

Time Planning

Managers who have developed a sense of time are able to create plans that not only incorporate provisions for delay, but also anticipate the seemingly inevitable obstacles. They are able to do so because they are aware of three time-related variables.

Processing time is the time it takes to perform or carry out a process. Inherent in every process are the limitations imposed by the technology of the process as it is now practiced. Prudent managers learn to avoid committing their departments to projects or deadlines that exceed these limitations.

Start-up time is the time needed to set up, or to prepare an operation; a similar factor is the time needed to clean up after it is over. These factors are what makes order changeovers and process interruptions so disruptive to schedules. These times are all prime targets for managerial planning and innovation.

Learning time is an extension of setup time, and it affects individuals and organizations. Just as an employee produces more slowly at the beginning of a new job, so do companies produce more slowly when they first take on new projects or contracts. Schedules must make allowances for these delays.

Personal Time Planning

Managers, first of all, must get a grip on their own time so as to plan for its optimum use. An analysis of managerial time shows that it can be categorized into several activities, which are engaged in to carry out several functions.

Activities include making personal contacts with employees and others; having telephone conversations, preparing paperwork, attending meetings, and doing necessary personal things such as traveling and having lunch.

Functions include assigning work; reviewing subordinates' performance; expediting orders and supplies; preparing and analyzing reports; preparing plans and schedules; conducting organization-level training and development, sales and customer development, and product development; doing creative work; and carrying out self-improvement projects.

A **personal time analysis** can be made by observing and recording time spent on these activities and functions at random intervals over a period of a week or month.

Once this analysis has been made, a **personal time budget**, or plan, can be constructed along the lines of that shown in Figure 11.2.

	Monday	Tuesday	Wednesday	Thursday	Friday
8	Routine	Routine	Routine	Routine	Routine
9	Inspection and supervision of operations	Individual work with staff Regular	Inspection and supervision of operations Regular	Individual work with staff Regular	Special work
10		Inspection and supervision of operations		Control studies and reports	Inspection and supervision of operations Regular
11	Regular	Regular	Division staff meeting Regular	Regular	Staff meeting Regular
12	L	U	N	C	H
1	Interviews and contacts Regular	Interviews and contacts Regular	Interviews and contacts Regular	Interviews and contacts Regular	Creative work
2					
3	Planning and organizing	Inspection and supervision of operations	Special work	Inspection and supervision of operations	
4	Regular	Regular		Regular	
5	Routine	Routine	Routine	Routine	Routine

Figure 11.2. Personal time budget.

Time Management and Control

In order for personal time planning to bring results, managers must also exert firm control over management of their own time. Many of the following techniques are effective in this regard.

1. *Control the telephone.* Many interruptive calls may be better handled by saying, "Please call back" or "I'll return your call in 15 minutes."

2. *Limit chitchat.* Irrelevant desk-side or water-cooler conversations are insidious time consumers. Better for a manager to say, "I'd love to hear it over lunch."

3. *Decide quickly on small matters.* Most problems are so routine as to have "programmed" solutions. If matters are small, a quick "yes" or "no" enables a manager to dispose of a query without having to return to it later.

4. *Start early.* By arriving at their desks a few minutes ahead of time,

many managers dispose of much of their routine paperwork, leaving the day ahead open for creative efforts.

5. *Avoid overcommitments.* Whether personal or organizational, time is extremely limited. When asked to exceed these limits, managers are better off saying, "No."

Practical Implications

The Situation. Homer William's department is charged with periodically updating circulation lists for a consumer magazine. Typically, however, his department fails to meet its deadlines. Updating is delayed, extra overtime is involved, and inevitably—in the rush—entry errors are made.

A consultant, Millicent Hodges, has been engaged to make recommendations for changes of procedures in Homer's department. The consultant's report has highlighted three problems, as follows: (1) delays while the computer waits for operators to input the coded tapes, (2) changes in the coding specifications each time the lists are updated, and (3) absence of the department supervisor when problems arise during entry time.

Question. What are the basic definitions of these problems and how might they be corrected?

Answer

1. The first is a problem of *start-up time.* Either this time can be shortened by improved procedures, or the necessary setup time must be anticipated by Homer and begun soon enough so that entry can begin the instant the computer is ready.

2. The second is a problem of *learning time.* Here again, either the importance of the coding being standardized must be made clear to the circulation director, or Homer must allow for learning time at each start-up period.

3. It is obvious that this is a *personal time-budget* problem. Homer must develop a personal time schedule that puts him on the floor supervising during critical start-up and entry periods.

Concept 53

The practice of delegation is a powerful technique for conserving managerial time and for adding leverage to a manager's talents.

Most authorities agree with one expert, Dr. Lawrence L. Steinmetz, on delegation: "Being proficient at the art and skill of delegating is probably the single most useful management tool for the person attempting to get work done through other people."[1] **Delegation** is the process of assigning tasks, usually associated with a manager's responsibility, to a subordinate—along with the necessary decision-making authority. Delegation provides managers with enormous opportunities for adding to the leverage of their jobs. In effect, a manager farms out work to a subordinate employee. As a consequence, the manager can spend more time on planning, special, and creative work. In return, the employee gets a chance both to learn a new skill and to demonstrate capabilities.

What Should Be Delegated

Managers face a puzzling choice about what should and should not be delegated. Delegated tasks should always contain an element of development for the subordinate: they should not be chosen to punish the subordinate or to enable the manager to shuck off unpleasant work. On the other hand, managers should attempt to delegate as many as possible of those tasks that are not purely management work. This often means that managers give up routine tasks they enjoy, or in which they excel, to subordinates. It may also mean that a manager entrusts to a subordinate a task in which the subordinate is not yet skilled. Figure 11.3 illustrates some useful guidelines for deciding what to delegate.

How to Delegate

Many managers are reluctant to delegate. They worry that the subordinate will make mistakes, or will do so well that the manager will look

---

[1]"Delegation," in *The Handbook for Professional Managers*, L. R. Bittel and J. E. Ramsey (eds.), McGraw-Hill Book Company, New York, 1985, p. 224.

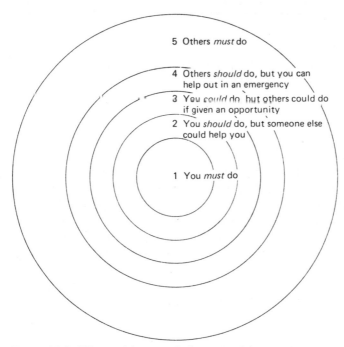

Figure 11.3. What to delegate and what not to delegate.

bad. Some managers also are concerned that they will appear to be lazy, or to be load dumpers. Many managers, however, do wish to delegate but do not go about it the right way. Effective delegation practices usually are based on the following guidelines:

1. The task must be clearly defined. Its goals, deadlines, and related authority should be specified in advance.

2. It must be appropriate for the subordinate. That is, its demands should not exceed either (a) reasonable expectations of capability or (b) limits imposed by a subordinate's job description.

3. The subordinate should have the right of refusal without reprisal. Acceptance of a delegated assignment should be voluntary; delegated assignments are not part of a subordinate's normal job duties.

4. The methods of monitoring, coaching, and control should also be established in advance. Managers always retain accountability for delegated tasks, but they should not oversupervise them. Additionally, since the delegated assignment usually represents a developmental

opportunity for the subordinate, the manager must be available for advice or guidance when it is requested.

Practical Implications

The Situation.   Carmen is a billing clerk in the office of the county tax collector. Carmen's boss Hank, the tax collector, has asked her to prepare a preliminary estimate of tax receipts from business licenses for the next year. Carmen's first reaction was to say, "I thought I was hired to prepare tax bills, not to do tax estimates. Isn't that what the tax collector is supposed to do?" The tax collector replied that this was a task he was delegating to Carmen. "What's in it for me?" asked Carmen.

Question.   How should the tax collector handle this situation?

Answer.   Hank should say something like this:
"You are right, Carmen. Preparation of tax-receipt estimates for submission to the town council is my responsibility. There are several parts to preparing these estimates, however. One important part is the preparation of a *preliminary* estimate for receipts from each tax source.

"I would like to delegate a portion of this task to you. That is, I would like you to calculate a preliminary estimate of receipts for business licenses only. I will make all the necessary information available to you.

"You have become an experienced billing clerk. The next logical advancement for you would be the position of clerk of accounts. This assignment will give you a chance to see what that work entails. It will also give you practice in tax estimating. All in all, it is an opportunity for you to expand your experience and to develop a new skill. That skill will make you more valuable in your present job and help to prepare you for advancement in a tax office, either here or elsewhere.

"As you know, right now is the slack season in your usual work. This will allow you time to handle this assignment. I think it should take you no more than the rest of the week to finish it. What is required is a preliminary, or rough, estimate — one that I can use as the basis for further adjustment. I'll need the estimate by Friday noon. And I'll be available all week if you have any questions as you proceed.

"Does this put the assignment into a different light? I hope that it does. Estimate preparation time is *my* busiest period, and I'll appreciate your helping me out."

Concept 54

Participative skills enable managers to enlist the energies of an entire organization in the pursuit of mutually understood and accepted goals

---

Rensis Likert, a noted researcher into behavior in organizations, characterized "participative group managers" as those who have total confidence in subordinates; whose relationships are friendly and marked by mutual trust; whose decision making is highly decentralized; and whose communications are both two-way and lateral. Such managers obviously subscribe to McGregor's Theory Y of human behavior. Some researchers describe this managerial style as "employee-centered." In its simplest terms, it is called **participative management**, and its essential ingredient is a sharing of responsibilities and decision making with employees, especially groups of employees.

Participative Employees

When employees participate in an organization, their attendance and promptness are good. They stay with their jobs, instead of looking elsewhere for satisfying work. The principal unanswered question about participation, however, is whether or not it increases employees' effort and productivity. Research conclusions are somewhat uncertain here. Other factors that also strongly influence productivity include an individual's personal capabilities and motivation, the nature of the work itself, and the degree to which the manager focuses the employee's attention on the tasks to be performed.

It is safe to say, however, that a participative management style sets the stage for a positive influence of any or all of these factors on a group's productivity. Given the wide choice of jobs available to employees today, if frequent and genuine opportunities for employees to participate are not provided, effort and productivity will *not* improve; they may very well slacken.

It has also been convincingly shown that a participative management style reduces employees' resistance to change and increases cooperation.

Quality of Work Life

Employees' expectation of, if not an outright demand for, work that is meaningful has led to an increasing interest in the **quality of work life**

(QWL). This is the process by which an organization attempts to unlock the creative energies of its employees by involving them in decisions that affect their work life. QWL invites such innovations as **flextime**, wherein schedules are adjusted to fit the personal needs of employees. Under flextime, employees arrange their own arrival and departure times within certain established limits. The benefits of flextime are similar to those associated with other forms of participative management.

Theory Z and Japanese Management

Many participative schemes emulate the "consensus" style of Japanese management. While highly autocratic in some areas, Japanese managers tend to invite extensive employee participation in arriving at decisions that will affect the long-term welfare of the organization. An American author, William G. Ouchi, has suggested that American companies develop a Japanese-like style of management he calls **Theory Z**. It would be characterized by long-term employment, relatively infrequent evaluations and slow promotions, considerable job rotation, self-imposed responsibilities and self-discipline, consensual decision making, and a concern for each person as a whole rather than just as an employee.

Requirements for Participation

Not every manager is adept at participative management, which requires of managers a high degree of confidence, not only in themselves but also in others. Effective participation is based upon mutual trust. Without that trust, offers of shared decision making will be rejected.

For participation to be effective, the following considerations must be observed.

- There must be mutual trust between manager and employees.

- Employees must want to participate. There are always some employees whose work interests are so low that they would rather not be bothered.

- Employees must be knowledgeable about the facts and conditions that affect their contributions.

- Employees must have the competence for making the required knowledge and skills-related contributions. There is a discouraging tendency on the part of managers, however, to underestimate their employees' competence.

- Enough time must be allowed for genuine participation. The participative process is slow; that's why it is most successful when applied to longer-range problems.

- Finally, the manager who invites participation must (1) value the inputs received and (2) implement the decisions arrived at.

Practical Implications

The Situation. Roger heads an excavation crew at the construction site for a high-rise apartment building. His crew is made up of skilled workers — forms carpenters, backhoe operators, etc. — and unskilled laborers. Roger is notoriously hard-nosed. He has to be, he says, working with rough-and-tough construction crews. The work of Roger's crew is generally acceptable, if not outstanding, but he experiences a high degree of turnover, especially among the unskilled laborers. Nor could Roger's crew be described as "a happy lot."

This week, Roger's crew ran into a difficult problem at the site. Instead of the soft dirt that the engineers had predicted, they encountered a massive rock shelf. Roger's first inclination was to call the home office for a blasting team to remove the rock. One of Roger's older crew members, however, suggested that the rock appeared to be a relatively soft sandstone. If so, the excavation could be completed with the crew's air hammers. "It's a good idea, a money-saving idea," thought Roger, "but I'll lose face if I accept it."

Question. What advice would you give Roger now?

Answer. Obviously, Roger is not practicing participative management, and he is suffering because of it. Turnover among his unskilled laborers is evidence of that. So is the absence of apparent job satisfaction among his crew. It would appear that Roger's older crew members are competent and willing to participate, if given a chance. Can Roger change his style? Perhaps this incident presents him with the perfect opportunity to do so. All he really need say is, "Hey, that sounds like a great idea! What do you air-hammer operators think about it? Can it be done that way?" Roger and his crew will have plenty of time to work out the details, since calling in a blasting unit might cost a day or more of delay before the job could go ahead.

Not everyone can change his or her style, but often the mechanics of making the change are so simple that all that is needed is to make the effort.

Concept 55

In order to avoid debilitating stress, managers must maintain a sense of proportion and balance in respect to both their capabilities and their responsibilities.

As almost every layperson knows, "stress" is pressure that makes a person feel anxious or depressed, and ultimately not able to perform up to par. Scientists break this process down into several terms that help us to better understand it. **Stress** is a physiological condition that sends adrenaline rushing into the bloodstream and then to the muscles and the organs. **Stress reactions** are mental and physical responses to stress. These reactions can be physiological, as when displayed as high blood pressure, or psychological, as with depression. Stress reactions manifest themselves in the workplace in terms of job dissatisfaction, absenteeism, high turnover, and other undesirable reactions and behavior.

Stress is not all bad. At lower levels, it helps to activate the human body so that it can handle danger and crises. At excessive levels, however, it causes the body and mind to malfunction, or underfunction, as described above. Such **distress** is costly and disruptive to organizations, and damaging to the individual who undergoes it.

Recognizing Stress

The causes of stress—**stressors**—are conditions in an individual's environment. These conditions can include tight deadlines, excessive noise, disorganized procedures, too many rules to follow, job insecurity, office politics, a disagreeable boss, tasks beyond one's capabilities, and all sorts of personal problems and family worries.

The extent of the impact of these stressors on an individual is influenced by three factors:

1. *The degree of change the person is facing.* Changes can be for better or worse, but change of any kind tends to raise an individual's stress reactions. Furthermore, the pressure felt from change is cumulative. Such pressure from a number of minor causes can build up to an unbearable level. We've all heard the expression, "This is the last straw!"

2. *The degree of uncertainty and conflict that the individual is encountering.* Much of this may occur outside the workplace, but much of it is present in work situations. Role conflict and role ambigu-

ity, discussed in Chapter 3, are common sources of such uncertainty. Stress is aggressively present in jobs without clearly defined objectives and in jobs in which the evaluation criteria change from rating to rating.

3. *An individual's behavior pattern.*   Scientists have been able to classify individuals as having either a **type A behavior pattern** (hyperactive) or a type B (relaxed) pattern. Type A individuals attack work aggressively, find themselves constantly struggling under their work loads, and — as a consequence — are impatient and excessively aware of time pressures. Type B persons, on the other hand, seem not to be aware of these pressures, even under similar conditions. They are relaxed and "laid back," and they take things as they come, working at an even pace.

It is the type A person who is more likely to experience high stress levels and to exhibit dangerous stress reactions. Type A individuals, for example, are far more prone to coronary heart disease than are type B people.

Stress Management

Managers must deal not only with their own stress reactions but also with those of their subordinates.

In minimizing stressful conditions for their subordinates, managers can try to establish an environment that lessens conflict and uncertainty — for example, by avoiding issuance of conflicting instructions. Managers can also create greater stability in the workplace by introducing change only when necessary and by being consistent in their methods of direction and discipline. It is especially important, too, to have enough resources on hand to enable employees to accomplish the work assigned. Otherwise, frustration and stress are sure to set in.

When it comes to managing one's own stress, medical experts have a number of suggestions to offer, including those listed below.

- *Understand your limitations and live with them.*   This calls for you as an individual to (1) be realistic about your true capabilities, (2) exploit them only as far as they can carry you, (3) try not to move too far too fast, and (4) accept that it is usually more satisfying to do well at a lesser job than to feel relentlessly pressured at one slightly beyond your capacity.

- *Get more genuine exercise.*   Tensions are reduced when blood circulation improves. Even an individual who is not athletically inclined can find half an hour a day to loosen up the body with some sort of relaxing exercise. It need not be vigorous. Walking, bike riding, bowling, or lawn mowing may help as much with relaxation as jogging, tennis, or swimming.

- *Select and pursue at least one diversion.* Your pastime should be enjoyable, whether it's stamp collecting, woodworking, local politics, gourmet cooking, card playing, or needlepoint. The test of a true diversion is that you find yourself lost in it, that time flies, and that you forget your cares during your involvement.

- *Take time to look at the world around you.* This will help you to gain perspective about what is truly important to you and what is not. This means that your thoughts should be turned outward occasionally, as opposed to being endlessly concerned with your own successes and failures.

Practical Implications

The Situation. Rebecca Teller, a cataloging librarian at the Center City Library, is about to blow all her fuses. John Carter, the library director, has just made an announcement that will negate a good deal of the work that Rebecca has been doing for the past 3 months. In place of the present "FastCat" system, which makes books immediately available to borrowers, even before cataloging is complete, an entirely new, computerized system will be introduced. The new system is, admittedly, better than the FastCat system, since it greatly reduces the typical delay between a book's receipt and its placement on the shelves. Nevertheless, Rebecca, who has been working under great pressure to keep up with the FastCat system, is very annoyed. "This is the fourth time the cataloging system has been changed in the past 3 years. Now I'll have to run even harder to keep up with the computerized system," she complains to herself.

It was at the very moment of Rebecca's internal complaints that John stopped by her desk and remarked, "I've been disappointed that you were not able to keep up with the FastCat system, Rebecca. Perhaps your work will be more satisfactory under the new system."

"More satisfactory! I've been working like a dog under FastCat. I don't know what it is that you expect from me!" was Rebecca's response. Rebecca did not report for work the next day and called in saying that she had a dreadful headache.

Question. How would you diagnose Rebecca's headache and the reasons for it?

Answer.   Rebecca is suffering from *stress* caused by (1) the cumulative effect of changes in the work she is required to do and (2) uncertainty about how much she is expected to do in order to achieve satisfactory performance. Her headache is a *stress reaction,* a negative one that causes *distress.* It would also appear that Rebecca is inclined toward a *type A behavior pattern.*

Question.   What improvements might be made in Rebecca's work environment to reduce the chances of her headache returning?

Answer.   The *stressors* in Rebecca's work environment might be lessened by (1) involving her in the planning of new cataloging systems, (2) introducing change less often and more gradually, and (3) establishing clear-cut performance objectives and measurements for Rebecca's job.

Comprehension-Check Case for Chapter 11

The Case of the Lively Advertising Agency

For easy reference, the text of the comprehension-check case is numbered to correspond to the assignment questions that follow.

Life at the Lively Advertising Agency is nothing if not exciting. "Something new and challenging every day," says Billy Webster, the creative director. "It's more like something new and upsetting every day," says George Wilson, the production director. Whether working at this agency is challenging or upsetting apparently depends upon the individual person's viewpoint. For example, here are five situations that have arisen at Lively during the past month.

1. The agency's president, Tanya Arthur, complains that Billy is "fabulous when it comes to artwork, but he has put us weeks behind on the Regina Perfume account. We'll never have his completed art in time for the campaign to begin in January. I've got to stay on his back continually. If you gave people like him their head, production in this shop would simply fall apart. We make money by running a tight ship, not by tolerating a lot of prima donnas."

2. When Billy heard about Tanya's criticism, he remarked, "Her trouble is that she doesn't understand that it takes a prescribed amount of time to go from an artist's roughs through several other steps until the art is camera-ready for the printer. And that's not all. We get practically no re-

peat jobs here. Every account is different, and it takes time to set it up and work the bugs out."

3. George, from the standpoint of production, agreed with the creative director. "I'm up to my hips in work right now. If I didn't put in a 12-hour day, 6 days a week, nothing would be completed on time. And when I do rely upon one of my air-headed assistants to take care of something, what happens? I'll tell you. Last week I asked Randy Flynn to take over the Fast Fax job. He must have bothered me with questions every half hour. In the end, I had to do it myself."

4. Randy had a different version of his experience with the Fast Fax job. "George simply wouldn't let go of that job. He had to make every little decision. We could be just as innovative in production as the people in the creative department, but that's not the way George sees it. Instead, he has made work here at Lively a real downer for me. You know, most of the work builds up in the late afternoon. I suggested to George that it would make my life a lot simpler if he allowed me to come in to work at 10:30 a.m. and leave at 6:30, rather than our standard 9-to-5 day. George turned that idea down cold!"

5. When these complaints filtered back to Tanya, as they inevitably did, her comment was, "If these guys don't like the heat, let them stay out of the kitchen. In the advertising business, it's the client who calls the tune. We can do all the planning we want, but then we have to wait for ages for a decision from the client. And that can go either way, yes or no. Our creative director has a hard time living with these conditions. He gets so wound up at times that I expect him to burst into tears."

Assignment Questions

1 (a)   Based upon Tanya's comments about the creative director, his shortcomings have to do with his _____ for controlling work.
- _____ *a.* mode
- _____ *b.* competency
- _____ *c.* style
- _____ *d.* technique

1 (b)   Tanya's leadership style would appear to be _____ , and as a result this establishes the organization's _____ .
- _____ *a.* democratic; culture
- _____ *b.* participative; climate
- _____ *c.* laissez faire; climate
- _____ *d.* autocratic; culture

2 (a)   When Billy refers to the time it takes to go from an artist's roughs to camera-ready art, he is referring to _____ time.
- _____ *a.* start-up
- _____ *b.* processing

_____ *c.* learning
_____ *d.* lost

2 (b)   That there are few "repeat" jobs at the agency and that it takes time to "work out the bugs" indicates that considerable _____ time is involved.

_____ *a.* learning
_____ *b.* negotiating
_____ *c.* cleanup
_____ *d.* processing

3 (a)   Based upon his comments about the Fast Fax incident, George is reluctant to engage in:

_____ *a.* planning.
_____ *b.* organizing.
_____ *c.* directing.
_____ *d.* delegation.

3 (b)   What management practice might allow George to reduce his work load?

_____ *a.* Planning
_____ *b.* Organizing
_____ *c.* Controlling
_____ *d.* Delegation

4 (a)   From what Randy said about George, one would judge that George was not a believer in _____ management nor in _____ .

_____ *a.* participative; Theory Z
_____ *b.* scientific; Theory Y
_____ *c.* precautionary; Theory X
_____ *d.* contingency; path-goal theory

4 (b)   Randy's request for an adjustment in his reporting and quitting times is called _____ , and he believes that this would improve his _____ .

_____ *a.* start-up time; motivation
_____ *b.* free time; satisfaction
_____ *c.* flextime; quality of work life
_____ *d.* release time; quality assurance

5 (a)   The conditions that are typical of the advertising business, as described by Tanya, are _____ , and they apply _____ to those people employed in the industry.

_____ *a.* stressors; stress
_____ *b.* stress; stressors
_____ *c.* motivators; stressors
_____ *d.* demotivators; stress

5 (b)   Tanya describes Lively's creative director as a person with a(n) _____ behavior pattern.

_____ *a.* indifferent
_____ *b.* irrational
_____ *c.* type A
_____ *d.* type B

12
Productivity Improvement

Productivity improvement is an everyday battle for most organizations. For some, it is a life-and-death struggle. More often than not, productivity spells the difference between profit and loss, survival and failure. Mostly, however, productivity is the consequence of dealing forthrightly with reality: the output of a firm must equal or exceed its inputs. Productivity also puts a premium on conservation: waste is an enemy. Common sense plays a valuable role, too—as do the newest of productivity's handmaidens: automation and computer systems. Finally, like all important concerns of an organization, productivity improvement rests on the quality and motivation of the human resources employed in the endeavor.

Key Concepts Regarding
Productivity Improvement

Figure 12.1 shows the five key concepts that relate to productivity improvement. They are:

56. Resources should be available in sufficient quantity and quality to meet the stated objectives.

57. Management of resources is directed toward their optimum usage and, thus, toward their conservation.

58. Application of commonsense principles helps to improve productivity by systematizing and simplifying work.

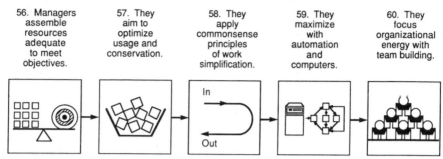

| 56. Managers assemble resources adequate to meet objectives. | 57. They aim to optimize usage and conservation. | 58. They apply commonsense principles of work simplification. | 59. They maximize with automation and computers. | 60. They focus organizational energy with team building. |

Figure 12.1. Concepts 56–60.

59. Introduction of automation and computer systems aims at maximizing the productivity of resources.

60. Team building focuses the energy of an organization on attainment of its objectives.

Key Terms

To make best use of the five concepts, you should understand the following terms:

Productivity

Percentage of capacity utilized

Throughput

Materials usage report

Capital usage report

Employee productivity

Downtime

Yield

Defect report

Leakage

Layout

Work simplification

Flow-process chart

Flow diagram

Value analysis

Automation

Feedback

Labor-intensive process

Capital-intensive process

Robotics

Office automation

Organization development (OD)

Change agent

Team building

Quality circle

Concept 56

Resources should be available in sufficient quantity and quality to meet the stated objectives.

You should recall, from Chapter 1, that management is concerned with the conversion of resources (or inputs) into results (outputs.) This is the same as saying that managers are responsible for the productivity of their organizations. **Productivity** is the ratio of outputs to inputs. The greater the ratio, the higher is the productivity. Exact productivity measurements are elusive; the most popular consider only the input of labor and the dollar value of the output. A comprehensive measurement of productivity would compare the value of *all* inputs and outputs.

Matching Resources to Targeted Results

Most organizations force managers to look at productivity in reverse. That is, a manager is given an objective, or target result to be obtained, then told to reach it. Unless there are sufficient resources available, however, the objective cannot be met. Accordingly, managers must assess their resources in light of the results desired. Adjustments must then be made to match the resources to the results, with neither too few nor too many resources.

The principal resources to be evaluated in terms of their adequacy are as follows:

1. *Facilities.* Is there enough space to carry out the process, and to allow for storage?

2. *Equipment.* Does the facility have the necessary capacity to handle the volume of output scheduled? Can it meet the quality specified for product or service?

3. *Utilities and auxiliary services.* Are the services that are available powerful and flexible enough? Consider electricity, steam, compressed air, waste disposal, transportation, telephone lines, computer systems, etc.

4. *Materials and supplies.* Are inventory levels high enough, alternate vendors available, and quality as specified?

5. *Capital.* Is funding strong enough to see the project to its conclu-

sion? Will cash flow in at a rate that will keep the organization solvent?

6. *Human resources.* Are there enough of the right kinds of skills? Are the employees properly trained and motivated?

7. *Information.* Have schedules been prepared? Are instructions and procedures clear, blueprints and other specifications on hand, and reference sources available as needed?

Practical Implications

The Situation. The forms reproduction unit of the Ultra Real Estate Agency had generous floor space. In the eyes of Wanda Brown, unit supervisor, there was no crowding of her or her employees during the course of normal work. Recently, however, Wanda agreed to produce, in-house, a large supply of forms that had previously been purchased from an outside vendor. All went well until the supply of forms produced began to overflow the department's storage capacity. Wanda had the forms piled into cases and cartons and stacked to the ceiling, but there was still an almost unbearable overcrowding. When Wanda brought this to the attention of Wilton McCormick, her boss, and asked if storage space might be made available, he said: "If we have to go out and find storage space, it will cost us all the money we have saved by producing the forms ourselves. As it is, it will take months to work down the supply that you have produced. You'll just have to live with it."

Question. Where does that leave Wanda now?

Answer. It leaves her having to live for a long while with a situation that will not only be uncomfortable but also interfere with the unit's productivity. In retrospect, Wanda should have anticipated the need for storage space when she accepted the project. At that time, she could have requested extra space or rejected the project because of insufficient facilities.

Concept 57

Management of resources is directed toward their optimum usage and, thus, toward their conservation.

Increased productivity is achieved by either (1) getting greater results from the same resources or (2) reducing the amount of resources to get the same results. Either way, a manager's objective is to strive for optimum utilization of resources as well as their conservation.

Utilization Measurements

How do managers find out how well their resources are being utilized? They do so by applying a number of measurements, such as the ones discussed below.

Percentage of Capacity Utilized.   For example, if a bottling machine has the capacity to fill 2000 bottles an hour but fills, on average, only 1500, its **percentage of capacity utilized** is 75 percent. Or, suppose a word processing unit has 5 operators available for 40 hours a week each, or a total of 200 hours. If the unit bills out only 180 hours of time, then its capacity utilization is 90 percent. In both examples, the capacity would be said to be underutilized.

Throughput.   The amount of a raw material that actually goes through the process, whether or not the output is 100 percent acceptable, is **throughput.** A textile printing mill may speak of a throughput of 100,000 square yards per week, a chemical plant of 30 million gallons of product per month, etc.

Materials Usage Reports.   Many companies report daily on the usage of key materials and supplies as compared with a projected, or budgeted, standard. These are **materials usage reports.**

Capital Usage Reports.   Many financial statements and ratios — **capital usage reports** — measure how productively the funds of a firm are employed. Important among such ratios are asset turnover ratio (sales revenues divided by assets), inventory turnover ratio (sales revenues divided by average inventory on hand), and accounts receivable ratio (sales revenues divided by accounts receivable.)

Employee Productivity.   Dividing the total output of an organization (expressed in units or dollars) by the total labor input (in terms of labor-hours) provides a measure of **employee productivity.** Thus, a cannery that packed 10,000 cases of peas, using 100 labor-hours, would be said to have a productivity of 100 cases per labor-hour. This measure takes on importance, of course, only when it is compared with a standard.

Conservation Measurements and Methods

Conservation efforts are aimed mainly at avoiding waste of an organization's resources. This effort goes hand in hand with greater utilization, and both contribute to increased productivity. Here again, there are many measurements of conservation, as well as many techniques for reducing waste. Some of the more common measurements are discussed below.

Downtime. Somewhat like a capacity-utilization measure, **downtime** reports the number of hours, or the percent of available time, that a piece of equipment is unusable and waiting for repair. Downtime may be reduced by (1) preventive maintenance, (2) operator training, or (3) machine replacement.

Yield. The percentage of usable raw materials that actually end up in the finished product is **yield**. Yield is calculated by subtracting damaged products and salvage from total throughput, and then dividing the remainder by total throughput. See Figure 12.2. Yield may be improved by (1) better process design, (2) greater operator care, and (3) improved machinery.

Defect Report. A **defect report** measures the number or percentage of units damaged during processing. Defects may be further classified as (1) repairable (rework), (2) nonrepairable (discard), or (3) nonre-

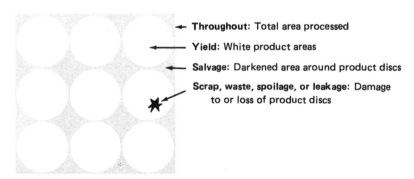

Figure 12.2. Yield relationship in materials usage.

pairable (salvage, or utilize discount sales potential as "secondary quality"). Defects may be reduced by a combination of (1) better operator training and instruction, (2) higher-quality equipment and improved equipment maintenance, (3) better raw-material specification and inspection, and (4) improved product and process design.

Leakage. Leakage measures the amount, or percentage, of valuable supplies, finished goods, or merchandise that is lost or damaged in storage, pilfered by employees, or stolen. Leakage may be reduced through closer inventory control and better security measures.

Absence, Tardiness, Accident, and Employee Turnover Reports. Each of these factors is considered to be a waste of human resources. Each can be reduced by participative management, improved motivation, and closer controls.

Practical Implications

The Situation. Something has been wrong with productivity at the Botany Apparel Company for the past year. Throughput of materials has been about the same. Yet, the percentage of salable, first-class finished goods produced is way down. A check of the percentage of capacity utilized for the major presses looks good, however. There has been little or no unusual downtime. Employee productivity, as measured by total yardage produced per labor-hour, is also in line.

Question. Where else should the management of Botany Apparel Company look for the source of the trouble?

Answer. If throughput, capacity utilization, and "raw" productivity figures are in line, there must be "slippage" somewhere in the quality or yield of what is being produced. In this case, management examines its defects report and also looks closely at the yield it is getting from its raw materials.

The *defects report* shows that the percentage of cloth yardage damaged during processing has risen to 5 percent; this compares poorly with the company standard of 2 percent.

The *yield* figures confirm the defects report: instead of a yield of nearly 98 percent, present figures show a yield of about 95 percent.

The company's quality-control people pinpoint the cause of the problem as a faulty die-locking mechanism that allows the imprinting dies to slip in the press during the latter part of long runs. After the locking mechanism is repaired, defects drop to less than 2 percent, yield rises to better than 98 percent, and productivity based upon production of salable finished goods returns to normal.

Concept 58

Application of commonsense principles helps to improve productivity by systematizing and simplifying work.

The underlying secret of process productivity is to prepare for, and maintain, a sense of order. To grasp the significance of this statement, think of what happens under the opposite extreme—chaos. When conditions are chaotic, confused, and disorganized, movements occur at random. We speak of "going around in circles." Little or no progress is made. Scientific managers, during the early part of this century, directed their thinking toward developing ways to establish order in the workplace. As a consequence of their efforts, the basic steps that managers take in seeking to improve productivity are to (1) systematize and (2) simplify the arrangement of processing operations wherever they take place.

Systematizing the Workplace

The physical arrangement of a process greatly affects its efficiency. Materials to be processed should flow smoothly from machine to machine, from workstation to workstation, or from desk to desk. The physical arrangement of a process is called its **layout**. A good layout:

- *Is orderly.*   Its sequences follow a logical succession.
- *Is uncluttered.*   No obstacles lie in the path of flow.
- *Is free from backtracking.*   The work in progress always moves forward; it does not retrace its steps to return to an area or operation.
- *Keeps handling and movement to a minimum.*   Handling time is wasteful and nonproductive. Movement of materials, too, is time-consuming and costly.

Design of a layout includes the placement of machinery and equipment, workstations, and support services. Layouts are arranged so that the work flow is as continuous and uninterrupted as possible. For prac-

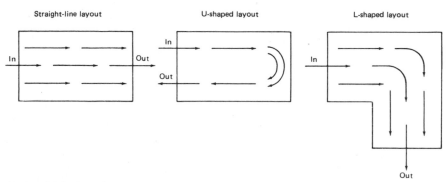

Figure 12.3. Basic layout patterns.

tical reasons—to conform to the configuration of a an existing building or work area—layouts may be arranged (1) in a straight line or (2) in a U shape or L shape, as shown in Figure 12.3.

Simplifying the Work Itself

Work simplification is an extension of systemization. **Work simplification** is an approach that (1) analyzes a process by breaking it down into simple segments, (2) identifies which segments are most costly and time-consuming, and (3) seeks to find a better way of performing these segments by using either (a) known techniques that are shorter or quicker or (b) known equipment and devices that are faster and more efficient.

Work simplification employs two important tools, as follows:

A **flow-process chart** portrays the process in terms of numbers, symbols, and words. The symbols identify operations that are truly productive, and separate them from handling and storing operations and delays.

A **flow diagram** is similar to a blueprint in that it traces and measures the actual physical flow of the work as it moves through a department.

Work simplification also engages in three analytical approaches: (1) process analysis, (2) process simplification, and (3) value analysis.

Process Analysis. Accomplished through a study of the flow-process chart and the flow diagram, process analysis asks six key groups of questions about each segment of the process:

1. *What* is the purpose of this operation or activity? Does it accomplish what it is supposed to do?

2. *Why* is it done? Should it be done at all? Could the same result be accomplished without it?

3. *When* is it done? Why is it done then? Is the process being done in the right sequence? Would another sequence be better? Can all or part of it be done at a different time?

4. *Who* does it? Why does that person do it? Is he or she the right person to do it? Would it be better to have someone else do it?

5. *How* is it done? How might it be done better? With a different layout? With different tools or equipment? With different methods?

6. *Where* is it being done? Is it being done in the right place? Where might it be done more conveniently or more efficiently?

Process Simplification. This proceeds somewhat along the lines of the idea checklist on page 217. After asking the six systematic and unrelenting groups of questions listed above, analysts seek ways to remove flaws in, or to simplify, the existing process by searching these classes of opportunities:

1. *Eliminate.* The first search is for nonproductive job segments that can be dropped from the sequence. It make no sense to try to improve something that is unnecessary to begin with.

2. *Combine.* Whenever two things can be done at once, time, motion, and effort are saved. Combining is accomplished by working with two hands rather than one, or by having a machine perform two operations simultaneously, such as filling and sealing a box of cereal.

3. *Change sequence.* Despite the saying, "The process dictates the sequence," many times the process was not in the right order in the first place. Scheduling of parallel operations often invites a "hurry up and wait" situation; such waiting and storage time can be reduced by postponing a job segment until it is needed.

4. *Simplify.* After each of the three previous possibilities has been explored, the emphasis shifts to a search for ways to improve each and all of the remaining job segments. Improvement, or simplification, can be accomplished by use of the following techniques:

- Improving the orderliness of the work flow
- Cutting down on waste motions of materials, documents, and people
- Replacing hand operations with mechanical or electronic ones

- Using material-handling equipment (like conveyors, cranes, and lift trucks)
- Providing positioning fixtures, chutes for feeding materials, and workstation consoles arranged to make the work easier to manage

Value Analysis. This technique focuses simplification efforts on the product or service, rather than on the method used to produce it. **Value analysis** is an approach that (1) identifies the functions the user (or customer) wants a product or service to perform and then (2) seeks to change the elements of a product or service so as to provide those functions at the least cost. Very often, the change involves replacing a material or part with a less costly one. Or the product or service may be stripped of all nonessential and decorative features so as to perform only the bare essentials of the functions desired.

Practical Implications

The Situation. Sales orders at Ivanhoe Industrial Distributors have been handled the same way for years. This way seemed efficient enough when orders flowed in at the rate of 50 a day. Now, however, Ivanhoe's business has grown, and sales orders arrive at the rate of 500 or more a day.

This is the way they are presently processed: (1) The order is received by a salesclerk, who acknowledges it with a typed letter and forwards it to (2) a pricing clerk, who calculates its total price and sends the order to (3) a credit clerk, who verifies the customer's credit standing and sends the order back to (4) the salesclerk, who assigns an order number to it and forwards it to (5) a registry clerk, who posts the order in a control file and gives the order to (6) a production-control clerk, who prepares a warehouse order with six copies and staples a copy of the customer order to it, and then routes this to (7) a mail clerk who inserts it in an envelope, addresses it, and mails it to the warehouse.

Question. How can this process be improved?

Answer. A *flow-process chart* and a *flow diagram* — techniques of work simplification — would highlight the extent of unnecessary handling and movement. They would also point to places where job segments could be combined or methods improved and backtracking eliminated.

A better way to process the sales order would be as follows: (1) The salesclerk receives the order, selects an appropriate form letter, and prepares it on a word processor, making whatever particularized entries are needed in the spaces provided. (This saves 4 minutes per order.) The routing of the order to (2) the pricing clerk and (3) the credit clerk remains the same, but the salesclerk no longer assigns an order number (saving another 2 minutes per order); this is done by (4) the registry clerk, who, instead of posting numbers and details in a log book, picks up the necessary data via carbon on a form, a copy of which goes to (5) the production clerk, whose job has been combined with that of the mail clerk. Using a snap-out form enables the production clerk to cut order-typing time from 12 to 6 minutes. Having the production clerk also handle mail preparation (by accumulating warehouse orders in a tray and then inserting them in one self-addressed bulk-mail envelope at the end of the day) saves another 2 minutes per order.

The need for the mail clerk has been eliminated, as has backtracking of the order to the salesclerk. The improved methods cut total processing time from 52 labor-minutes per order to 38. At an average wage rate of $9 per hour, or $0.15 per minute, that is a savings of $2.10 per order. With 500 orders a day to process, the savings comes to $1050 per day. The cost of word processing equipment and snap-out forms equates to about $0.25 per order, or $125 per day. This yields a net savings of $925 on sales-order processing.

Concept 59

Introduction of automation and computer systems aims at maximizing the productivity of resources.

Automation and computer systems are advanced stages of work systematization and simplification.

Automation is a modern extension of mechanization. It is a collection of methods for controlling machinery and processes by automatic means, often with computerized electronic equipment. An essential element of automation is **feedback**. This is a method of two-way communication between the machine and a control device that instructs the machine to perform in a certain manner based upon the results being reported.

Automation is typically applied to **labor-intensive processes** — those that have a high degree of labor inputs relative to capital, or equipment, inputs. As a result, automated and computerized processes are usually **capital-intensive processes**. That is, they require relatively large infusions of costly equipment, which reduces the proportion of labor required.

An increasingly popular form of automation is **robotics**. This is the use of mechanical devices that duplicate certain motions of the human hand. They are especially good for dirty, dull, repetitive, precise, or hazardous work. Robotics are often associated with automation and computerized controls.

Until recent years, office and clerical work have been notable for their low productivity. Increasingly, however, the labor-intensive hand operations of the office are giving way to office automation. **Office automation** encompasses aspects of traditional clerical work and administration that automation puts together, in building-block style, of such computer-oriented devices as electronic mail, voice message systems, electronic filing, advanced telephone systems, and personal workstations.

Practical Implications

The Situation.   Refer back to the simplified sales-order-processing system of the Ivanhoe Industrial Distributors, as described in the solution of the "Practical Implications" section under concept 58.

Question.   What can now be done now to improve the system's productivity dramatically?.

Answer.   In all probability, the entire process—receiving, entering, acknowledging, and pricing the order; verifying the customer's credit; posting the sales order; and preparing and mailing the warehouse order—could be performed by a single clerk in a computerized operation. The *office automation* equipment would be more expensive and the software programming more sophisticated than at present. The clerk would also have to be more knowledgeable, skilled, and versatile than any of the clerks who currently perform their relatively narrow specialities. The process would become far less *labor-intensive* and far more *capital-intensive*.

Concept 60

Team building focuses the energy of an organization on attainment of its objectives.

As discussed in Chapter 5, organizations are created by managers and are designed to provide the most effective way for people to work together toward common goals. The structure of an organization, unfortunately, tends to become increasingly rigid as it ages. As a consequence, many organizations have difficulty in dealing with change. A structure that was once highly productive loses that edge.

Organization Development

An approach called "organization development" has been conceived to help an organization to renew its vigor and to become more flexible and productive. **Organization development (OD)** is (1) a planned effort (2) initiated from the top of the organization (3) to improve the effectiveness of the organization as a whole (4) through "intervention" and (5) by applying knowledge and methods of the behavioral sciences.

Intervention implies the employment of someone who is not a member of the organization (usually a specialized consultant) to act as a change agent. During the OD process, the **change agent** performs a number of functions and roles, including:

- Identifying a need for change, such as to increase productivity, improve quality, or reduce conflict
- Selecting a technique to assist in bringing about the needed change
- Supervising and facilitating the change process

During the course of an extended OD process, an organization may radically restructure itself, its goals, and its culture.

Team Building

Among several techniques that may be used during the OD process are such approaches as attitudinal surveys and feedback, education in interpersonal skills, consultation and coaching by the change agent, third-party peacemaking, group planning and goal setting, and—most often—team building.

Team building consists of a number of planned activities designed to help people who work in small groups to develop a sense of teamwork. These activities focus on (1) identifying problems within the group or that confront it, (2) improving problem-solving, goal-setting, and decision-making processes within the group, (3) understanding and improving interpersonal relations within the group, and (4) clarifying and defining roles.

Team building lays the foundation for groups to find their own ways of improving productivity. It also makes them more receptive to innovative technology.

Quality Circles

Quality circles are not the same as team building. Some of the characteristics of quality circles, however, are derived from OD and the team-building concepts. **Quality circles** require a participative approach, in which small groups of employees meet regularly under management sponsorship to examine work-related quality problems, as well as production problems, and to suggest solutions. A quality circle is aided by a "facilitator" who plays a role similar to a change agent. Membership in a quality circle is voluntary, although meetings are held on company time.

Circle members are provided with instruction in skills such as problem analysis, statistical analysis, ABC analysis, cause-and-effect diagrams, value analysis, motion economy, and work simplification.

Practical Implications

The Situation. Bettina B. was recently appointed manager of a medium-sized branch of a national discount chain. This particular branch was labeled a "problem" because of low sales volume and high labor costs. Bettina was chosen for the assignment because of her reputation as a team builder. When Bettina arrived at the branch store, she found that conditions were worse than expected. The store was cluttered, merchandise was soiled and improperly priced, the employees' morale was low, and there was endless bickering among the staff.

Question. What specific steps should Bettina take to build a team at the branch?

Answer. Bettina can set about team building by taking the following steps.

1. She should first call a meeting of employees, so that she can introduce herself and state her qualifications for becoming the store manager. Next she should say that she will spend the next month or two getting to know the employees, and that she has no preconceived ideas about any changes in the way things are being done now. This way, Bettina can make it clear that she has come to the branch as a team member, not as a critic.

2. Bettina should subsequently meet privately with each employee to

discuss that individual's background and experience, career expectations, and thoughts about what is good or bad about the present job. The purpose of this interview is to gather information about facts and feelings. She should make no value judgments and should avoid making comments—either good or bad—about anything or anybody. This will give evidence of Bettina's willingness to listen and not to sit in judgment.

3. A second meeting of all employees will enable Bettina (a) to report her impressions of the store's operation and problems, based upon her interviews, (b) to reiterate that she has no preconceived ideas about changes that should be made, and (c) to invite each employee to participate in identifying critical problems and helping to solve them.

4. She should make a habit of circulating freely during the store's operation: observing, listening, being seen, and helping out in operations that seem to need an extra hand. This will continue to reinforce Bettina's presentation of herself as a team member.

5. At a third meeting, using the nominal group technique (discussed in Chapter 9), she should gather a list of problems that employees believe are important, and ask the employees how these problems ought to be solved. Bettina can then suggest a method for approaching these problems that maximizes group participation. (A variation of a quality circle might be one way.) This meeting is the time when Bettina begins to gain her employees' acceptance of her as their leader.

6. Following the third meeting, she should continue to emphasize her concern for employees' welfare by using (a) private interviews, (b) group meetings, and (c) visibility on the floor.

7. In her accepted role as leader of the team, Bettina may introduce problems of performance and productivity that may not be evident to rank-and-file employees. These problems should always be talked about, however, in the context of the employees' interests as well as those of the company.

The cumulative effect of these seven steps, taken over a period of from 3 to 6 months, will build a team, for which Bettina is the acknowledged leader. This team can attack and solve the problems of the store's poor performance and appearance, and bring productivity up to a reasonable level.

Comprehension-Check Case for Chapter 12

The Case of the Declining Productivity at Carrie's Crafts

For easy reference, the text of the comprehension-check case is numbered to correspond to the assignment questions that follow.

Carrie's Crafts Company is a small manufacturer of cardboard "novelty" boxes. These boxes are fashioned in a number of shapes and imprinted with a variety of designs and options that include several different colors. All boxes are of the folding variety, so that they can shipped flat, or "knocked down." Upon receipt of a knocked-down box, the customer assembles the box and its lid by folding and fitting them along prescored markings on the cardboard. Carrie's was originally a one-woman, one-press operation, originated and run by Carrie H., who is still the owner and president. Today, the company employs more than 50 people and makes several thousand boxes a week. Along with the growth have come competition and its companion—productivity problems.

1. In the pressroom, there is a small stamping machine run by a single operator. When it was first purchased, it easily turned out 100 boxes an hour, but lately it has had to be nursed along, and it now turns out only 90 per hour. Carrie has bought an additional stamping machine, rated by the manufacturer to turn out 300 pieces per hour. Its motor, however, required installation of an electrical supply of 220 volts. ·

2. The new machine has not been living up to the promise of 300 units an hour, mainly because the drive mechanism connecting the motor to the stamper keeps getting loose. Each time this happens, the operator has to shut off the motor and wait until a mechanic can come to repair the drive mechanism. Carrie estimates that the operator has lost 15 units an hour, on average, because of this problem. Carrie is also disappointed to find that, of every 100 boxes put through the machine, only 97 are in good enough shape to be salable. The rest have to be scrapped.

3. Carrie's box designer and pressroom supervisor got together, looking for ways to save money and improve productivity. The previous procedure for making the boxes was to cut them on one machine, prescore the folding marks on a machine called a "bending brake," and then stamp the design with a third machine. Each machine had its own operator—a total of three machines run by three operators for each box produced. The boxes in process were moved in bundles from machine to machine on a hand truck. The box designer and pressroom supervisor found out that a single machine could be purchased that would cut and prescore the boxes in a single operation, and that could be operated by a single person. Carrie was sold on the idea and traded in the two old machines for the new one.

The designer also came up with an idea that shortened the lip on each box lid. The lids fit just as snugly as before, and the savings in materials for box lids adds up to more than $100 per week.

4. Despite the machine in the pressroom, most of Carrie's operations are handwork done by craftspeople and artists who personalize many of the novelty boxes. While only 3 people work in the pressroom, there are more than 50 people working at benches in the decorating room. Recently, Carrie has bought a word processor and a minicomputer for the office, where sales orders and invoices are processed.

5. While productivity has been getting back on track in the pressroom, performance in the decorating room has been anything but good. The artists and craftspeople are a temperamental lot and don't get along well with one another or with the decorating supervisor. Nor does the decorating department get along well with the designer or the pressroom people. Reggie R., an organization development consultant, called on Carrie and suggested that he might improve matters by helping the decorating-room supervisor to build a more unified and cooperative team. Carrie didn't buy that idea, but she did invite employees in the decorating room to meet regularly with the consultant to identify production and quality problems, and to suggest ways to improve them.

Assignment Questions

1 (a)   The productivity of the small stamping machine has_____
to a point where it is _____ percent of what it used to be.
- _____ *a.* increased; 90
- _____ *b.* declined; 90
- _____ *c.* increased; 110
- _____ *d.* neither increased nor declined; the same

1 (b)   The new stamping machine that Carrie bought has a_____
of 300 pieces per hour, and its motor must be _____ by a utility supply of 220 volts.
- _____ *a.* capacity; matched
- _____ *b.* potential; balanced
- _____ *c.* facility; matched
- _____ *d.* input; balanced

2 (a)   The utilization measure of the new machine when it is waiting for repairs is called _____ , and it comes to _____ percent of the machine's rated time, or capacity.
- _____ *a.* "a defect report"; 5
- _____ *b.* "throughput"; 15
- _____ *c.* "leakage"; 15
- _____ *d.* "downtime"; 5

2 (b)   The _____ of the materials processed by the new machine is 97 percent.
- _____ *a.* capacity utilization

_____ *b.* throughput
_____ *c.* yield
_____ *d.* productivity

3 (a)   The box designer and pressroom supervisor used_____
to _____ two operations.
_____ *a.* work simplification; combine
_____ *b.* work simplification; eliminate
_____ *c.* layout planning; combine
_____ *d.* flextime; merge

3 (b)   The box designer applied _____ to save on cardboard used
on the box lids.
_____ *a.* layout planning
_____ *b.* elimination
_____ *c.* simplification
_____ *d.* value analysis

4 (a)   The decorating-room process is _____ , while the
pressroom process is _____ .
_____ *a.* labor-intensive; capital-intensive
_____ *b.* capital-intensive; labor-intensive
_____ *c.* simplified; not simplified
_____ *d.* productive; nonproductive

4 (b)   Carrie intends to install _____ for handling sales-order
processing.
_____ *a.* robotics
_____ *b.* logistics
_____ *c.* office automation
_____ *d.* distributed data processing

5 (a)   The organization development consultant suggested that he might play
the role of _____ in the decorating room.
_____ *a.* inventor
_____ *b.* protagonist
_____ *c.* change agent
_____ *d.* stimulator

5 (b)   The productivity improvement approach that Carrie adopted for the
decorating room is *most* like:
_____ *a.* quality circles.
_____ *b.* team building.
_____ *c.* organization development.
_____ *d.* office automation.

Answer Key to
Comprehension-Check Cases

The comprehension-check cases can be found at the ends of the chapters.

Chapter 1
The Case of the Harrassed Plant Superintendent

1 (a)   *b*
1 (b)   *d*
2 (a)   *b*

COMMENT: While all three (*a*, *b*, and *c*) are culpable, the company president should hold Brady responsible for all work performed under his management.

2 (b)   *a.* Planning   *d.* Staffing
        b. Not managerial work   *e.* Controlling
        c. Directing   *f.* Organizing

3 (a)   *a.* Decisional (negotiator)
        b. Interpersonal (spokesperson)
        c. Informational (disseminator)
        d. Interpersonal (liason)
        e. Decisional (crisis handler)
        f. Decisional (innovator)

3 (b)   *a.* Human relations   *d.* Technical or conceptual
        b. Human relations   *e.* Technical
        c. Human relations or technical *f.* Conceptual or technical

COMMENT: Answers may vary here due to interpretation. What is important is to observe the range of skills needed to handle the situation.

4 (a)   *c*

COMMENT: 400,000 units × $5 per unit = $2,000,000 gross output
Less 20,000 defective units × $5   =   100,000 scrapped
                              Results = $1,900,000 net output

4 (b)   *c*

COMMENT: Results ($1,900,000) divided by resources ($2,000,000) = 0.95 = 95 percent effectiveness.

5 (a) *c*
5 (b) *a*

Chapter 2
The Case of the Underflown Airline

1 *a*

COMMENT: Managers who run their departments as if they were closed systems try to make their own operations look good, at the expense of other departments and the organization as a whole. This seems evident at FFA, where results will not improve until its managers recognize that theirs should be open systems.

2 (a) *c*

COMMENT: The operations manager's goal, which appears to be maximum cost efficiency, is at odds with the president's strategy, which is based upon gaining passenger miles with better service. The operations manager is at the administrative level of the hierarchy, while the president is at the strategic level.

2 (b) *c*

COMMENT: Partisanship can be expected and accepted at the operational level, but when it leads to factionalism and conflict, then it is damaging to the company's effectiveness, which is the case with FFA.

3 (a) *c*

COMMENT: FFA's schedules don't suit customer convenience, and those of its competitor, Commuter Sky, do. Both of these forces are in the company's directly interactive environment.

3 (b) *c*

COMMENT: The Denver hub evolved as a consequence of deregulation—a legal and political force in the indirectly interactive environment. Because the indirectly interactive environment appears remote to insiders, they often fail to anticipate correctly the impact of changes in it. Apparently FFA also not anticipate correctly.

4 *c*

5 (a) *c*

COMMENT: Allocating resources is one of the things mentioned in the text that management sciences does well.

5 (b) *d*

COMMENT: It would appear that employees' performance is more closely related to human than to technical factors here; accordingly, a behavioral management approach seems the best one to begin with.

5 (c)   *a*

COMMENT: Measurement of the time needed to perform a task is a strength of the scientific management approach.

Chapter 3
The Case of the Contrary Claims
Department

1 (a)   *b*
1 (b)   *d*

2 (a)   *a*
2 (b)   *d*

COMMENT: We don't know for sure, but the evidence throughout the case suggests that George tends to underestimate and undervalue employees' capabilities and potential.

2 (c)   *a*

COMMENT: Personality, of course, sums up perceptions and attitudes and reflects motivation; the text classifies self-discipline as a personality trait.

3   *c*

COMMENT: In George's case, his desire for improved status, as indicated by a promotion to a higher-level position, shows his need for greater esteem from the organization.

4 (a)   *c*
4 (b)   *c*

COMMENT: George might try to involve Marge in planning schedules and setting work goals, provided that it becomes a shared, rather than a unilateral, activity for Marge. Marge needs to be challenged by her work, too.

5 (a)   *d*
5 (b)   *a*

COMMENT: There are a great variety of roles that may be played in an informal work group, just as norms may take many forms and for a variety of reasons.

Chapter 4
The Case of the Burgeoning
Cosmetics Company

1 (a)   *d*

COMMENT: Some mission statements are even more detailed, and may include acquiring, preparing, packaging, and marketing.

1 (b)   high-quality; upper-income

COMMENT: These specifications narrow down the mission but give it sharper focus.

1 (c)   *b*

COMMENT: Only *b* offers any concrete opportunity for measurement.

2 (a)   *b*
2 (b)   *d*
2 (c)   *c*

3   *d*

4 (a)   *b*
4 (b)   *c*

COMMENT: $40,000 \times 50 = \$2,000,000$; $\$2,000,000 + 50\% = \$3,000,000$.

4 (c)   *d*

COMMENT: This is a typical one-of-a-kind project and highly complex in its variables, which makes it a natural for CPM or PERT.

5 (a)   *b*

COMMENT: Knowledge of the organization's hierarchy of goals is often difficult to obtain, since there is a tendency to declare that "all goals are equal and must be met." In actual practice, some goals are naturally at the top of the hierarchy, and others are assigned a low priority after it becomes clear that not all goals are likely to be met.

5 (b)   *d*

COMMENT: The MBO approach offers subordinates an opportunity to clarify misunderstandings about goals, and the psychology of involvement in the goal-setting process induces commitment.

Chapter 5
The Case of the Shrinking Lumber Company

1 (a)   *d*

COMMENT: Where there had been several jobs to accomplish the work of the stripping department, there are now only two.

1 (b)   *d*

COMMENT: The job was enlarged by giving the operator many things to do; it was enriched by requiring more judgment and assigning more responsibility. Job enhancement consists of either, or both, of these two job improvements.

1 (c)   *d*

COMMENT: Choice *a* is enlargement; *b* is enrichment; *c* improves working conditions. All three add to the quality of the work itself.

2 (a)   *a*
2 (b)   *c*
2 (c)   *b*

COMMENT: Spreading out the selling responsibilities from one office at headquarters to six in the field creates a flatter, more decentralized organization.

3 (a)   *d*
3 (b)   *b*

4 (a)   *d*
4 (b)   *a*

COMMENT: Managers were expected to handle more activities (a broader span), which leads to the flatter organization structures of decentralization (as in 4*a*).

5 (a)   *c*

COMMENT: This is the strongest kind of authority that can be granted a staff department, so that its advice must be accepted.

5 (b)   *d*

Chapter 6
The Case of the Expanding World of
Kits 'n' Games

1 (a)   *c*
1 (b)   *a*

2 (a)   *d*

COMMENT: She has 350 employees and needs 50 more, for a total payroll of 400 at year end. Total new hires = 50 to increase staff + 10 to fill absences + 70 to replace quits + 20 to replace retirements = 150.

2 (b)   *c*

COMMENT: While "job evaluation" is the correct answer, job evaluation often emerges from a process of job analysis and its two attendent documents, the job description and the job specification.

3 (a)   *a*
3 (b)   *c*

COMMENT: It is true that the job specification contains information drawn from the job description, but the latter is targeted at the qualifications needed to fill the job rather than at the job requirements themselves.

4 (a)   *a*
4 (b)   *d*

COMMENT: Coaching and interactive training are the *methods* used in many management development programs.

5 (a)   *c*

COMMENT: Increasing care is given to the way in which employees' performance is monitored and recorded in formal performance appraisal programs. Without systematic and written reviews of performance, decisions regarding either failure to promote or termination are not likely to be supported by EEOC.

5 (b)   *c*

Chapter 7
The Case of the Take-Charge CEO

1 (a)   *b*

COMMENT: By wearing a jacket and tie, Jones was telling his staff that the easy-going days of blue-jeans management were over. This is an effective use of body language.

1 (b)   *c*

2 (a)   *d*

2 (b)   *b*

COMMENT: Jones's reliance on downward communications and a restricted network, over which he had central control, tended to stifle the kind of coordinated problem solving the company needed.

3 (a)   *a*

3 (b)   *c*

COMMENT: He was motivated by short-range, attainable goals and frequent feedback about his performance. We know little about either his affiliation or his power needs.

4 (a)   *d*

COMMENT: Expectancy leads to performance; performance then becomes the instrumentality for obtaining the outcome.

4 (b)   *c*

COMMENT: Nonreinforcement led to the extinction of Hopkin's complaining behavior.

5 (a)   *a*

COMMENT: It was Jones's knowledge and performance that gained him followers. Most of them were not attracted to his personality and did not think he had charisma, both of which are included in referent power.

5 (b)   *b*

COMMENT: While Jones's position power gradually grew, his relationships were never strong. The complexity of the research job would indicate a relations-oriented style. Because manufacturing and purchasing activities were more routine and structured, Jones's task-oriented style would appear to be more appropriate there, but it might be argued either way.

Chapter 8
The Case of the Spectacular Ski
Company

1 (a)   c
1 (b)   c

COMMENT: It may appear that measurement and comparisons are made simultaneously, but they actually take place in sequence.

2 (a)   a
2 (b)   d

COMMENT: Any *type* of control might be placed at a key, or strategic, point.

3 (a)   a

COMMENT: In most instances, the variable budget is combined with the overhead budget, with some items representing fixed and others variable expenses.

3 (b)   c

COMMENT: As a matter of convenience, flexible budgets are not issued on separate sheets; the data are simply placed on a single sheet in columns with headings representing different volumes of activity.

4 (a)   c
4 (b)   d

COMMENT: Inspection during statistical quality control may be made either by looking, feeling, measuring, etc. (nondestructive testing), or by breaking, opening, etc. (destructive testing).

5 (a)   b

COMMENT: Measurement of employee turnover (a comparison of separations and hirings with total employment) may be made to control the high costs associated with employing and training new personnel, not necessarily to limit growth.

5 (b)   d

COMMENT: Employees and managers, alike, are very resourceful in finding ways to resist, deflect, or destroy control measures that they believe to be unreasonable or threatening.

Chapter 9
The Case of the Puzzled Bank
Manager

1 (a)   b

COMMENT: As a matter of fact, Dan skipped, or poorly approached, several steps. He did not specify the problem, consider a number of possible solutions, or evaluate them. He was guilty of jumping to conclusions.

1 (b)   d

COMMENT: Most of all, Dan did not perform a complete rational analysis, which would include *all* the items listed.

2 (a) *c*

2 (b) *a*

COMMENT: The heart of problem solving is identification of causes; otherwise, proposed solutions are not likely to be "cause removers."

3 (a) *c*

3 (b) *d*

COMMENT: Nominal group technique is a form of brainstorming, and the idea checklist is an extension of brainstorming.

4 (a) *b*

COMMENT: MAU stands for "multiattribute utility," or the process of placing values (or utility) on each of the attributes of the solution criteria.

4 (b) *a*

5 (a) *b*

COMMENT:

$$\$2,000,000 \times 0.20 = \$ \quad 400,000$$
$$1,000,000 \times 0.30 = \quad 300,000$$
$$1,500,000 \times 0.50 = \quad \underline{750,000}$$
$$\$\,\overline{1,450,000}$$

5 (b) *d*

Chapter 10
The Case of the Coleman Memorial Hospital

1 (a) *a*

COMMENT: The data from the hospital association would probably also be considered secondary data.

1 (b) *c*

COMMENT: While the hospital association probably provides a "service" that comes from a "library," the assumption is that their data is compiled into an electronic library, or database.

2 (a) *b*

COMMENT: The system may require electronic data processing, but the principal definition of it is a management information system.

2 (b) *d*

3 (a) *a*

3 (b) *a*

4 (a) *b*

4 (b) *d*

5 (a) *d*

COMMENT: A time series is simply a special arrangement of an array; both are considered to be descriptive statistics.

5 (b) *b*

COMMENT: The key words in the question were "would need *now* to examine the information." Inferential statistics is an extension of descriptive statistics; it interprets the information provided by descriptive statistics.

Chapter 11
The Case of the Lively Advertising Agency

1 (a) *b*
1 (b) *d*

COMMENT: Tanya is certainly autocratic in her style. Note that organizational "climate" and "culture" are sometimes used interchangeably, although "climate" is more closely related to morale, and "culture" to "the way things are done here."

2 (a) *b*
2 (b) *a*

COMMENT: Learning time would be closely related to start-up time in this instance, had the option been offered.

3 (a) *d*
3 (b) *d*

COMMENT: George is a classic example of a manager who is overloaded, but who is reluctant to obtain the relief and assistance that delegation would provide.

4 (a) *a*

COMMENT: George compounds his problems by not leaning toward a participative management style when a key employee indicates that he would respond productively to it. Theory Y, incidentally, is akin to Theory Z, but scientific management is far removed from participative management.

4 (b) *c*
5 (a) *a*

COMMENT: *Stressors* are the conditions that apply *stress* and draw from an individual a *stress reaction*, which, when it is negative, is called *distress*.

5 (b) *c*

COMMENT: Type A reactions may be dysfunctional, but to the human physiological system, they are *rational* and they reflect the normal circulatory process of pumping adrenaline into the body.

Chapter 12
The Case of the Declining
Productivity at Carrie's Crafts

1 (a)   *b*

COMMENT: The past productivity rate was 100 an hour; the present is 90 per hour. Present compared with past is 90 ÷ 100 = 0.90 = 90 percent.

1 (b)   *a*

COMMENT: It is important to think of capacity, rather than "potential" or "facility." Many times, as in this case, it works out that the actual performance does not live up to the potential promised by the capacity listed by a manufacturer. If so, the owner — for productivity measurement purposes — respecifies the capacity to what the machine can actually do when operating perfectly.

2 (a)   *d*

COMMENT: Production lost because of downtime was 15 per hour. Compared with a rated capacity of 300 per hour, this is 15 ÷ 300 = 0.05 = 5 percent.

2 (b)   *c*

COMMENT: Yield is throughput (100) minus scrap (3) = 97, or 97 out of 100, or 97 ÷ 100 = 0.97 = 97 percent.

3 (a)   *a*

COMMENT: One machine was eliminated by combining the operations previously handled by two into a one-machine operation.

3 (b)   *d*

4 (a)   *a*

COMMENT: Answers *c* and *d* are not appropriate, for if anything, the decorating-room process has not been simplified, and it does not appear to be productive, when compared with pressroom processes.

4 (b)   *c*

5 (a)   *c*

5 (b)   *a*

COMMENT: Neither *b* nor *c* is a correct answer, because Carrie's approach is *most* like quality circles, even though quality circles are somewhat similar to, or are derived from, OD and team building.

Index

ABC analysis, 213
Absence, 196
Absence reports, 275
Accident reports, 275
Accountability, 109–110
Accountant, 5
Achievement motivation theory, 164
Achievement need, 165
Affiliation need, 164
Affirmative action program, 127
Age Discrimination in Employment Act
  (1978), 126
Alderfer, Clayton, 164
Application blanks, 134–135
  restricted subjects for, 135
Appraisals (see Performance appraisals)
Apprenticeship programs, 140
Aptitude tests, 136
Array, 242
Arrow diagram, 87
Assessments:
  of personality, 138
  of technical competence, 137–138
Attitudes, 54–55
  related to perceptions, 54
  toward risk, 219–220
Attributes, weighting of, 218–219
Authority, 108
  delegation of, 109–110
  modified, 115–116
Automation, 280–281
  office, 281
Average, 243

Balance sheet, 187
Batch processing, 238
Behavior modification, 168–169
Behavioral management, 37–38

Behaviorally anchored rating scales
  (BARS), 144–145
Blake, R., 172
Boundary spanning, 34
  in managerial activities, 34–35
Brainstorming, 215, 216
Budget, 79, 187
  flexible, 187–188
  overhead, 187
  personal time, 254, 256
  variable, 188

Capacity and time planning, 85
Capital-intensive processes, 280–281
Capital structure, 186–187
Capital usage reports, 273
Cash flows statement, 187
Causes, identification of, 212–213
Central value, 243
Centralization, 112
Chain of command, 109, 110, 114, 160
Change agent, 282
Civil Rights Act (1964), 126
Client group, 31
Cliques, 62
Closed systems, 26–27
Coaching, 140
Collective bargaining, 128
Command, unity of, 108–110
Communications, 155–156, 159
  channels in, 160
  downward, 160
  grapevine, 166
  interpersonal, 159–160
  networks in, 160–161
  sideways, 160
  upward, 160
Compensation, 131

Competency, 251–252
Competitor group, 32
Computer networks, 239
Computer systems, 229, 237
Concurrent controls, 184, 186
Conservation measurements and methods,
    274–275
Contingency management, 18
Controlling, 8, 179–200
    budgets, 187
        flexible budgets, 187–188
    capital structure, 186–187
    concepts regarding, 180, 181, 184, 186,
        191, 195
    definition of, 179
    economic order quantity, 191–192
    effectiveness of, 180
    financial statements, 186–187
    human problems with controls, 196–197
    human resources controls, 180
    just-in-time inventory control, 192
    key-point (strategic) controls, 185
    locus of control, 184–185
    as management function, 8
    materials controls, 191–192
    materials requirements planning, 192
    network planning methods, 193
    parallel scheduling, 193
    perpetual inventory control, 192
    quality control, 193
    sequential scheduling, 192
    steps in, 181–182
    variance reports, 188
Controls (see Controlling)
Conversion process, 13
Cooperation, 47–48
Corrective action, 182–183
Correlation analysis, 244
Cost-benefit analysis, 219
Cost benefits, 16
Cost containment, 16
CPM (critical path method), 87, 193, 195
Creative process, 215
Critical path method (CPM), 87, 193, 195
Cultural forces, 32–33
Culture, 252
Customer, departmentation by, 104, 106
Customer group, 31

Data, 231
    classes of, 232

Data collection, 231
    external sources, 231–232
    internal sources, 231
Data processing functions, 237–238
Data processing modes, 238
Decentralization, 112
Decision, 208
Decision making (see Managerial problem
        solving and decision making)
Decision support systems, 229, 239, 240
Decision trees, 222–223
Defect report, 274–275
Delegation, 108–109, 249
    choices in, 257
    methods of, 257–259
Departmentation:
    by customer, 104, 106
    by function, 103–105, 107
    by location, 104–107
    by product, 104, 107
    by service, 104
Department schedules, 87
Descriptive statistics, 242–244
Directing, 8
    advanced concepts of leadership, 172
    behavior modification, 168–169
    components of, 155–156
    concepts regarding, 153–155, 159, 162,
        166, 170
    content theories of motivation, 163–165
    continuum of leadership styles in,
        171–172
    equity theory, 168
    expectancy theory, 166–168
    interpersonal communications, 159–160
    leadership traits, 170–171
    as management function, 8
    organizational communications,
        160–161
    path-goal leadership theory, 173–174
    self-fulfilling prophecies, 156–157
    situational leadership, 173
    two-dimensional leadership, 172
Directly interactive environmental forces,
    31–32
Dispersion, 243–244
Dissatisfiers, 59
Distress, 263
Distributed data processing, 239
Division of labor, 99, 100
Downtime, 274

Downward communication, 160

Economic order quantity (EOQ), 191–192, 195
Economy, 32
Educational institutions as source of employees, 134
Employee benefits program, 131
Employee productivity, 273–274
(*See also* Productivity; Productivity improvement)
Employee training programs, 139–140
Employee turnover reports, 275
Employees' performance, measurements of, 46–47
Employment agencies, private and public, 134
Employment interviews, 135, 136
restricted subjects for, 135
Engineer, 5
Environment:
international, 33
legal, 32
managerial (*see* Managerial environment)
physical, 33
political, 32
Equal Employment Opportunity Act (1972), 126, 131
Equal Employment Opportunity Commission, 126
Equal Pay Act (1963), 126
Equity theory, 168
Escape conditioning, 169
Ethical value, 55
Evaluation criteria, 218
Exception reports, 240–241
Executive-search firms, 134
Executives, 5, 6
Existence-relatedness-growth (ERG) theory, 164
Expectancy, 167
Expectancy theory, 166–168
Expert power, 170

Factionalism, 30
Fair Labor Standards Act (1938), 127
Fair treatment as self-fulfilling prophecy, 156
Feedback, 159, 280
Feedback controls, 184–186

Fiedler, Fred, 173
Financial controls, 180
Financial officers, 186
Financial statements, 186–187
First-level managers, 5
Five-point checklist, 79, 80
Flexible budgeting, 187–188, 190
Flextime, 261
Flow of funds, 187
Flow diagram, 277, 279
Flow-process chart, 277, 279
Forced-choice method, 144
Forced distribution, 145
Forecasting methods, 84–85
historical-trends forecast, 85
statistical-analysis forecast, 85
survey-method forecast, 84–85
Formal work groups, 61
Friction, minimizing, 30
Function, departmentation by, 103–105, 107

Gaming theory, 224
Gantt chart, 87, 88
Gap analysis, 211, 233
Goals, 73–74
characteristic features of, 74–75
superordinate, 116
Goals statement, 73–74
Grapevine, 161
Groups:
characteristics of, 62–63
creativity in, 215–216
formal work, 61
homogeneous, 62
informal work, 61–62
small work, 63
harnessing power of, 64–65
norms and roles in. 63–64
stable, 62–63

Halo effect, 145
Headhunters, 134
Herzberg, Frederick, 59
two-factor theory of, 59–60, 163–164
Hierarchical spheres of influence:
administrative influence, 28
operational influence, 28–29
strategic influence, 28
Hierarchy of needs theory, 53–54, 163
Historical-trends forecast, 85

Homogeneous groups, 62
Human needs, 52–53
Human resources, 43
  attitudes of, 54–56
  concepts regarding, 43–45, 49, 52, 57, 61
  cooperation, 47
  human needs in, 52–54
  job enhancement, 59–60, 100–101
  leadership of, 171–174
  motivation of, 57–58
    (*See also* Motivation)
  performance of, 46–47, 49
  personality in, 50
  potential in, 50
  values in, 55–56
  work groups in, 61–65
Human resources controls, 180
Human resources management:
  activities, 125
  appraisal format and methods, 144
  compensation, 131
  employee training programs, 139–140
  goals of appraisals, 144–145
  induction, 139
  job analysis, 130–131
  and labor unions, 128
  legal aspects of, 126–127
  management development programs,
    140
  orientation, 139
  placement and movement within an
    organization, 136–137
  selecting most qualified individual,
    134–136

Income statement, 187
Index numbers, 244
Indirect labor ratio, 196
Indirectly interactive environmental
  forces, 32–33
Individual creativity, 215
Individual schedules, 87
Induction training, 139
Inferential statistics, 244
Informal work groups, 61–62
Information, 231
Information management, 229–246
  classes of data, 232
  computer networks, 239
  concepts regarding, 229–231, 233, 237,
    239, 242

Information management (*Cont.*):
  data collection, 231–232
  data processing functions, 237–238
  data processing modes, 238
  databases, 232
  decision support systems, 240
  descriptive statistics, 242–244
  exception reports, 240–241
  index numbers, 244
  inferential statistics, 244
  management information system, 233
    criteria for effective, 235
  measurement, 242
  sampling, 242
  time series, 244
Input functions, 237
Inspection, 193
Instrumentality, 167
Integrative approach, 38
Interactive method, 140
Internal factions, 29–30
International environment, 33
Interpersonal communications, 159–160
Interpersonal skills:
  concepts regarding, 249–250, 253, 257,
    260, 263
  delegation, 249, 257–259
  managerial skills and competencies, 251
  participative management, 261–262
  participative skills, 249–250
  personal time planning, 254–255
  recognizing stress, 263–264
  stress management, 264–265
  styles of, 252
  Theory Z, 261
  time management and control, 255–256
  time planning, 253–254
Interviews, employment, 135–136
Inventory control, 192
IQ tests, 136

Job, 100
Job analysis, 130–131
Job content, 100
Job description, 131, 132
Job duties, 100
Job enhancement, 59–60, 100–101
Job enlargement, 101
Job enrichment, 101
Job evaluation plan, 131
Job instruction training (JIT), 140

Job specification, 131
Just-in-time inventory control, 192

Kanban, 192
Key-point controls, 185

Labor contract, 128
Labor-intensive processes, 280
Labor unions and human resources
    management, 128
Landrum-Griffin Act (1959), 127
Lateness, 196
Layout, 276
Leadership, 156, 170
    advanced concepts of, 172–174
    basic concepts of, 171
    continuum of styles in, 171–172
    path-goal theory of, 173–174
    situational, 173
    traits in, 170–171
    two-dimensional, 172
Leakage, 275
Learning time, 254, 256
Legal aspects, 126
Legal environment, 32
Likert, Rensis, 260
Line, conflict between staff and, 116
Line activities, 114
Line-and-staff organizations, 114–115
Linear programming, 224
Location, departmentation by, 104, 106,
    107
Locus of control, 184–185
Long-range plans, 78

McClelland, David, 164, 165
McGregor, Douglas, 57–59, 157, 260
Management:
    behavioral, 37–38
    contingency, 18
    definition of, 5, 25
    human resources (*see* Human resources
        management)
    information (*see* Information manage-
        ment)
    participative, 260, 261
    production and operations (POM), 192
    scientific, 36–37, 46
    situational, 18
    span of, 111
    stress, 264–265

Management by exception, 240
Management by objectives (MBO), 71, 89,
    92
    advantages of, 92
    disadvantages of, 92
    variants on, 89, 92
Management control, 180
Management development programs, 140
Management information system (MIS),
    229, 233
    applications of, 233, 235
    components of, 234
    criteria for effective, 235
Management process, 9–10
Management sciences, 37
Managerial environment:
    boundary spanning in, 34–35
    closed systems, 25–26
    concepts regarding, 23–25, 28, 31, 34,
        36
    directly interactive environmental
        forces, 31–32
    hierarchical spheres of influence, 28–29
    indirectly interactive environmental
        forces, 32
    internal factions, 29–30
    open systems, 26–27
Managerial Grid, 172, 173
Managerial levels, 5–6
Managerial motivation, content theory of,
    164
Managerial problem solving and decision
    making:
    concepts regarding, 205–207, 210, 214,
        217, 221
    criteria for judgment, 217
    decision trees, 222–223
    gaming theory, 224
    gap analysis, 211
    generating possible solutions, 215–216
    identification of causes, 212–213
    linear programming, 224
    managerial information system (MIS),
        229, 233–235
    problem screening, 213
    problem-solving process, 208–210
    problem specification, 211–212
    programmed solutions, 214
    simulations, 224
Managerial resources, 14–15
Managerial roles, 11

Managerial roles (*Cont.*):
  decisional, 11
  informational, 11
  interpersonal, 11
Managerial skills, 11–12
  conceptual, 12
  human relations, 12
  technical, 12
  (*See also* Interpersonal skills)
Managerial work, 3–4, 5
  concepts regarding, 7, 11, 13, 17
Managers:
  effectiveness of, 13–14
  first-level, 5
  functions of, 7–9
  middle, 5–6
Market research, 232
Maslow, Abraham, 53, 59, 163
Master schedule, 86–87
Materials controls, 191–192
Materials requirements planning (MRP),
  192
Materials usage reports, 273
Matrix organizations, 116–117
Mayo, Elton, 156
Mean, 243
Measurement, 242
Median, 243
Middle managers, 5–6
MIS [*see* Management information system
  (MIS)]
Mission, 73
Mission statement, 73
Mode, 243
Money as self-fulfilling prophecy, 156
Motivation, 59, 156, 162
  achievement motivation theory,
    164–165
  ERG theory of, 164
  hierarchy of need theory, 53–54, 163
  two-factor theory of, 59–60, 163–164
Mouton, J., 172
Multiattribute utility, 218–219

National Labor Relations Act (1935), 127
National Labor Relations Board, 127
Network planning methods, 193
  CPM (critical path method), 87, 193,
    195
  PERT (program evaluation review
    technique), 87, 193, 195
Network plans, 87

Newspaper advertisement as source of
  employees, 134
Noise, 159–160
Nominal group technique (NGT), 217,
  284
Nonmanagerial work, 7
Nonreinforcement, 169

Objective standard, 143
Objectives, 73
Occupational Safety and Health Act
  (1970), 127
Occupational Safety and Health Commis-
  sion, 127
Office automation, 281
Off-the-job training, 139
Open systems, 26–27
Operating controls, 180
Operating plans, 79
Operating schedules, 86
Operations research, 37
Organization charts, 109
Organization development (OD) process,
  282
Organizational communications, 160–161
Organizational productivity, 45
Organizing, 97
  accountability, 109
  authority, 109
  centralization, 112
  concepts regarding, 98, 99, 103, 108,
    111, 114
  decentralization, 112
  delegation, 108–110
  departmentation, 103
    by customer, 104, 106
    by function, 103–105, 107
    by location, 104, 106, 107
    by product, 104, 107
    by service, 104
  division of labor, 99, 100
  job content, 100
  job enhancement, 100–101
  line-and-staff organizations, 114–116
  as management function, 8
  matrix organizations, 116–117
  modified authority, 115–116
  responsibility, 109
  span of management control, 111
  specialization, 99–100
Orientation, 139
Osborn, Alex, 216

Ouchi, William G., 261
Output, 16
Output functions, 238
Output standards, 183
Overhead budgets, 187
Overlap plans, 87

Parallel plans, 87
Parallel scheduling, 193
Pareto's law, 213
Participation, requirements for, 261–262
Participative employees, 260
Participative management, 260, 261
Participative skills, 249–250
Partisanship, 29–30
Path-goal leadership theory, 173–174
Payoff tables, 222
Percentage of capacity utilized, 273
Perception, 49
    relation of, to attitudes, 54–55
Performance, 46–47
Performance appraisals, 143–144, 196
    format for, 144–145
    goals of, 144
    methods of, 144–145
    problems with, 145
    rating form for, 146
Performance standards, establishment of,
    181
Perpetual inventory control, 192
Personal time analysis, 254
Personal time budget, 254–256
Personal time planning, 254–255
Personality, 50
    assessment of, 138
PERT (program evaluation review
    technique), 87, 193, 195
Physical environment, 33
Planning, 81–83
    capacity and time planning, 85–86
    concepts regarding, 71–73, 76, 81, 84,
        89
    department scheduling, 87
    five-point checklist, 79, 80
    forecasting methods, 84–85
    goals, 73–75
    historical-trends forecast, 85
    individual scheduling, 87
    management by objectives, 71, 89, 92
    as management function, 7–8
    master scheduling, 86–87
    operating plans, 79

Planning (*Cont.*):
    operating schedules, 86
    scheduling techniques, 87–92
    statistical-analysis forecast, 85
    steps in, 81–85
    strategic plans, 77–79
Planning premises, 82
Plans, 76
    conception of, 76–77
    operating, 79
    point-to-point, 87
    strategic, 77–79
Point-to-point plans, 87
Policy, 78
Political environment, 32
Positive reinforcement, 168
Postperformance controls, 184–185
Potential, 50
Potential problems, 211
Power need, 164–165
Pragmatic value, 55
Pregnancy Discrimination Act (1978),
    126
Preliminary controls, 184, 186
Preventive controls, 184
Primary data, 232
Private employment agencies, 134
Probabilities, statistical, 194
Problem, 207
Problem screening, 213
Problem solving, 207–210
    (*See also* Managerial problem solving
        and decision making)
Problem specifications, 211–212
Procedures, 78–79
Process analysis, 277–278
Process capacity, 85
Process simplification, 278–279
Processing functions, 237–238
Processing time, 254
Product, departmentation by, 104, 107
Production controls, 192
Production and operations management
    (POM), 192
Production scheduling, 183, 192–193
Productive relationships, formation of,
    58–59
Productivity, 16, 271
Productivity improvement:
    automation, 280–281
    concepts regarding, 269–270, 272, 276,
        280, 281

Productivity improvement (*Cont.*):
  conservation measurements and
      methods, 274–275
  matching resources to targeted results,
      271–272
  organization development, 282
  process analysis, 277–278
  process simplification, 279
  quality circles, 283
  systematizing the workplace, 276–277
  team building, 282–283
  utilization measurements, 273
  value analysis, 279
  work simplification, 277–279
Profitability, 16
Program evaluation review technique
    (PERT), 87, 193, 195
Programmed decisions, 214–215
Programmed solutions, 214–215
Project, 79
Promotions, 137
Public employment agencies, 134
Punishment, 168–169

Quality, 16
Quality of work life (QWL), 260–261
Quality assurance, 193
Quality circles, 283
Quality control, 193–194
Quality standards, 183

Rational analysis, 208, 215
Real-time processing, 238
Recency, 145
Recruiting, 133–134
Reference checks, 136
Referrals, 134
Referrent power, 170
Regulations, 78–79
Reports:
  absence, 275
  accident, 275
  defect, 274–275
  employee turnover, 275
  exception, 240–241
  materials usage, 273
  variance, 188, 240–241
Resources, 14
  matching of, to targeted results,
      271–272
Responsibilities, 100

Results, 15–16
  matching of resources to targeted,
      271–272
Risk, 219
  attitude toward, 219–220
Risk averters, 219
Risk seekers, 219–220
Robotics, 281
Roles, 63–64
Rule, 78–79

Sabotage, 197
Sample, 242
Sampling, 242
Satisficing, 219
Scalar chain, 109
Scheduling:
  parallel, 193
  sequential, 192–193
Scheduling techniques, 87
Schmidt, Warren, 171
Scientific management, 36–37, 46
Secondary data, 232
Section schedules, 87
Self-fulfillment:
  and hierarchy of needs theory, 53–54,
      163
  prophecies of, 49, 50, 156–157
  and the work ethic, 55–56
Separations, 137
Sequential scheduling, 192–193
Service, departmentation by, 104
Sideways communication, 160
Simulations, 224
Situational leadership theory, 173
Situational management, 18
Skills:
  interpersonal (*see* Interpersonal skills)
  managerial, 11–12
  participative, 249–250
Skinner, B. F., 168, 169
Slowdowns, 197
Smith, Adam, 100
Social forces, 32–33
Span of control, 111
Span of management, 111
Specialization, 99–100
Stable groups, 62
Staff, conflict between line and, 116
Staff activities, 114
Staff authority, types of, 115

Staffing, 8, 123–124
  activities, 125–126
  concepts regarding, 124, 125, 129, 133, 138, 143
  (See also Human resources management)
Start-up time, 254, 256
Statement(s):
  of cash flows, 187
  financial, 186–187
  income, 187
Statistical analysis, 230, 242
  forecast, 85
Statistical quality control (SQC), 193–195
  approach based on the statistics of probabilities, 194
Statistics, 242
  descriptive, 242–244
  inferential, 244
Steering controls, 184
Steinmetz, Dr. Laurence L., 257
Stereotyping, 49
Strategic controls, 185
Strategic plans, 77
Stress, 263
  reactions to, 263
  recognizing, 263–264
Stress management, 264–265
Stressors, 263
Subjective judgments, 143–144
Superordinate goals, 116
Supplier group, 31
Survey-method forecast, 84–85
System, 25

Table of organization, 196
Taft-Hartley Act (1947), 127
Tannenbaum, Robert, 171
Tardiness reports, 275
Tasks, 100
Taylor, Frederick W., 156
Team building, 270, 282–283
Teamwork, 47
Technical competence, assessments of, 137–138
Technology, 32
Test reliability, 136
Test validity, 136
Testing, 136

Tests:
  aptitude, 136
  IQ, 136
Theory X, 57–59, 157, 171
Theory Y, 57–59, 157, 171, 260
Theory Z, 261
Thomas Register of American Manufacturers, 216
Throughput, 273
Time management and control, 255
Time planning, 253
  and capacity, 85
Time series, 244
Time studies, 85
Tolerances, 194
Training programs, employee, 139–140
Trait approach, 144
Traits in leadership, 170–171
Transactional processing, 238
Transfers, 136–137
Two-dimensional leadership, 172
Two-factor theory, 59–60, 163–164
Type A behavior pattern, 264
Type B behavior pattern, 264

Uncertainty, dealing with, 221–222
Unity of command, 108–110
Upward communication, 160
Utilization measurements, 273–274

Valence, 167
Value analysis, 279
Values, 55
Variable budgets, 187
Variance reports, 188, 240–241
Vestibule training, 140
Vietnam-Era Veterans' Readjustment Assistance Act (1974), 126
Vocational Rehabilitation Act (1973), 126
Vroom, Victor, 166

Work ethic and self-fulfillment, 55–56
Work groups:
  formal, 61
  harnessing power of, 64–65
  informal, 61–62
  norms and roles in, 63–64
Work simplification, 277–279

Yield, 274

About the Author

LESTER R. BITTEL, professor of management and Virginia Eminent Scholar at James Madison University, has devoted his entire career to management. He is the recipient of numerous awards, including the Frederick W. Taylor Award for his contributions to management literature and the Centennial Medal, both given by the American Society of Mechanical Engineers. An internationally respected writer, Professor Bittel is a five-time winner of the Jesse H. Neal Award for Outstanding Business Journalism. Among his many successful books are *What Every Supervisor Should Know*, Fifth Edition, and *Handbook for Professional Managers*, both published by McGraw-Hill.

Final Examination

The McGraw-Hill 36-Hour Management Course

Name_____

Address_____

City_____ State_____Zip_____

If you have completed your study of *The McGraw-Hill 36-Hour Management Course*, you should be prepared to take this final examination. It is a comprehensive examination, consisting of 200 questions. There are 60 questions covering the chapters in Part I, 100 for the chapters in Part II, and 40 for the chapters in Part III.

Instructions

1. If you like, you may treat this as an "open-book" exam and consult this and other textbooks while taking it. That approach will help to reinforce your learning and to correct any misconceptions. On the other hand, if you prefer to establish a superior understanding of the subject matter, you may choose to take the examination without reference to any textbook.

2. Answer each of the test questions directly on the examination sheets. Do so by circling the letter which indicates the answer you choose.

1

EXAMPLE:

   0. The first step in the problem-solving process is:
     a. decision making.   ⓒ problem finding.
     b. problem screening.   *d*. problem specification.

3. All questions are multiple-choice, with four alternative answers to choose from. Always select the answer that represents in your mind the *best* among the choices.

4. Each correctly answered question is worth ½ point on a scale of 100 percent. You must answer 140 questions correctly to have a passing grade of 70 percent (140 ÷ 200). A passing grade entitles you to receive a *certificate of achievement*. This handsome certificate, suitable for framing, attests to your proven knowledge of management.

5. Carefully fill in your name and address in the spaces provided at the top of this sheet, and send your completed examination to:

Alison Spalding—Certification Examiner
36-Hour Management Course
Professional & Reference Division
McGraw-Hill Book Company
11 West 19th Street
New York, NY 10011

PART 1 What's Expected of Managers
(Chapters 1–3)

   1. Which of the following activities is *not* the work of a manager?
     a. Finding out why this year's sales goal was not met
     b. Setting a goal for next year's sales
     c. Showing employees how to unload a truck shipment
     d. Helping employees to unload a truck shipment

   2. Management is best described as the process of:
     a. telling others what to do.
     b. planning and controlling.
     c. obtaining, deploying, and utilizing resources in support of an organization's objectives.
     d. directing the work of others in an organization so as to maximize profits.

   3. Managers are arranged in a hierarchy in an organization with_____ at the top.
     a. executives   *c*. department managers
     b. supervisors   *d*. nonmanagers

   4. The work of managers differs from that of nonmanagers in that:

a. managers work with their hands and others do not.

b. nonmanagers work with their hands but not their minds.

c. managers direct the work of others rather than perform the actual work themselves.

d. managers direct the work of others but are not held responsible for that work.

5. Muriel, a department head, is preparing a schedule for next week's production. Which of the five managerial functions is she performing?

    a. Planning   c. Directing

    b. Organizing   d. Controlling

6. A retail clerk, Joe, has just received instructions from his boss about how to ring up sales on the cash register. Which managerial function was his boss carrying out?

    a. Organizing   c. Directing

    b. Staffing   d. Controlling

7. John H., vice president for marketing, is currently concerned with performing the controlling function. Which of the following activities is he most likely to be engaged in?

    a. Hiring a new salesperson

    b. Establishing sales quotas

    c. Checking the number of sales made by the sales staff

    d. Giving a motivational talk to the sales staff

8. Usually, _____ is the first function and _____ is the last function performed during the management process (or cycle).

    a. planning; controlling   c. organizing; directing

    b. planning; organizing   d. directing; controlling

9. The three *roles* that managers are expected to play for an organization are:

    a. interpersonal, technical, and decisional.

    b. informational, decisional, and controlling.

    c. interpersonal, informational, and decisional.

    d. informational, situational, and decisional.

10. When Teresa J., manager of personnel administration for Home and Farm Insurance Company, presented the company's affirmative action plan to the Equal Employment Opportunity Commission, she was acting in a(n) _____ role.

    a. interpersonal, liason

    b. informational, spokesperson

    c. decisional, crisis handler

    d. decisional, negotiator

11. As a manager moves up the hierarchal ladder, his or her_____ skills become less important.

    a. technical   c. conceptual

    b. human relations   d. decisional

12. Ronald has just been promoted from maintenance supervisor to manager of the entire plant engineering department. He is likely to find that there

will be a higher demand for his _____ skills but no less a need
for his _____ skills.
  a. human relations; technical   c. conceptual; technical
  b. human relations; conceptual   d. conceptual; human relations

13. The effectiveness of managers is best judged by:
    a. the extent to which their results exceed the resources used to attain
       them.
    b. the extent to which they do not use up all their resources in seeking
       to attain results.
    c. how many resources are utilized.
    d. how many objectives are reached.

14. Linda, Joe, Ted, and Vera supervise nearly identical operations. Their
    boss has collected some figures to compare their effectiveness. These fig-
    ures are shown below. Which supervisor appears to be most effective?
    a. Linda, with expenses of $3000 and outputs of $3500
    b. Joe, with expenses of $2800 and outputs of $3400
    c. Ted, with expenses of $3200 and outputs of $3600
    d. Vera, with expenses of $2900 and outputs of $3400

15. David is in charge of setting up a service branch for a manufacturer of
    small appliances. He has rented a building, furnished it with the necessary
    benches and repair tools, and had the electricity turned on and telephones
    connected. He has also brought in a supply of spare parts and operating
    supplies. What three important resources has he still to acquire?
    a. Repair manuals, soldering irons, and petty cash
    b. Repair manuals, service personnel, and petty cash
    c. Miscellaneous bolts and washers, workbenches, and hand tools.
    d. Miscellaneous spare parts, soldering irons, and reels of solder

16. Of all the results that are expected of top-level managers, which one tends
    to put them all together?
    a. Cost containment   c. Output
    b. Profitability   d. Quality

17. Prudent managers seek not to _____ their results but to
    _____them.
    a. maximize; optimize   c. profit from; learn from
    b. optimize; maximize   d. worry about; work toward

18. The most effective managers are likely to be those who:
    a. treat every situation the same.
    b. never vary their approaches.
    c. vary their approaches only after finding that their usual techniques
       aren't working.
    d. vary their approaches contingent upon the factors that dominate a
       particular situation.

19. Which of the following statements is true?
    a. Most managerial methods will be effective under any circumstance.
    b. There is no single technique that works well in all situations.
    c. Situations may look different, but at their core, they are all alike.

    d. Situations differ only to the extent that a manager thinks that they are different.

20. In public agencies and not-for-profit institutions, the measure of managerial effectiveness that most closely resembles the profitibility measure is:
    a. optimizing.   *c.* cost benefits.
    b. maximizing.   *d.* results management.

21. Which of the following can be described as a system?
    a. An automobile engine
    b. A clock
    c. A business organization
    d. All of the above

22. When a set of interrelated elements functions as a whole, and is independent of its environment, it functions as a:
    a. closed system.
    b. open system.
    c. directly interactive force.
    d. indirectly interactive force.

23. If Sue, manager of a retail sporting-goods store, is troubled by the opening of a discount sporting-goods store nearby, she is acknowledging that she is operating in a(n) _____ system.
    a. closed   *c.* independent
    b. open   *d.* monopoly

24. An open system reflects the real world of most managers':
    a. ecosystem.   *c.* authority.
    b. environment.   *d.* responsibility.

25. The strategic sphere of influence in an organization is associated with managers at the _____ levels.
    a. upper   *c.* lower
    b. middle   *d.* operational

26. The supervisor of the accounts receivables section of a corporate accounting department is most likely to have control over:
    a. strategic influence.   *c.* operational influence.
    b. administrative influence.   *d.* departmental policy.

27. When factionalism dominates an organization, its operations are likely to:
    a. deteriorate.   *c.* stabilize.
    b. improve.   *d.* remain unchanged.

28. Factionalism and conflict can be reduced in an organization when its departmental managers:
    a. make it easy for other departments to cooperate.
    b. make other departments look good to upper-level managers.
    c. focus on the overall goals of the organization rather than solely on their own goals.
    d. do all of the above.

29. The two spheres of power in an organization's external environment consist of:

    a. the two top levels of its hierarchy.
    b. strategic and administrative influences.
    c. directly interactive and indirectly interactive forces.
    d. customers on the one hand and competitors on the other.

30. The forces in the environment that most closely affect an organization's daily operations consist of:
    a. customers, suppliers, and competitors.
    b. internal factions and technology.
    c. legal and political factors, social and cultural factors, and the economy.
    d. physical factors, technology, and the economy.

31. Since World War II, imports from overseas have made U.S. automakers increasingly aware of the _____ environment.
    a. social and cultural   *c.* economic
    b. legal and political   *d.* international

32. To an alert manager, changes in the external environment represent:
    a. unwarranted disruptions of the status quo.
    b. a source of opportunities as well as threats.
    c. unpredictable outcomes.
    d. nothing but trouble.

33. Managers who don't engage in active boundary spanning are likely to:
    a. conserve their resources better than their counterparts.
    b. find their results improving because of isolation.
    c. miss important changes in their environment.
    d. avoid interferences from environmental changes.

34. Developing informal relationships with managers in other departments is one good way to improve internal:
    a. partisanship.   *c.* closed systems.
    b. factionalism.   *d.* boundary spanning.

35. When monitoring a firm's directly interactive environment, a manager will be concerned mostly with customer groups, supplier groups, and _____ groups.
    a. international   *c.* professional
    b. trade   *d.* competitor

36. The most important outcome of effective boundary spanning will be:
    a. delay of the impact of changes on the organization.
    b. action taken to adapt the organization to change.
    c. improved knowledge of customers' needs.
    d. improved knowledge of competitors' actions.

37. Which of the following statements is true of the three management approaches of scientific management, behavioral management, and management sciences?
    a. Managers should always apply all three to a given problem.
    b. Managers should apply only one to a given problem.
    c. When in doubt, scientific management should be applied before trying another approach.

    d. Choice of the appropriate approach or approaches should depend upon the situation.

38. The manager of a hospital housekeeping department wishes to assign only enough cleaners to get the halls cleaned properly and on time. This manager is most likely to use a measurement technique that is associated with:
    a. scientific management.　　　*c.* management sciences.
    b. behavioral management.　　　*d.* contingency management.

39. Management sciences depend largely upon:
    a. scientific management.
    b. high-technology research.
    c. mathematical and statistical analysis.
    d. strategic and environmental analysis.

40. The development of behavioral management is dependent upon application of:
    a. the "one best way."　　　*c.* psychology and sociology.
    b. wage incentives.　　　*d.* operations research.

41. Specification of desirable employee performance has—in addition to cooperation—three important dimensions, or measures. They are:
    a. attendance, effort, and results.
    b. attendance, attitude, and effort.
    c. cooperation, self-discipline, and teamwork.
    d. cooperation, motivation, and self-discipline.

42. The two essential elements of the performance *results* that should be expected from employees are:
    a. attitudes and personality.　　　*c.* output and quality.
    b. attitudes and cooperation.　　　*d.* resources and results.

43. To make the specification of expected results complete, it should include:
    a. how many or how much to be produced.
    b. time allowed to attain the output.
    c. the quality of the expected output.
    d. all of the above.

44. Cooperation expected from employees includes three essentials: teamwork, commitment, and:
    a. a willingness to work overtime regularly.
    b. acceptance of reasonable orders and instructions.
    c. friendly attitudes.
    d. unquestioning loyalty.

45. If John tends to see opportunities in his work rather than threatening demands, this is a mainly a reflection of his:
    a. perception of the world of work.
    b. attitude toward his superiors.
    c. individual aptitude.
    d. working conditions.

46. A broad description of personality is that it is:
    a. how outgoing or introverted a person is.

    b. how socially responsible a person is.

    c. the sum total of everything a person is and does.

    d. the sum total of a person's potential.

47. Mary has become confused and frustrated because her boss must occasionally change the rules that guide her performance. It might be said that Mary's personality includes:

    a. a low tolerance of risk.

    b. a low tolerance of ambiguity.

    c. low self-discipline.

    d. a high degree of self-centeredness.

48. The biggest danger in assessing an employee's potential capabilities is that the manager may:

    a. undervalue it.

    b. overvalue it.

    c. give the employee the benefit of any doubts.

    d. believe that the employee can do everything.

49. The "hierarchy of human needs" is attributed to:

    a. Douglas McGregor.   *c.* John Gardner.

    b. Abraham Maslow.   *d.* Frederick Herzberg.

50. The lowest level of the hierarchy of needs is _____ , and the highest level is _____ .

    a. survival; socialization

    b. security; esteem

    c. survival; self-actualization

    d. security; self-actualization

51. One of Maslow's most important precepts is that:

    a. once a need has been satisfied, it will no longer serve as a motivator.

    b. satisfaction of needs always moves from the lowest level of the hierarchy to the highest.

    c. everyone has the same needs and in the same order of priority as everyone else.

    d. an individual's needs are constant; they never change in their relative importance to the individual.

52. Attitudes tend to be directed toward _____ persons, objects, or events, while values tend to be more _____ beliefs about what's truly important in one's life.

    a. all; selective   *c.* general; specific

    b. ordinary; religious   *d.* specific; general

53. The concept that human beings don't like to work and need to be closely supervised is labeled:

    a. "Theory X."   *c.* "contingency theory."

    b. "Theory Y."   *d.* "integrative management."

54. The theory that human beings like work, provided that it is meaningful and that they can exercise some control over it, is labeled:

    a. "Theory X."   *c.* "situational theory."

    b. "Theory Y."   *d.* "participative management."

55. Herzberg's "dissatisfiers" match up with:
    a. Maslow's psychological needs.
    b. Maslow's higher-level needs.
    c. McGregor's Theory X.
    d. McGregor's Theory Y.

56. Herzberg suggests that, in today's affluent society, most attempts to motivate employees should appeal to the higher-level needs. Changing job conditions to appeal to these needs is called:
    a. "job evaluation."   c. "job enhancement."
    b. "job specification."   d. "work simplification."

57. Managers establish _____ work groups; _____ work groups tend to emerge on their own.
    a. orderly; disorganized   c. formal; informal
    b. homogeneous; heterogeneous   d. stable; large

58. Small work groups are:
    a. the building blocks of an organization.
    b. established solely by management.
    c. infallibly productive.
    d. mainly a source of disruption.

59. The workers in the foundry room frown on anyone who doesn't begin washing up 20 minutes before quitting time. This practice is probably a(n):
    a. occupational privilege.   c. group norm.
    b. company regulation.   d. group role.

60. Informal work groups that are able to develop strong loyalties and enforce their norms upon members are probably:
    a. large.   c. heterogeneous.
    b. unstable.   d. cohesive.

PART 2 What Managers Do
(Chapters 4–8)

61. A mission statement should include a description of the organization's basic product or service, the functions it will perform, and:
    a. a hierarchy of objectives.
    b. a strategic plan.
    c. assignment of responsibilities.
    d. markets or clients to be served.

62. Goal statements tend to be more _____ than mission statements.
    a. general   c. flexible
    b. specific   d. verbose

63. A short-term goal covers:
    a. 1 week.   c. less than 1 year.
    b. 1 month.   d. all of the above.

64. Louise, manager of the records files, has most of her monthly departmental goals issued to her by her boss. There are other goals, however, such as

"having each employee in her department able to fill in on any other job," which she can set herself. These are called _____ goals.
- *a.* "controllable"
- *c.* "short-term"
- *b.* "dependent"
- *d.* "strategic"

65. Strategic plans differ from operating plans in that strategic plans are _____ while operating plans are _____ .
- *a.* tactical; mission-oriented
- *c.* long-range; short-term
- *b.* chronological; sequential
- *d.* short-term; long-range

66. A budget is a form of:
- *a.* operating plan.
- *c.* policy.
- *b.* strategic plan.
- *d.* regulation.

67. Which of the following is most likely to be a policy statement?
- *a.* No one may leave a workstation until 4:45 p.m.
- *b.* Assemblies will proceed in sequence from 1 to 25.
- *c.* The target output is for 100 units per day.
- *d.* Quality should take precedence over output.

68. A policy differs from a procedure in that a policy provides _____ while a procedure specifies _____ .
- *a.* strategic goals; operating goals.
- *b.* guidelines for action; the action to take.
- *c.* methods; guidelines.
- *d.* regulations; rules.

69. Which is the first step of the planning process?
- *a.* Assigning responsibility
- *c.* Determining goals
- *b.* Evaluating the situation
- *d.* Setting a timetable

70. When assessing a situation during the planning process, a company executive estimated that market demand was likely to rise but supplier's prices for raw materials were likely to fall. She assessed the first as an opportunity and the second as a threat in the company's:
- *a.* external environment.
- *c.* planning horizon.
- *b.* internal environment.
- *d.* strategic mission.

71. When Herbert H., the controller of the state water board, drew up his budgets for the next year, he did so on the assumption that there would be water shortages caused by a seasonal drought. This assumption is known as a planning:
- *a.* "horizon."
- *c.* "alternative."
- *b.* "environment."
- *d.* "premise."

72. Even a good plan may fail to reach its objectives if it is not staffed by:
- *a.* people capable of implementing it.
- *b.* well-motivated individuals.
- *c.* well-trained individuals.
- *d.* all of the above.

73. Forecasts for operating plans that are based upon projecting data gathered from past occurrences utilize the:

    a. survey method.   *c.* statistical-analysis method.
    b. historical-trends method.   *d.* intuitive method.

74. Which of the following represents a forecast based upon statistical analysis?
    a. The sales manager mails a questionnaire to 500 of the company's customers, asking them to estimate their next year's purchases.
    b. The sales manager makes a prediction based upon the fact that when highway construction decreases, the firm sells fewer replacement tires.
    c. The sales manager can show that sales have been increasing by 10,000 units a year for the last 5 years and will probably continue to do so next year.
    d. A panel of people who are well informed about the industry are polled for their opinions about next year.

75. Departmental, sectional, and individual operating schedules are derived from the:
    a. master schedule.   c. statistical analysis.
    b. point-to-point schedule.   d. hierarchy of objectives.

76. If a company has a large, complex project to perform and it will probably be done only once, the preferable schedule plan to be used would be:
    a. point-to-point.   c. Gantt chart.
    b. overlap.   d. network.

77. Schedules that are based upon an overlap or network plan are likely to _____ than those using a point-to-point plan.
    a. be longer   c. be easier to follow
    b. be shorter   d. involve fewer steps

78. The Gantt chart, or production scheduling board, is one of the most popular variations of the _____ schedule plan.
    a. point-to-point   c. network
    b. overlap   d. five-point

79. The concept underlying management by objectives is that:
    a. pay based upon attainment of objectives is a powerful incentive.
    b. subordinates perform with more dedication when coached by superiors.
    c. a person who sets his or her own objectives will set only those that can surely be attained.
    d. a person who participates in setting objectives is likely to be committed to attaining them.

80. A drawback of the MBO approach is that:
    a. goals are tailored to each subordinate.
    b. nontangible goals are likely to be overlooked.
    c. commitment to negotiated goals is weak.
    d. goals are likely to be too specific.

81. When the work of an organization is divided into work units, or jobs, the process is called:

   a. "departmentation."   c. "division of work."
   b. "decentralization."   d. "job enrichment."

82. Specialization enables jobs to be:
    a. more easily coordinated.
    b. learned more easily and performed more rapidly.
    c. less easily coordinated.
    d. confined to fewer people in the organization.

83. A job consists of three important elements. They are:
    a. tasks, responsibilities, and access to resources.
    b. tasks, authorities, and resources.
    c. duties, responsibilities, and authority.
    d. responsibility, authority, and accountability.

84. The manager of a supermarket changes the checkout-counter job so that it
    allows persons holding that job to use their own judgment about when to
    take their rest breaks. This is an example of:
    a. laxity on the store manager's part.
    b. application of Theory X management.
    c. job enlargement.
    d. job enrichment.

85. One supermarket divides up its store departments as follows: groceries,
    meats, frozen foods, vegetables, and dairy products. This is depart-
    mentation by:
    a. function.   c. location.
    b. product or service.   d. line and staff.

86. Another supermarket divides up its store departments this way: receiving,
    shelf stocking, customer checkout, and inventory control. This is depart-
    mentation by:
    a. function.   c. location.
    b. product or service.   d. matrix.

87. Both supermarket chains have six regional managers who report to a cen-
    tral vice president in charge of store operations. This is departmentation
    by:
    a. function.   c. location.
    b. product or service.   d. hierarchy.

88. Those departments that appear at the same level of an organization's hi-
    erarchy can be presumed to be:
    a. on an equal footing.
    b. independent of one another.
    c. on an unequal footing.
    d. independent of higher-level departments.

89. Authority has two important components, or rights—the right to take ac-
    tion and the right to:
    a. function independently.   c. direct the work of others.
    b. refuse assignments.   d. avoid accountability.

90. The process of distributing authority is called:

    a. "chain of command."   *c.* "division of work."
    b. "unity of command."   *d.* "delegation."

91. The principle that a subordinate should report to only one superior is called:
    a. "chain of command."   *c.* "line and staff."
    b. "unity of command."   *d.* "accountability."

92. Delegated responsibilities should always be accompanied by the appropriate:
    a. organization chart.   *c.* accountability.
    b. organization titles.   *d.* authority.

93. Span of management (or control) refers to the number of _____ a manager must coordinate.
    a. activities   *c.* resources
    b. employees   *d.* results

94. A midwestern state government has several levels in its hierarchy, with closely regulated procedures to be followed by all, from the capital to the lowest echelons in the counties. This is an example of a _____ organization structure.
    a. function-type   *c.* centralized
    b. service-type   *d.* decentralized

95. Flat organization structures are likely to be found in organizations where the span of management is:
    a. centralized.   *c.* broad.
    b. unified.   *d.* narrow

96. The more routine the tasks and activities to be managed, the _____ the span of control can be.
    a. broader
    b. narrower
    c. tighter
    d. Routine has no effect upon the possible span of control.

97. Staff departments usually provide either _____ or _____, or both, to line departments.
    a. responsibility; authority   *c.* plans; controls
    b. tasks; duties   *d.* advice; service

98. Which of the following grants the most authority to a staff department?
    a. Functional authority   *c.* Authority of consultation
    b. Traditional staff authority   *d.* Authority of concurrence

99. If, in order to resolve a conflict, two managers are asked to place the goals of the entire organization ahead of goals for their departments, these larger goals are called:
    a. "missions."   *c.* "compromise goals."
    b. "standards."   *d.* "superordinate goals."

100. In a matrix organization, specialists may receive instructions and orders from two superiors: (a) the manager of the functional specialty to which

they permanantly report and (b) the manager of a _____ to
which they are temporarily assigned.
    a. line department   *c.* project team
    b. staff department   *d.* subcontractor

101. The staffing process may be classified into three related activities:
_____ , _____ , and _____ of human
resources.
    a. recruiting; testing; selecting
    b. job analysis; job description; job specification
    c. appraising; training; improving
    d. acquiring; maintaining; developing

102. The federal agency that monitors compliance with laws affecting discrimination in employment and staffing is:
    a. OSHA.   *c.* EPA.
    b. EEOC.   *d.* NLRB.

103. _____ programs are intended to increase opportunities for females, minorities, and people in other protected categories so that they
may become more fairly represented in the work force.
    a. Affirmative action   *c.* The 40-hour week
    b. Assertiveness training   *d.* Self-awareness

104. The Fair Labor Standards Act established the principle of:
    a. equal employment opportunities.
    b. collective bargaining.
    c. the 40-hour week.
    d. equal pay for equal work.

105. The process of examining a job to determine its components and what it
will require of the person who fills it is called:
    a. "job analysis."   *c.* "job description."
    b. "job evaluation."   *d.* "job specification."

106. Job evaluation is a method used by human resource managers for:
    a. comparing pay rates.
    b. appraising performance.
    c. determining the relative worth of jobs.
    d. determining the components of a job.

107. ABC company, which now employs 100 people, expects that it will need to
fill 10 newly created jobs next year. It expects an absence rate of 5 percent
(which means it will need about 5 people to fill in), a turnover of 20 people
during the year due to quits and discharges, and 5 retirements. How many
new hires must it make next year?
    a. 10   *c.* 110
    b. 40   *d.* 5

108. Pay that is based upon hourly work is called _____ ; pay based
upon weekly or monthly work is called _____ .
    a. "salary"; "wages"   *c.* "regular"; "bonus"
    b. "wages"; "salary"   *d.* "compensation"; "incentive"

109. The employment recruiting source that is ordinarily most effective and least costly is:
    a. referrals from current employees.
    b. newspaper advertisements.
    c. private employment agency.
    d. public employment agency.

110. Employee testing for staffing purposes must meet the criteria for reliability and:
    a. fairness.　　c. difficulty.
    b. clarity.　　d. validity.

111. If a company's employees are represented by a labor union, the seniority principle may affect:
    a. promotions.　　c. layoffs.
    b. terminations.　　d. all of the above.

112. Which of the following groups of items may be requested on an application blank without being challenged by the Equal Employment Opportunity Commission?
    a. Height, weight, and strength
    b. Education and experience
    c. Spouse's occupation and number of dependent children
    d. Sex and marital status

113. During _____ , an employee is advised about unique company practices and introduced to coworkers.
    a. Job Instruction Training　　c. vestibule training
    b. apprenticeship training　　d. orientation training

114. The first step in Job Instruction Training is to:
    a. show how the job is done.
    b. tell how the job is done.
    c. advise the trainee of key points.
    d. prepare the trainee to learn.

115. During management development programs, emphasis is placed less on instruction and more on interactive learning and:
    a. coaching.　　c. listening.
    b. reading.　　d. observing.

116. Max W., supervisor of the assembly department, wants to make sure that all his employees know how to operate the new fastening machine. His best bet for this purpose is to:
    a. give a lecture.
    b. have employees read the instruction manual.
    c. conduct Job Instruction Training.
    d. initiate an apprenticeship program.

117. The format used by the Quality Printing Company for performance appraisals asks for ratings of how much each employee produces, the number of errors made, and the number of absences. These ratings are probably based upon:

    a. subjective standards.   *c.* supervisor's opinions.
    b. objective standards.   *d.* supervisors' judgments.

118. A behaviorally anchored rating scale used for performance appraisal tends to make appraisals:
    a. more consistent between raters.
    b. less consistent between raters.
    c. more subjective.
    d. less quantitative.

119. An important purpose of performance appraisals is:
    a. to encourage good behavior, and discourage and correct poor performance.
    b. to make certain that future actions involving either promotion or discipline can be justified.
    c. to provide a basis for immediate training and future training and development.
    d. all of the above.

120. Items such as "cooperation," "diligence," and "initiative," if they are to be evaluated on performance appraisal forms, lend themselves to bias because they depend upon:
    a. quantitative measurements.   *c.* subjective judgments.
    b. objective standards.   *d.* all of the above.

121. The three major components of the managerial directing function are:
    a. planning, organizing, and controlling.
    b. planning, organizing, and staffing.
    c. activating, motivating, and coordinating.
    d. motivating, communicating, and leading.

122. Frederick W. Taylor and other early pioneers of management believed that _____ was the strongest motivating factor.
    a. pride   *c.* respect
    b. money   *d.* job security

123. A principal founder of the human relations school of management, who believed that considerate treatment of employees was an essential motivator, was:
    a. Frank B. Gilbreth.   *c.* Elton Mayo.
    b. Henry L. Gantt   *d.* Frederick W. Taylor.

124. When managers accept McGregor's Theory X about employee motivation, those managers are likely to be _____ in their management style.
    a. autocratic   *c.* participative
    b. democratic   *d.* employee-centered

125. The distractions that commonly interfere with the communications process are known, technically, as:
    a. "filters."   *c.* "static."
    b. "radar."   *d.* "noise."

126. When a manager asks employees whether or not they have understood a particular communication, the manager is looking for:
    a. feedback.   *c.* noise.
    b. translation.   *d.* decoding.

127. The use of a departmental bulletin board is a popular channel of _____ communications in an organization.
    a. upward   *c.* horizontal
    b. downward   *d.* network

128. A restricted communications network is probably best for:
    a. managers who wish maximum participation from employees.
    b. managers who wish a free exchange of information in their departments.
    c. groups that must solve difficult, complex problems.
    d. groups with simple tasks, needing a precise exchange of information.

129. In Maslow's hierarchy, physiological needs closely resemble the _____ needs of Alderfer.
    a. existence
    b. relatedness
    c. growth
    d. none of the above resemble Maslow's physiological needs.

130. Motivation theories that attempt to explain *how* motivation takes place are called _____ theories.
    a. "content"   *c.* "situational"
    b. "process"   *d.* "contingency"

131. According to McClelland, managers in the western world are characterized by:
    a. moderate relatedness needs and strong growth needs.
    b. weak relatedness needs and strong growth needs.
    c. weak affiliation needs, moderate power needs, and strong achievement needs.
    d. strong affiliation needs, moderate power needs, and weak achievement needs.

132. Herzberg's "motivators" and Maslow's "self-actualization" tend to be reflected in:
    a. McGregor's Theory Y.
    b. Alderfer's "growth" need.
    c. McClelland's "achievement" need.
    d. all of the above.

133. Victor Vroom is closely associated with _____, and Fred Fiedler is closely associated with _____ .
    a. expectancy theory; situational leadership
    b. situational leadership; expectancy theory
    c. equity theory; reinforcement theory
    d. reinforcement theory; equity theory

134. John's boss has promised that John will get a raise of $10 per week if he produces 100 units each day. John's performance of 100 units a day is the _____ that will enable him to get the $10 raise.
    a. valence   *c.* instrumentality
    b. expectancy   *d.* motivation

135. If John rejects this proposal because the raise isn't attractive enough for him, the $10 raise is said to have:
    a. low valence.   *c.* low expectancy.
    b. high valence.   *d.* high expectancy.

136. Bob draws attention to himself by constantly bothering his boss, Letitia, with problems that he should solve himself. Letitia discourages this behavior by not offering any help with Bob's problems. She is using the Skinner behavior modification technique of:
    a. punishment.   *c.* negative reinforcement.
    b. positive reinforcement. *d.* nonreinforcement.

137. Leaders who are charismatic, with personalities that naturally attract followers, are said to have:
    a. "legitimate power."   *c.* "expert power."
    b. "referrent power."   *d.* "reward power."

138. In Tannenbaum's and Schmidt's continuum of leadership, the leader's style is expected to range from:
    a. autocratic to democratic to participative.
    b. autocratic to democratic to situational.
    c. people-centered to production-centered.
    d. relations-oriented to task-oriented.

139. The Managerial Grid© considers leadership as a combination of two dimensions: _____ and _____ .
    a. expert power; referrent power
    b. leader-member relations; task structure
    c. concern for people; concern for production
    d. task orientation; position power

140. In Fiedler's theory of leadership, a relations-oriented style is likely to be most effective in situations in which:
    a. position power is strong, leader-member relations are good, and the task is structured.
    b. position power is weak, leader-member relations are poor, and the task is unstructured.
    c. position power is weak, leader-member relations are good, and the task is unstructured.
    d. a relations-oriented style would not be effective for any of these situations.

141. The following important elements of the controlling process are derived from organizational goals:
    a. Tolerances   *c.* Specifications
    b. Standards   *d.* Variances

142. Comparison is the step that determines whether or not there is a need to take corrective action in the _____ process.
    a. planning   c. directing
    b. organizing   d. controlling

143. If, during the controlling process, a significant deviation between expected and actual performance is detected, a manager should:
    a. initiate corrective action.
    b. wait until the deviation is repeated.
    c. immediately change the standard.
    d. discipline the guilty parties.

144. The more quickly that _____ of actual conditions in, or performance of, an operation is made, the more quickly deviations can be corrected.
    a. standardization   c. specification
    b. measurement   d. improvement

145. Inspection of incoming raw materials is an example of:
    a. preliminary control.   c. postperformance control.
    b. concurrent control.   d. feedback control.

146. Which of the following illustrates a concurrent control?
    a. Testing of employment applicants
    b. Analysis of customer complaints
    c. Year-end profit-and-loss statement
    d. Pressure-control gauge on a chemical process

147. When adjustments to a situation are made continuously so as to keep it on course, but not to stop it, these controls are called:
    a. "steering controls."   c. "slippage controls."
    b. "go, no-go controls."   d. "preventive controls."

148. In the operation of a motel, revenues from food and drinks are almost wholly dependent upon the number of rooms occupied. Furthermore, about half of a motel's profits come from food and drink sales. Accordingly, a control that monitors room occupancy would be designated as a:
    a. "feedback control."   c. "special control."
    b. "strategic control."   d. "standard control."

149. A firm's income statement is an example of a(n):
    a. preliminary control.   c. financial control.
    b. concurrent control.   d. operating budget.

150. A budget is, essentially, a(n):
    a. financial control standard.   c. cash reserve.
    b. operating specification.   d. credit reserve.

151. A company typically makes a distinction between _____ and _____ expenses in its budgeting process.
    a. past; present   c. financial; nonfinancial
    b. justified; unjustified   d. variable; overhead

152. Wilma, supervisor of the spinning department in a textile mill, was given a budget that listed different expenditure allowances according to the number of spools wound during the month. This was a _____ budget.
    a. fixed   c. flexible
    b. variable   d. elastic

153. The EOQ inventory control balances the cost of acquiring materials against the:
    a. cost of storing and holding them.
    b. cost of processing the materials.
    c. eventual sales price of the materials.
    d. discount obtained by quantity purchasing.

154. The concept of requiring suppliers to hold a company's inventory and to deliver it exactly when needed is called:
    a. "materials requirements planning."
    b. "perpetual inventory control."
    c. "just-in-time inventory control."
    d. "periodic inventory control."

155. In planning and scheduling the construction of an ocean liner, which of the following techniques is most appropriate?
    a. Sequential scheduling   c. Gantt charts
    b. Parallel scheduling   d. PERT or CPM

156. The high and low limits set for the standards used in statistical quality control are its:
    a. allowance.   c. assurance conditions.
    b. tolerance.   d. acceptance variables.

157. A human resources control standard that specifies how many people should be employed at any one time in a department or activity is called a(n):
    a. "load limit."   c. "development blueprint."
    b. "employment roster."   d. "table of organization."

158. If the superintendent of a factory that makes refrigerators is criticized for letting the indirect labor ratio get too high, the chances are that the factory employs a relatively high number of _____ workers as compared with _____ workers.
    a. line; staff   c. staff; production
    b. advisory staff; service staff   d. production; staff

159. An employee performance appraisal is an example of a(n) _____ , _____ control.
    a. human resources, feedback
    b. preliminary, operating
    c. concurrent, financial
    d. concurrent, human resources

160. Which of the following statements is true?
    a. Employees readily accept standards and controls that affect their jobs.

    b. Managers usually welcome controls that apply to their own performance.

    c. It is only natural for employees and managers to occasionally object to, or resist, controls.

    d. Employees and managers who resist controls are either poor performers or malcontents.

PART 3 Skills that Managers Develop and Apply (Chapters 9–12)

161. Problems occur when there is a difference between _____ and _____.
    a. causes; effects
    b. causes; solutions
    c. expected conditions; actual conditions
    d. standards; objectives

162. In making a decision, a manager must:
    a. engage in some sort of problem solving.
    b. evaluate alternative solutions.
    c. make a choice among alternatives.
    d. deal with all of the above.

163. The first thing Alma, the department supervisor, does each morning is to check the time-card rack to see if there are any empty slots in the "in" rack. As a problem solver, Alma engages in:
    a. gap analysis.   *c.* cause identification.
    b. decision making.   *d.* cause removal.

164. A good way to separate trivial problems from vital ones is to apply _____ during problem screening.
    a. ABC analysis   *c.* change analysis
    b. MAU analysis   *d.* gap analysis

165. Robert, the manager of the files department, refers to the company's standard operating procedures manual to find answers to many routine problems. When John does that, he is probably making _____ decisions.
    a. postperformance   *c.* programmed
    b. predictable   *d.* nonprogrammed

166. In a brainstorming session, Thelma interrupts to criticize a suggestion that has just been made. This is:
    a. an acceptable practice, since anyone can say whatever is on her or his mind.
    b. encouraged, so that evaluation of ideas can be made on the spot.
    c. all right, since it prevents the session from being distracted by bad ideas.
    d. against the rules, since it inhibits idea generation and free association.

167. Many decisions represent a compromise that falls short of an optimum solution. This is called:
    a. "satisficing."
    c. "programmed decision making."
    b. "risk aversion."
    d. "nonprogrammed decision making."

168. The use of multiattribute utility approaches during the evaluation of alternatives in decision making involves:
    a. separating the vital few from the trivial many.
    b. assigning weights to the various decision criteria.
    c. forecasting future conditions.
    d. removing uncertainty as a factor.

169. Which of the following statements is true?
    a. Almost all decisions are made without any concern for the risk involved.
    b. Very few decisions are made in which a manager allows intuition to play a part.
    c. Most decisions rarely require that a manager deal with uncertainty.
    d. Most decisions can benefit from a formal or informal estimate of the uncertainty involved.

170. If, when evaluating possible outcomes of a decision, a manager creates a graphic representation of the process, with different branches representing different outcomes, the manager is using _____ to aid decision making.
    a. linear programming
    c. gaming theory
    b. simulations
    d. decision trees

171. The distinction between data and information is that data:
    a. are more useful than information.
    b. form the raw material of information.
    c. consist of numbers and information of facts.
    d. are derived from statistical information.

172. Data are said to be collected from two sources: _____ sources and _____ sources.
    a. internal; external
    c. corporate; government
    b. reliable; unreliable
    d. printed; electronic

173. The ABC company has collected data not previously published in usable form for their own particular and exclusive purpose. This is called:
    a. "privileged information."
    c. "primary data."
    b. "proprietary data."
    d. "secondary data."

174. The American Society of Stamp Collectors has compiled a great deal of information and stored it in a computer file, where the information is available to members for retrieval and analysis. This file is called a:
    a. "management information system."
    c. "memory."
    b. "distributed data system."
    d. "database."

175. Many managers rely upon an organized set of processes, called _____ , to provide information that helps them to discharge their responsibilities effectively.
    a. "management by objectives"

b. "management by exception"
c. "management information system"
d. "management sciences"

176. In the _____ processing mode, a salesclerk enters data in a point-of-use terminal, and the data processing system takes over immediately from there.
    a. batch
    b. transactional
    c. real-time
    d. distributed

177. When an airlines reservation clerk books a seat on a flight, and that transaction automatically updates the reservation file, this is an example of:
    a. batch processing.
    b. transaction processing.
    c. real-time processing.
    d. decision support processing.

178. A _____ system is designed especially to help answer a manager's "What if?" questions.
    a. distributed processing
    b. management-by-exception
    c. decision support
    d. None of these systems is designed for that purpose.

179. In statistical measurement, a(n) _____ is a subgroup that is representative of an entire group, or universe.
    a. sample
    b. array
    c. index
    d. central value

180. Here is an array of numbers: 5, 10, 6, 8, 5, 13, 7, 5, 1, 15, and 2. In this array, the mean is _____ , the median is _____ , and the mode is _____ .
    a. 6; 5; 7
    b. 5; 6; 7
    c. 7; 5; 6
    d. 7; 6; 5

181. Competence, in describing an individual's personal qualities, means:
    a. the style of leadership chosen by that person.
    b. the individual's capacity to employ a particular skill.
    c. the nature of the individual's personality.
    d. the extent of the person's intelligence.

182. Managers may choose from a range of management styles. Whatever style is chosen, however, it is important for the manager to be:
    a. consistent.
    b. opportunistic.
    c. compromising.
    d. open-minded.

183. When a processing plant that makes crayons has to shift from making dark-colored crayons to light-colored ones, the crayon press cylinders must be cleaned out before the light colors can be run. This is an example of _____ time.
    a. start-up
    b. process
    c. backup
    d. cycle

184. A personal time budget should be based upon:
    a. payoff tables.
    b. motion study analysis.
    c. linear programming.
    d. personal time analysis.

185. Mary is a manager who can't find time to handle all her responsibilities effectively. One good way to reduce her work load would be for her to assign some of her tasks, along with the necessary authority, to subordinates. This is known as the _____ process.
    - *a.* "participative"
    - *b.* "directing"
    - *c.* "delegation"
    - *d.* "staffing"

186. When asked to accept a delegated task, a subordinate should:
    - *a.* be expected to accept it without question.
    - *b.* be allowed to refuse it without recrimination.
    - *c.* not expect any personal benefit from the assignment.
    - *d.* expect either a promotion or extra pay.

187. Mark Smith is head of purchasing for a major department store. His relationships with his staff are characterized by mutual trust, communications are two-way and lateral, and decision making in his department is highly decentralized. His style of management is:
    - *a.* autocratic.
    - *b.* democratic.
    - *c.* situational.
    - *d.* participative.

188. Research makes it clear that employees under employee-centered managers are _____ than those under task-centered managers.
    - *a.* more productive
    - *b.* less productive
    - *c.* more satisfied with their jobs
    - *d.* less satisfied with their jobs

189. An individual's behavior in response to stress:
    - *a.* is dependent upon the degree of change the person is facing in his or her life.
    - *b.* is dependent upon the degree of uncertainty encountered in the situation.
    - *c.* is dependent upon the individual's behavior pattern in response to stress.
    - *d.* is dependent upon a combination of all three of the above factors.

190. Persons with type A behavior patterns are likely to be:
    - *a.* relaxed, easygoing, and evenly paced.
    - *b.* impatient, and excessively aware of time pressures.
    - *c.* responsive mainly to opportunities for self-actualization.
    - *d.* motivated only by monetary rewards.

191. The productivity of an organization, process, or individual is stated by comparing the _____ with the _____ .
    - *a.* profits; expenses
    - *b.* costs; revenues
    - *c.* inputs; outputs
    - *d.* outputs; inputs

192. In order for the productivity ratio of a process to be 1.0 or better, it is important that there be sufficient _____ available to meet the process's _____ .
    - *a.* controls; standards
    - *b.* controls; goals
    - *c.* resources; target results
    - *d.* resources; profits

193. An office copying machine is rated to copy 2400 sheets an hour. As a practical matter, however, the office usually makes only about 1500 copies an hour; all 1500 sheets are good. The _____ of the machine is 2400 sheets and hour and its _____ is 1500 sheets an hour.
    a. throughput; capacity   c. capacity; downtime
    b. capacity; throughput   d. capacity; yield

194. The Roadway Repair Shop keeps close track of its accounts receivables ratio (or turnover), to make sure that payments are received from their customers promptly. This utilization measure is called a _____ report.
    a. "materials usage"   c. "yield"
    b. "leakage"   d. "capital usage"

195. The arrangement of a process or workplace is called a _____ ; it may flow in a straight line, or it may be L-shaped or _____ .
    a. "layout"; U-shaped   c. "blueprint"; systematic
    b. "floor plan"; rectangular   d. "layout"; star-shaped

196. Productivity improvement that focuses on the process is called _____ ; productivity improvement that focuses on the product's design is called _____ .
    a. "methods improvement"; "ABC analysis"
    b. "work simplification"; "value analysis"
    c. "learning time"; "cleanup time"
    d. "layout improvement"; "product improvement"

197. An essential element of automation is _____ , which aids in communications and control of a machine or process.
    a. a modem   c. feedback
    b. robotics   d. indexing

198. The mail room of a large publishing company employs dozens of people to hand-sort incoming and outgoing mail. In the company's printing plant, huge, expensive presses print books with hardly an operator in sight. The mail room represents a(n) _____ process, and the printing plant a _____ process.
    a. open-shop; captive
    b. inexpensive; expensive
    c. labor-intensive; capital-intensive
    d. capital-intensive; labor-intensive

199. A "change agent" is likely to be encountered in a company undergoing:
    a. reconstruction after a fire.
    b. a revised way of collecting bills.
    c. work simplification.
    d. organization development.

200. Organizations frequently use _____ when trying to improve productivity and reduce defects by inviting participation from voluntary employee groups.
    a. quality circles   c. group norms
    b. suggestion boxes   d. Theory Y teams